SCOTLAND'S QUEST
FOR THE
WORLD CUP

Alex Ferguson,
Scotland's team manager
in Mexico, 1986.

Jock Stein, Scotland's World Cup manager from 1978 until his tragic
death in 1985.

SCOTLAND'S QUEST FOR THE WORLD CUP
A Complete Record
1950 – 1986

CLIVE LEATHERDALE

Foreword by
ALEX FERGUSON

JOHN DONALD PUBLISHERS LTD
EDINBURGH

I would like to express my thanks for the cooperation of the Scottish Football Association, and to Tony Griffin, who kindly put his encyclopaedic knowledge of Scottish soccer at my disposal.

Clive Leatherdale

© Clive Leatherdale 1986

All rights reserved. No part of
this publication 'may be reproduced
in any form or by any means
without the prior permission of
the publishers, John Donald Publishers Ltd.,
138 St Stephen Street,
Edinburgh, EH3 5AA

ISBN 0 85976 149 5

By the same author

So you want to teach English to foreigners
(Abacus Press, 1980)

Britain and Saudi Arabia 1925–1939: The Imperial Oasis
(Frank Cass, 1983)

England's Quest for The World Cup — A Complete Record
(Methuen, 1984)

Dracula: The Novel and the Legend
A study of Bram Stoker's Gothic Masterpiece
(Aquarian Press, 1985)

Photoset by Quorn Selective Repro Ltd.
Printed in Great Britain by Bell & Bain Ltd., Glasgow

Foreword

It is a great pleasure to be asked to write a Foreword for a book which embraces the magic and achievements of Scotland's World Cup history and success story – which must not be devalued. For a small country of five million people we have managed to compete in six World Cup Finals going back to Switzerland in 1954, Sweden in 1958, West Germany in 1974, Argentina in 1978, Spain in 1982 and now Mexico 1986, which makes this book a collector's gem.

As a small boy with heroes of these earlier sojourns I well remember the humiliation by Uruguay 7-0 in Switzerland when the players of that era were household names: Tommy Docherty, Willie Fernie, Jimmy Davidson and Johnny McKenzie and when they were beaten 7-0 I just couldn't believe it. It is interesting to note that Scotland took only thirteen players to the World Cup Finals in 1954, and only a trainer (no manager) in 1958 and when you think of the number of players we take now, plus technical and medical staff, it shows how much the game has advanced from those early days. In 1958 we did not reach beyond the first stage in a group which consisted of Paraguay, France and Yugoslavia. A small insight into the planning of those days was that Archie Robertson, then a player, was actually doing the spying on the opponents in the World Cup and no doubt this contributed later to his success as a Manager.

We then had a big lapse and it wasn't until 1974 in West Germany that we managed to reach the Finals again; here we set something of a record by not losing a game in the World Cup Finals yet still being knocked out. Of that team Kenny Dalglish was an emerging international and the great Denis Law was reaching the twilight of his career; it was to be his last appearance in a Scotland jersey. So as one great player came, another went. The Manager at that time, Willie Ormond, proved that the gift of balancing and picking players was as important as any aspect of management.

1978 was again a World Cup Final year and we were rather downcast. I felt that the Manager Ally MacLeod did a great job in giving hope to the people. Unfortunately that hope did not materialise and Ally was left to face the disappointment. However, sometimes progress is made through failure and if Argentina was to be a lesson then it was surely a watershed for Scottish International football, because the next man brought a humility and orderliness to the job which was just a part of himself.

Jock Stein was Scotland's most successful Club Manager of all time and it was only fitting that he should eventually attain the highest position in football – the Manager of the National Team. And, as expected, he once again proved how good he really was by taking them to two World Cup Finals – Spain in 1982 and Mexico in 1986. I had the great pleasure of working with him for a year until that tragic night in Cardiff and found him to be the most humble of men. Considering he had achieved such success he was always reluctant to discuss or elaborate upon any of his achievements, always turning the conversation on his players who he said made his success. Jock Stein had the quality of greatness. Few people have it. In Jock's time he was prepared to recognise a home based player and if you examine his teams in the period he was Manager you will appreciate that he did a lot for Scottish football. But more than that he gave some young players a start in international football: Jim Leighton, Alex McLeish, Jim Bett, Charles Nicholas, Paul McStay, Gordon Strachan and many others who have become household names.

I could go on and on and wax lyrical about all of the great players we have had and all of the great names that Scotland has played in the past but the best piece of advice I can give you is to read the book which will fully elaborate the achievements of World Cup football.

Alex Ferguson, 1986

Contents

Introduction

For Scotland – as for England, Wales and Ireland – active involvement in the World Cup did not commence until after the Second World War. By then three tournaments were already part of history, those of 1930, 1934 and 1938. The four Home soccer Associations, however, had spent most of the inter-war years disaffiliated from FIFA and so were ineligible to compete – even if they had a mind to. Differences of opinion over allowing official fixtures with defeated First World War enemies; mistrust at the motives of continental professionalism eating into the amateur ethos; and general suspicion towards foreign interference in a game considered to be British to the bootlaces all contributed to prolonged periods of estrangement between British and world football.

It took a more enlightened attitude regarding international cooperation, brought about by the ending of the Second World War, before permanent reconciliation was effected. The British Associations rejoined FIFA in 1946 and expressed their preparedness to compete in the first post-war World Cup competition, to be held in Brazil in 1950 – where the scheduled 1942 tournament would have been staged but for the War.

It is difficult to gauge how Scotland would have fared had they taken part in the World Cups of the 1930s. It was not until 1929 that Scotland ventured to play their first international against non-British opposition. By then England had been playing, and beating, continental sides regularly for over twenty years (albeit with a twelve-year gap between 1909-21). Scotland's undisputed supremacy in the Home International Champion-ship throughout the 1920s – winning it no less than seven times – would not necessarily have benefited them against the unfamiliar styles and tactics employed by the emerging continental teams.

Even so, Scotland's record against foreign teams between 1929-39 was impressive enough. A total of fifteen fixtures produced just two defeats, both recorded in the space of four days in May 1931, when they lost 0-5 and 0-3 in Austria and Italy respectively against two of the dominant teams of the decade.

Unaccountably, Scotland's international form deteriorated in the immediate post-1945 period. Of their first ten peacetime fixtures only two were won, with defeats being registered in Brussels, Berne and Paris, not to mention Wrexham and Belfast – and worst of all at Hampden against the English. In fact, no British opposition were beaten until the seventh post-war attempt. By then it was October 1948, and three months later the qualifying procedures for the 1950 World Cup were announced.

CHAPTER 1

The 1950 World Cup

FIFA evidently wanted to express its goodwill towards the four British footballing nations, in recognition of their historical influence on the game and their decision to rejoin its ranks. FIFA's qualifying arrangements were generous, to say the least. At the demand of the British Associations FIFA spared the home countries the indignity of the preliminary rounds. British footballers would not be asked to soil their boots against 'foreign' opponents. Instead, the Home Internationals of season 1949-50 were constituted as Britain's World Cup qualifying zone. The champions would qualify automatically for Brazil.

Even then FIFA's beneficence was not spent. They invited Britain's top *two* teams to travel to Brazil, only to be rebuffed by the Scottish FA. Nowadays, appearing in the finals of the World Cup is accorded the status almost of a national imperative, with no effort being spared to attain that objective. But in those days there was no great enthusiasm in Britain – especially in Scotland – for dabbling in what were felt to be sub-standard foreign competitions. The SFA reiterated its earlier declaration, that a Scottish playing party would not journey to Brazil unless they did so as British champions. In other words, if Scotland finished as British runners-up they would forfeit FIFA's invitation to compete.

At the time, the SFA's decision did not arouse much comment. The Welsh and Irish FAs had made similar declarations, though in their case with possibly greater justification. Should either of them qualify for Brazil there would be an obvious strain on their financial and playing resources. Neither Wales nor Ireland were at all prepared or equipped for the rigours of a World Cup. Wales' sum experience of non-British football amounted to two visits to Paris in 1931 and 1939. They had not played across the English Channel, let alone in South America, since the War. And as for the Irish, they had not yet played anybody outside Britain. Even when the qualifying rounds for the 1958 World Cup came around, their total previous continental experience was confined to a 1-3 defeat in France in 1952.

Scotland's decision, however, could not so easily be explained away. It was probably taken in part through false modesty: the belief that Scotland were not yet strong enough to do themselves justice – though they had emerged from their post-War trough to register a clean sweep in the British Championships of 1948–49. The rebuff was also insensitive and impolite:

the SFA apparently expected FIFA to wait until after the conclusion of the Home Internationals before knowing whether Britain would be sending one representative or two. A last-minute replacement might need to be found, but by then the World Cup finals would be just two months away.

England were unruffled by the whole charade. They, it seemed, would be going to Brazil whatever, either as British champions or as the second British team in company with the British champions.

In fact, FIFA's arrangements were unfair as well as generous. It is standard practice that in World Cup eliminating rounds teams play each other twice – home and away – or, in the event of a play-off, on neutral territory. The Home Internationals in any given season were not so arranged. The four countries played each other once only, and in the season in question Scotland and Wales would enjoy the unmerited advantage of two home fixtures out of three – one of which would be against England. Despite the SFA's self-imposed restrictions, the fixture schedule smiled on Scotland.

The Qualifying Rounds

Saturday, 1 October 1949
NORTHERN IRELAND v SCOTLAND   Belfast 56,000

All things considered, Scotland journeyed to Windsor Park for the first international of the new season in good spirits. They had followed up their triple British success the previous season with a 2-0 Hampden win over France, and were now looking for a fifth straight victory. Scotland had been beaten in Belfast, 0-2, on their last visit in 1947, but with the creation of the neighbouring Irish Republic the following year the Irish team were unable to call upon those players from the South who remarkably had beaten England at Goodison Park a fortnight previously. Only three players – Vernon, Cochrane and Smyth – remained from the 1947 winning Irish side, with seven of the remaining places being filled by new 'caps'.

The Scottish team was a near-replica of that triumphant at Wembley the previous April. Jimmy Cowan of Morton had worn the green jersey for eighteen months, and would remain first-choice goalkeeper until 1952. In front of him were the Rangers full-backs George Young and Sammy Cox, and centre-half Willie Woodburn. There was only one 'Anglo' in the side – Billy Steel of Derby County. The solitary newcomer, earning his one and only international cap – replacing Billy Houliston – was East Fife centre-forward Henry Morris. He had a difficult game in prospect, being opposed by the worthy Irish pivot Jack Vernon of West Bromwich Albion. Scotland had every incentive to win: if they wanted to retain the British championship and compete in Brazil, they simply had to beat Ireland.

The game proved to be a walkover for the Scots. Irish goalkeeper Pat Kelly (once of Aberdeen, then of Barnsley), experiencing the pressures of international football for the first time, must have suffered nightmares for many a night to follow. He was responsible for as many as five of the Scottish goals, and was probably the major factor separating the teams. The match, declared the *Glasgow Herald*, 'was the most remarkable International of our time', mainly because Scotland, despite the score, 'were inferior in several positions and played less combined football than the opponents they routed'.

Scotland were two goals up before four minutes had elapsed. Morris' international call-up was instantly justified with a headed goal from Waddell's centre. Vernon would have comfortably headed clear, but Kelly, enthusiastically leaping for the ball, succeeded only in knocking his centre-half to the ground, leaving Morris an unguarded net. Immediately afterwards Waddell scored a splendid solo goal, bearing down on Kelly along the goal-line. The goalkeeper expected a pull-back which never came. He edged outwards and left ample room for Waddell to score.

Ireland had apparently absorbed these setbacks and had their opponents on their heels during the critical phase of the match. Cowan changed direction in mid-air to keep out a goal-bound Brennan header, and then gratefully parried a Cochrane shot. But the outcome of the match was sealed when Scotland scored another pair in the 24th and 25th minutes. Steel's floated lob from the edge of the area totally perplexed Kelly, who clutched spectacularly at an illusory football. The agonised goalkeeper must have felt almost relieved when, from the restart, Lawrie Reilly took Waddell's pass to score emphatically. No-one could blame Kelly for that one!

The total was five just before half-time. The ball was driven hard against Vernon's arm from a couple of yards and the referee awarded Scotland a ludicrous penalty, converted by Waddell. No fewer than four of Scotland's goals could be put down either to one man in black or another swathed in red blushes.

Ireland commenced the second half as if the score was as they thought it should be, 0-1, not how it was, 0-5. Within five minutes the best move of the match saw six Irish players involved in the build-up which led to Smyth pulling a goal back. The tall inside-forward with his delicate skills was giving Bobby Evans and George Aitken a torrid afternoon. After fifty-nine minutes he scored again, powering home McKenna's corner. Despite their three-goal cushion, there were unmistakable signs of Scottish unease, which persisted until Kelly once again came to the rescue. With twenty minutes left the ball was belted downfield towards the Irish goal. Morris started to chase but soon gave it up as a lost cause. It would have been except that Kelly, coming out to collect, inexplicably stopped in his tracks. Morris spurted forward and scored with ease.

Ten minutes from time Jimmy Mason embarked on a jinking run which culminated in his walking the ball into the net. But Pat Kelly's day of horrors was not yet finished. This is how the *Glasgow Herald* described Scotland's eighth goal, in the last minute: 'Morris off his balance swung his boot and just managed to trundle the ball at Kelly, whose lamentable effort to save was received in complete silence. Not even the most raucous-voiced of the tartan-bedecked Scots desired any such goal'. At the end Jimmy Cowan generously tried to console his distraught opposite number. Not since 1901 had Scotland scored more goals in an international, when they had thumped in eleven – against Ireland.

NORTHERN IRELAND (0)2   SCOTLAND (5)8
  Smyth 2   Morris 3, Wadell 2 (1 pen), Steel,
                                       Reilly, Mason

NORTHERN IRELAND: Kelly, Bowler, McMichael, Banchflower, Vernon, Ferris, Cochrane, Smyth, Brennan, Crossan, McKenna.

SCOTLAND: J Cowan (Morton), G Young (Rangers, capt.), S Cox (Rangers), R Evans (Celtic), W Woodburn (Rangers), G Aitken (East Fife), W Waddell (Rangers), J Mason (Third Lanark), H Morris (East Fife), W Steel (Derby), L Reilly (Hibs).

Wednesday, 9 November 1949
SCOTLAND v WALES   Hampden 74,000

The following month it was Wales' turn to try to put a stop to Scotland's winning sequence. Although the Welsh had just suffered a heavy 1-4 home defeat at the hands of England, they had proved to be, of late, more than a handful for the Scots. Matches between the two nations dated back to 1876. Of these, the Welsh tally of victories was a meagre dozen – although six of them had come from the past ten meetings. Wales had won 2-1 on their first post-War visit to Scotland, in 1947, and – with a better recent record against the Scots than even England could manage – had come to be regarded as something of a Scottish bogey team.

The Welsh retained seven of the 1947 Hampden winning eleven. These included the powerful Trevor Ford in attack, but several other positions were filled by players earning their bread and butter in the obscurity of reserve or lower-division football. In goal, twenty-one year old Keith Jones of Aston Villa was making his debut, and in his prayers must have been pleading for greater divine protection than had been granted Ireland's debutant, the luckless Pat Kelly.

Scotland's Nos 7, 8 and 9 shirts found new occupants, the wearers in Belfast all having to vacate them through injury. Alec Linwood of Clyde, called up at the last moment, pulled on the centre-forward jersey for the first time. He was not a bustling type of player, eschewing brawn for skill, and he would not relish the attentions of veteran Welsh stopper, Trevor Jones. A further newcomer to international football, John McPhail, became Celtic's second representative, teaming up with Bobby Evans. For this match a second Anglo was also selected, Liverpool's experienced Billy Liddell stepping in for regular right-winger Willie Waddell.

Hampden was dank and misty. Its terraces were charged with noise, yet the game was unexceptional. Scottish aggression was unleashed from the first whistle to the last, yet with so much at stake goalscoring opportunities were at a premium. Pick of the Scottish players was the fleet-footed, diminutive Billy Steel, but he could not carry the home attack single-handed on a day when both wingers, Liddell and Reilly, were largely contained by the Welsh full-backs.

At the other end, Woodburn's muscle occasionally upset Mr Law – the English referee. Perhaps the key to the result came when, from a Welsh corner, Woodburn lunged at the ball, missed, and clattered Ford instead. Mr Law's silent whistle on this occasion did not endear him to the red shirts, especially when Scotland scored shortly afterwards. Midway through the first half Steel went past Barnes to despatch an awkward cross. It proved too awkward for the young goalkeeper who mishandled it on to the crossbar. The ball fell neatly for McPhail to sweep home.

The longer the game went on, the more dominant Scotland became. Cowan was not overtaxed by a punchless Welsh attack, where the eye-catching duel between Woodburn and Ford tended to cancel out both players. Yet Trevor Ford was involved in the game's second, and decisive, turning point. It was in the 62nd minute that his powerful volley looped off George Young's boot, spun high in the air and plopped sweetly against the face of the crossbar. Griffiths was first to the ball, controlling it instantly. The angle was tight but the goal was empty. Perhaps he was trying to score: perhaps to centre to a colleague, but Griffiths could only watch mortified as he side-footed the ball inches beyond the far post. The Hampden sigh was audible. The Welsh challenge was now exhausted, but one Scottish paper was later moved to concede: 'Scotland had all the luck of this hard, gruelling struggle'.

Twelve minutes from time Linwood escaped from centre-half Trevor Jones for virtually the first time, although he needed a fortuitous break of the ball to do so. Linwood seized his opportunity to hook an excellent goal. Wales were hanging on now, and at the death McPhail missed a clear opportunity to increase the lead. Scotland fully deserved their victory, but not by three goals.

Alec Linwood had taken his effort well, but he now suffered the fate of his predecessor, Henry Morris – scoring on his debut but becoming an international outcast thereafter. Young Keith Jones had not disgraced himself either, but he too would never be picked for his country again. On the other hand, it came as no surprise to Pat Kelly to learn that he was not included in the Irish team to face England later in November. A namesake – Hugh Kelly – won his first cap hoping for better things. He was to be disappointed. England cocked a snook at the Scots and went one better. They scored nine.

SCOTLAND (1)2   WALES (0)0
  McPhail, Linwood

SCOTLAND: J Cowan (Morton), G Young (Rangers, capt.), S Cox (Rangers), R Evans (Celtic), W Woodburn (Rangers), G Aitken (East Fife), W Liddell (Liverpool), J McPhail (Celtic), A Linwood (Clyde), W Steel (Derby), L Reilly (Hibs).

WALES: K Jones, Barnes, Sherwood, Powell, T G Jones, Burgess, Griffiths, Paul, Ford, Clarke, Edwards.

Saturday, 15 April 1950
SCOTLAND v ENGLAND   Hampden 134,000

By the following April the full implications of the SFA's policy of conditional participation were embarrassingly apparent, and were earning them condemnation throughout football. Now, as the climactic moment drew near, honourable defence of the original statement was hard to find. Instead, it was rumoured that following Scotland's 'grand slam' the previous season the SFA had been encouraged in its 'champions or nothing' edict in the arrogant belief that the team would obviously finish top in 1950, and had nothing to fear from England or anybody else.

If FIFA's initial proposal had been accepted, the issue would now have been settled: Wales and Northern Ireland were already eliminated and

Scotland and England could prepare for the trip. But the SFA's intransigence meant that the coming match assumed high drama. 'The Match of the Century' it was billed – the 68th meeting between Scotland and England, and the most vital. The world's oldest soccer fixture had traditionally been a private affray designed solely for British consumption. But not now. The eyes of the world were turned on Hampden. There was the unedifying spectacle of representatives from FIFA, Brazil and the English FA trying to plead with the SFA for a change of heart *before* the match. It seems almost comic now: Scotland were being paid the compliment of an unconditional invitation to compete in the world's greatest soccer festival – and were refusing.

England journeyed north with both teams having four points. Goal figures in those days played no part in the British Championship or World Cup, so for Scotland the issue was starkly simple. They must at least draw with England, for that would enable both countries to share the championship with five points each. Only if Scotland avoided defeat would they accompany England to Brazil for the World Cup finals.

All the pressure was on Scotland: none on England, who even if they lost could not finish lower than second and so had already qualified for Brazil. To the Scots' habitual relish of beating the auld enemy were now added extra, unwanted, pressures that could hardly assist their cause. England had won at Hampden on their last two visits – in 1939 and 1948 – and the previous month nine of the current England eleven had been included in an English League team which comprehensively disposed of the Scottish League, 3-1, at Middlesbrough. That Scottish setback, allied to all the other factors, made bookies unanimous in their expectation that Scotland – defending champions or not – would lose.

The English team were a settled crew. Stanley Matthews was out of favour, but Tom Finney was there, and stylish full-back Alf Ramsey would be making his inaugural Hampden appearance – marking Billy Liddell.

There were several enforced changes to the Scottish line-up. Three players were asked to win their first caps in the cauldron of Hampden Park on the occasion of Scotland's biggest match in memory. The occupants of the Nos 8 and 9 shirts changed again. At inside-right came Willie Moir of Bolton Wanderers, who had topped the scoring sheets in the English First Division in the season just completed. Alongside him was Willie Bauld of Hearts. Ian McColl came in at right-half to boost the Ibrox contingent to five. This time there were as many as four Anglos – Alec Forbes of Arsenal being the fourth – in a side clearly weighted in favour of battlers.

The match was all-ticket: 134,000 bodies crammed into Britain's largest stadium. Within two minutes Bauld pounded a shot straight at Bert

Williams, England's goalkeeping successor to Frank Swift. As the match wore on it was apparent that both defences were well in charge, and that any goals were likely to stem from rare defensive errors. By the interval Scotland seemed the more disorganised team, particularly on the right flank, where Moir's contribution was totally invisible and the doubts about Waddell's fitness were fully vindicated. Every time he tried to cross the ball he had to pull it back on to his left foot. Steel was also having a quiet game. By no stretch of the imagination did England look an accomplished side: it was simply that Scotland looked worse. But there was no need to fret: England, too, appeared incapable of scoring.

Early in the second half an English 'goal' was rightly disallowed for offside. Bauld then sizzled a shot the wrong side of Williams' post, but after sixty-three minutes England took the lead – slightly against the general run of play at that point. The Scottish defence expected Langton to pass wide to Mannion, but he slipped it square to Bentley. The Chelsea forward had hitherto been well-marshalled, but now he turned and shot before Woodburn could tackle, and from twelve yards the ball cannoned off Cowan into the net.

Hampden was transformed instantly into a morgue. Somehow a Scottish equaliser needed manufacturing, but England would not cooperate. In the last quarter of an hour Liddell's savage volley was miraculously kept out by Williams, and near the end poor Willie Bauld, clean through the English defence and able to pick his spot, lashed the ball wildly against the underside of Williams' bar. The ball bounced out, not in, and Scotland had lost. The *Scotsman* confessed: 'The Englishmen were just value for their win', and the *Glasgow Herald* went further, being unable to 'recall any international side so superior to another in ground passing and in accurate head work as Saturday's England eleven ... We should not now be too proud to learn; we are no longer the masters'.

SCOTLAND (0)0   ENGLAND (0)1
                                  Bentley

SCOTLAND: J Cowan (Morton), G Young (Rangers, capt.), S Cox (Rangers), I McColl (Rangers), W Woodburn (Rangers), A Forbes (Arsenal), W Waddell (Rangers), W Moir (Bolton), W Bauld (Hearts), W Steel (Derby), W Liddell (Liverpool).

ENGLAND: Williams, Ramsey, Aston, Wright, Franklin, Dickinson, Finney, Mannion, Mortensen, Bentley, Langton.

The begging did not cease with the final whistle. Efforts were continued to persuade the Scottish FA to reconsider. Whatever the private thoughts of its members, pride was now at stake, and the SFA would lose credibility if it now repudiated its earlier and oft-repeated declarations solely as a result of the team being beaten. So Scotland knocked themselves out of the 1950 World Cup.

The Scottish public was not in the mood for forgiveness. The amateurish organisation of Scottish international football came in for vituperation. It transpired that Willie Moir, the most inconspicuous player on the field, had been picked despite several members of the selection committee never having seen him play for Bolton. FIFA was likewise ill-inclined to be indulgent with the SFA, and in due course the Scottish Vice-President of FIFA failed to be re-elected to his post. Scottish wounds, entirely self-inflicted, would not be quickly healed.

The only consolation to the Scots was that England were heading for even greater humiliation, beaten 1-0 by the no-hopers of the United States and then by Spain, and sent crashing out of the Brazil World Cup. It is a mischievous thought: if Scotland had triumphed at Hampden it would have been they – as British champions – who would have been allocated to play the United States.

World Cup Qualifying Group 6:

	P	W	D	L	F	A	PTS
ENGLAND	3	3	0	0	14	3	6
Scotland	3	2	0	1	10	3	4
N.Ireland	3	0	1	2	4	17	1
Wales	3	0	1	2	1	6	1

Other group results

Wales v England	1-4
England v N.Ireland	9-2
Wales v N.Ireland	0-0

Scotland appearances (A) and goal-scorers (G):
World Cup qualifying rounds 1950

	A	G		A	G
Cowan J	3	–	Waddell W	2	2
Cox S	3	–	Bauld W	1	–
Steel W	3	1	Forbes A	1	–
Woodburn W	3	–	Linwood A	1	1
Young G	3	–	Mason J	1	1
Aitken G	2	–	McColl I	1	–
Evans R	2	–	McPhail J	1	1
Liddell W	2	–	Moir W	1	–
Reilly L	2	1	Morris H	1	3
18 players			caps	33	10 goals

Scottish League	26
English League	7
	33

Laurie Reilly represented Scotland in the Qualifying rounds of the 1950 and 1954 World Cup. This picture shows Laurie wearing one of his Scottish Caps and looking at a picture of himself scoring his last-minute equaliser against England at Wembley, 1953. The score finished 2-2.

CHAPTER 2

The 1954 World Cup

FIFA saw no reason to change the qualifying procedure assigned to the four British nations for the following, 1954, World Cup. Two qualifying places were again on offer and this time Scotland – to no-one's surprise in view of their chastening experience in 1950 – quietly agreed to accept FIFA's terms.

Of course, circumstances in 1954 also happened to be somewhat more enticing. The World Cup finals would not be staged on the opposite side of the world but in nearby Switzerland, with all the advantages in preparation and travelling arrangements which that entailed.

Results had not gone well for Scotland in their three and a half year interlude between World Cup commitments. They had – somewhat to their chagrin – recorded a six-point maximum a year too late in claiming the 1950-51 British championship, but in the midst of those victories had suffered a major setback. Back in 1931 Austria had been the first country to defeat Scotland on foreign soil. Then, in December 1950, they achieved the more impressive distinction of becoming the first non-British team to win in Scotland. Cowan picked the ball out of his net only once but that was enough to send the powerful continentals home victorious. It was no fluke: five months later Scotland tasted Austrian hospitality and shooting prowess, being thumped 0-4.

Sweden were the next European side to complete the double – winning 3-1 in Stockholm in 1952, and then 2-1 at Hampden in May 1953. This latter reverse was Scotland's last scheduled fixture before the new season, when they would be pitched into the World Cup eliminators. Scotland entered their new campaign without an international victory for a year.

The Qualifying Rounds

Saturday, 3 October 1953
NORTHERN IRELAND v SCOTLAND   Belfast 52,000

Despite the passing of four years, no fewer than four Scottish players turned out for a second time against Northern Ireland in the World Cup – Young, Cox, Evans and Waddell. John McPhail was also recalled for his second World Cup campaign, having faced Wales in 1949. The team had a new goalkeeper, George Farm of Blackpool, who had taken over from Cowan a year previously. The general complexion of the side, and especially the attack, had an experimental, makeshift quality about it, as the selectors struggled to find an effective blend. Only one player, East Fife's Charlie Fleming, was making his international debut, but – excluding the five players embarking on their second World Cup – the other six could scrape up only ten previous caps between them.

Since the Irish dark days of 1949 when they had lost eight goals to Scotland, then nine to England, there had evidently been some stiffening of their powers of resistance. They had kept the Scottish total down to six in 1950, three in 1951, and the following year actually had the temerity to draw 1-1 at Hampden – and come perilously close to winning. Ireland were desperately in need of a win: they hadn't recorded a victory over anybody for six years, since they had beaten Scotland in 1947.

Yet all the signs were that Ireland were on the up. Shrewdly coached by Peter Doherty, they couldn't keep losing, not with the trio of exceptional young players now at their disposal. Danny Blanchflower had been only a child when winning his first cap in the 8-2 horror of 1949. Now with Aston Villa, he was developing into one of Britain's classic half-backs. He would shortly be snapped up by Tottenham and go on to greater things. Wilbur Cush and Billy Bingham were of similar age and not far short on talent. All three, despite their youth, had been permanent fixtures in the Irish side for some years, and would provide the backbone of the national team till well into the 1960s. With Ireland improving all the time, and Scotland bedevilled by a slump, few Scotsmen were banking on a certain victory.

If the navy shirts had been flattered by events in Belfast in 1949, they were entirely in the debt of the gods in 1953. The Irish had Scotland on the ropes from the start and kept them there for practically the whole match. Scotland scarcely managed to cross the half-way line as Blanchflower and Cush held the Irish half-back line together. Bingham repeatedly skipped round Cox, and Charlie Tully's delicate skills provided Celtic team-mate Evans with a wretched forty-five minutes until a knock forced Tully into semi-activity. A large, heavy Scottish eleven were being brushed aside by Irish speed and touch-play.

Attacks rained down on Farm, the busiest man on show. The goalkeeper leapt this way and that, down at Irish feet, and brought gasps from the crowd as he kept out scorching shots from Simpson (of Rangers) and McIlroy. Defenders unceremoniously hacked clear when he was beaten, but Tully and McIlroy were also guilty of glaring misses.

Two minutes into the second period Scotland broke into the Irish half. McPhail headed on to Fleming, who survived Cush's tackle to send an instant drive past Smyth. According to the *Glasgow Herald*, even the Scottish supporters were embarrassed by a goal so hard on Ireland: the scorer 'did a dance of delight and made more noise than all the thousands of his fellow countrymen, who found the occasion suitable for nose-blowing, scarf-adjustment and shoe-lace tieing'. Ireland returned to bombard the Scottish defence, producing overall 'a dozen shots worthy of a goal'.

After seventy minutes Scotland raced upfield to score a second. Fleming's header from Waddell's centre was saved by Smyth's legs. In keeping with the run of the ball that day the rebound went not to a defender but back to Fleming, who gleefully scored again.

The two-goal advantage lasted barely five minutes. Brennan impeded Simpson with a bear-hug which did not go unnoticed, and Lockhart scored Ireland's penalty. Not many Scots would have given odds on holding out now, but near the end the ball was again played upfield towards an underpopulated Irish defence. McCabe's miscued clearance was his one and only memorable mistake, but it gave Jackie Henderson the chance to shoot inside Smyth's near post – a goal which, claimed the *Scotsman*, 'made the score almost farcical'.

The Scottish press were unanimous in their assessment of Scotland's play and the ill-fortune of the Irish. The Aberdeen *Press and Journal* described Scotland as 'slow, inept, unenterprising, and altogether a very unimpressive lot'. The *Scotsman* admitted 'in every respect but the vital one of finishing, Ireland enjoyed much the better of the play'. The *Glasgow Herald* put matters into truer perspective: 'Not one of the thousands of Scots who attended the Windsor Park match will disagree with the view that if ever there was a travesty of justice this was it ... Had Scotland lost 1-3 and yet played as well as Ireland did all of us would have been in a much happier frame of mind'.

NORTHERN IRELAND (0)1   SCOTLAND (0)3
   Lockhart (pen)   Fleming 2, Henderson

NORTHERN IRELAND: Smyth, Cunningham, McMichael, Blanchflower, McCabe, Cush, Bingham, McIlroy, Simpson, Tully, Lockhart.

SCOTLAND: G Farm (Blackpool), G Young (Rangers, capt.), S Cox (Rangers), R Evans (Celtic), F Brennan (Newcastle), D Cowie (Dundee), W Waddell (Rangers), C Fleming (East Fife), J McPhail (Celtic), J Watson (Huddersfield), J Henderson (Portsmouth).

Wednesday, 4 November 1953
SCOTLAND v WALES   Hampden 71,000

Scotland had to wait only a month for the opportunity to secure qualification for Switzerland. Victory over Wales – if followed a week later by an Irish defeat in England – would mean that Scotland were guaranteed at least second position in the British league table. And that would be good enough.

Wales, however, could be expected to take defeat no more lightly than had Ireland. They had been grotesquely hard done by against England, mesmerising their more illustrious opponents with their spirited play, and leading 1-0 until their defence was disrupted by injury shortly before half-time. The final result – 4-1 to England – was as nonsensical as Scotland's scoreline in Belfast. For the present match, Wales fielded an unchanged team. Trevor Ford was still unfit, which meant that the redoubtable 6'2" John Charles of Leeds retained the No 9 shirt.

The Welsh 'Indian sign' on Scotland had not dissipated following their World Cup defeat of 1949. Indeed, they had returned in 1951 to snatch a late winner, and could boast two Hampden wins out of three since the War. A Welsh victory now – with only Ireland still to face, in Wrexham – would leave Wales well poised for qualifying.

The Scottish selectors had been no more deceived than the press by the result in Belfast. Six players were axed, including the entire forward line. Charlie Fleming became the latest in a growing list of Scottish centre-forwards who scored on their debuts and were dropped thereafter – permanently. For Jimmy Watson and John McPhail, too, it was the end of the international trail. The players brought in were a mixture of the old and new. Experienced hands – Lawrie Reilly and Bobby Johnstone of Hibs, Billy Liddell, and Allan Brown of Blackpool – were recalled to the front line. But another veteran, Willie Waddell, made way on the right wing for Partick's John McKenzie – one of two new caps. The other was St Mirren's powerful and reliable centre-half Willie Telfer, expecting to mark Trevor Ford, but being confronted by John Charles instead.

Scotland began the stronger in an entertaining game played at high speed. They might have scored as early as the first minute, but Brown couldn't capitalise on McKenzie's created opening. But a goal did fall to the home side after nineteen minutes. A fluid move involving McKenzie and Reilly was highlighted by the latter's through pass to Brown. The Blackpool forward had only recently returned to action after breaking a leg, but there was no sign of his injury as he confidently shot past Howells. Four minutes from half-time Scotland scored a second, and even better, goal. Johnstone switched the ball from one foot to the other before hooking home a cracking shot. The scorer deservedly milked the applause.

Wales had defended stubbornly, with their wing-halves – Paul and Burgess – always prominent, yet the visitors had been clearly second best on the first-half performance. Three minutes after the turnaround, however, they climbed back into the match with a stunning goal. John Charles, for all his reputation, had looked less impressive than Lawrie Reilly at the other end – though Charles was being deprived of comparable service. But now he collected Foulkes' right-wing centre, swivelled, and hit a thunderbolt past the hapless Farm into the far corner.

With the game rattling along, it was with a huge roar of relief that Hampden greeted Scotland's third goal, nine minutes later. Liddell slipped the ball through for Reilly, Daniel converged to challenge, only to lose his footing and present the Hibs No 9 with a clean shot at goal. But Wales, despite being under the cosh for most of a thrilling game, once more demonstrated their resilience at Hampden. Bobby Evans had been taking good care of the blond Ivor Allchurch, but was nowhere to be seen as the Welshman picked up the ball on the half-way line and survived one, two, three, four determined challenges before rounding off his audacity by hammering his shot into the net from twenty yards. It was, by any standards, a scintillating goal.

The final two minutes were packed with incident and controversy. The ageless Welsh full-back Wally Barnes awkwardly chested the ball back to his goalkeeper. The contact was sufficiently near the arm to provoke a spontaneous roar of 'penalty'. The referee did not think so, and was already racing upfield to follow the belted clearance. The ball sailed deep into the Scottish half. Telfer was possibly prematurely congratulating himself on a flawless international baptism as he casually prepared to pass back to Farm. But the lightning-fast Charles whipped the ball off him and, with Farm caught in no-man's land, scored a dramatic Welsh equaliser. Telfer, desperately trying to retrieve his error, ended up in the back of the net with the ball.

If Scotland had cause to feel aggrieved, in view of their earlier good work, they felt doubly sore from the restart. Reilly outstripped Daniel for pace as he burst clear, only to have his heels clipped from him just outside the Welsh penalty box. To use a well-worn cliché, Scotland had played much worse and won – and had done so the previous month.

SCOTLAND (2)3   WALES (0)3
  Brown, Johnstone, Reilly   Charles 2, I Allchurch

SCOTLAND: G Farm (Blackpool), G Young (Rangers, capt.), S Cox (Rangers), R Evans (Celtic), W Telfer (St Mirren), D Cowie (Dundee), J McKenzie (Partick), R Johnstone (Hibs), L Reilly (Hibs), A Brown (Blackpool), W Liddell (Liverpool).

WALES: Howells, Barnes, Sherwood, Paul, Daniel, Burgess, Foulkes, R Davies, Charles, I Allchurch, Clarke.

Saturday, 3 April 1954
SCOTLAND v ENGLAND   Hampden 134,000

A week later England unconvincingly beat the gallant Irish at Goodison Park, but the outcome of Scottish qualification dragged on to the following spring. Four days before England were due at Hampden, Wales would entertain the Irish. If Wales won, as expected, it would mean Scotland would have to avoid defeat against England, and all the tension of 1950 would be reactivated. Yet to undisguised Scottish relief the Irish chose that occasion to put an end to their seven-year sequence without a win. The World Cup aspect of the British Championship was now settled: Scotland and England were uncatchable. There was nothing at stake at Hampden except prestige – and the British title.

Actually, this was not entirely true. As in 1950, the British champions were to be seeded in the World Cup finals. The draw had already taken place, without waiting for all sixteen qualifying places to be finalised. In the first round the seeded British champions were scheduled to play the modest opposition provided by Belgium and Switzerland, while the British runners-up would be left with the daunting prospect of Uruguay and Austria. Scotland's dropped point against Wales now meant that nothing less than a victory over England would do – to head the Home International table and tread the gentler path in Switzerland.

England had troubles enough. Against Wales and Ireland they had looked quite dreadful. Disaster was brewing. Massacred by the Hungarians at Wembley in November, the England team was promptly despatched to the knacker's yard. There was no international future for Alf Ramsey, Stanley Mortensen, and many others. An England eleven containing four new caps emerged into the unfamiliar and intimidating atmosphere of Hampden, intent on seizing the first opportunity to recapture lost pride – at Scotland's expense.

The hosts, too, made several changes. These included George Young missing his first ever World Cup game, providing a first (and last) cap to his Celtic rival Mike Haughney; and Hibernian's Willie Ormond making his debut at outside-left. Willie Telfer was left to ponder that agonising moment which had let in Wales for their late equaliser. In all probability it had helped consign him to international oblivion, and Newcastle's Frank Brennan returned for what was to be his own last cap. It was as well that Bobby Johnstone was versatile: he had previously worn the Scottish No 7 shirt and the No 11. Now he turned out wearing No 9 against England's untried 6'3" centre-half Harry Clarke.

In preparation for the World Cup finals the SFA had recently appointed a team manager to minister to Scotland's affairs. Andy Beattie – full-time boss of Huddersfield Town – must have been encouraged as his team enjoyed the early supremacy and the early goal. It was scored in the eighth minute at the second attempt by Brown, the ball bouncing off Merrick and squeezing through Staniforth's legs. With an almost entirely untried defence, the visitors could not at that moment have felt confident about extending their winning ways at Hampden. England were in line for a fifth successive victory: Scotland had not beaten them at home since 1937.

Playing into pounding wind and rain Scotland maintained their early ascendancy. But, out of the blue, England equalised on the quarter-hour. Tom Finney, back in the English side after a lengthy spell out of favour, returned the ball to Ivor Broadis, who accelerated past Cox – Scotland's acting captain – to thump an unstoppable shot high and wide to Farm's right. Undismayed, Scotland returned to the attack, on one occasion forcing Roger Byrne to head off the line.

As England's new boys gradually grew accustomed to one another, the flow of play towards their own goal was stemmed, then reversed. The supply to McKenzie and Ormond was throttled and Finney increasingly stamped himself as the game's principal authority.

For the second half one team wore white, the other brown – several Scottish players had not changed out of their mud-soaked kit. Within six minutes Finney rebuked them for their untidiness, leaving Cox for dead and crossing for the incoming Nicholls. Farm might have claimed the cross, but he didn't and Nicholls headed England in front. The scorer formed part of the West Brom partnership with Ronnie Allen which had between them just scored over sixty goals in the season. Midway through the second period it was Allen's turn, climbing unmarked to head in England's third from Mullen's free kick.

Hampden had already been quiet for some time. Now the trickle for the exits became a stampede. The remaining twenty-odd minutes were superfluous. The *Glasgow Herald* complained of Scotland's lack of fight:

'Half-way through the second half Scotland were disheartened, disillusioned and defeated'. Those who left the ground early missed two more goals. Eight minutes from the end Finney rubbed salt into the Scottish wounds, taunting Cox from one end of the pitch to the other. He crossed at leisure on to Mullen's head for number four. It was a landmark in itself: England had never before scored four goals in Scotland. In the final seconds Ormond's swirling centre under the English crossbar saw Merrick and Byrne collide, leaving the ball to squirm gently over the line.

The Scottish verdict was depressing. The *Glasgow Herald* could 'recall no worse forward line, as a line, having worn Scottish colours ... England, a far from brilliant England, have exposed our deficiencies to the full'. The *Scotsman* resorted to poetry: 'shiver'd was fair Scotland's spear and broken was her shield'.

SCOTLAND (1)2   ENGLAND (1)4
   Brown, Byrne O.G.   Broadis, Nicholls, Allen, Mullen

SCOTLAND: G Farm (Blackpool), M Haughney (Celtic), S Cox (Rangers, capt.), R Evans (Celtic), F Brennan (Newcastle), G Aitken (Sunderland), J McKenzie (Partick), R Johnstone (Hibs), J Henderson (Portsmouth), A Brown (Blackpool), W Ormond (Hibs).

ENGLAND: Merrick, Staniforth, Byrne, Wright, Clarke, Dickinson, Finney, Broadis, Allen, Nicholls, Mullen.

World Cup Qualifying Group 3:

	P	W	D	L	F	A	PTS
ENGLAND	3	3	0	0	11	4	6
SCOTLAND	3	1	1	1	8	8	3
N.Ireland	3	1	0	2	4	7	2
Wales	3	0	1	2	5	9	1

Other group results

Wales v England	1-4
England v N. Ireland	3-1
Wales v N. Ireland	1-2

World Cup Finals – SWITZERLAND – *June/July 1954*

Scotland were now set to taste the fruits of the World Cup finals, though hardly in the most confident frame of mind. The competition would be held in the congenial surroundings of Switzerland, a suitable venue in those Cold War years in view of her long-standing political neutrality.

But if the host country was inviting, FIFA was determined to leave a bad taste with indefensible organisation. Half the sixteen finalists were seeded, two put into each group, and were then asked to play only the two non-seeds. Although the groups comprised four teams, each would play only two matches. The seeded teams avoided each other, so did the non-seeds. Never in the history of the World Cup had the status of being seeded carried greater rewards. In Group 3 the two seeded countries were defending world champions Uruguay and the immensely powerful Austrians. Theoretically making up the numbers were Scotland and Czechoslovakia, neither of whom would be given the opportunity to pick up points at the other's expense. The top two teams from each group would proceed to the quarter-finals.

Adding further to FIFA's stock of eccentricities was the official denunciation of drawn games. For no obvious reason, if the scores in group matches at the end of ninety minutes were level, a mandatory thirty-minute period of extra time would be enforced to try to break the deadlock. Extra time for knock-out matches has its logic – but not for league games.

The Scottish players could do with some winning practice before departing for Switzerland. Three games were played against feeble Scandinavian opposition: Scotland beat Norway 1-0, unconvincingly, at Hampden; were then held 1-1 in Oslo; before going on to win 2-1 against Finland in Helsinki. Nothing emerged during these matches to suggest that Scotland would do other than struggle against Uruguay and Austria.

The Scottish Football Association had recovered from its humiliation of 1950, only to try new variants in absurdity four years later. The eighteen players called upon in Oslo and Helsinki were evidently going to provide the basis of the travelling party. Twenty-two players were permitted. The SFA, however, had already announced a decision to send only *thirteen* players – thirteen players who might, perchance, have to survive five matches if Scotland were going to reach the final. They would have to play despite injury or loss of form, for only in an emergency could any replacements be flown out and inserted 'cold' into the team. The most plausible explanation for the small size of the squad was the SFA's expectation that Scotland hadn't an earthly chance of staying on in Switzerland once their two group matches were completed. The thirteen-man squad which finally departed to set up base in Lucerne on 12 June was as follows:

Name	Position	Club	Age	Caps	Goals
Fred Martin	goalkeeper	Aberdeen	25	2	–
Willie Cunningham	full-back	Preston	29	3	–
John Aird	full-back	Burnley	28	2	–
Bobby Evans*	wing-half	Celtic	26	17	–
Tommy Docherty	wing-half	Preston	26	5	–
Doug Cowie	wing-half	Dundee	28	6	–
Jimmy Davidson	centre-half	Partick	28	2	–
John McKenzie	winger	Partick	28	4	1
Willie Ormond	winger	Hibernian	27	3	1
George Hamilton*	forward	Aberdeen	36	5	4
Allan Brown	forward	Blackpool	27	12	6
Neil Mochan	forward	Celtic	27	1	–
Willie Fernie	forward	Celtic	25	1	–
		Averages	27.7	4.8	

*Players who would not appear in the 1954 World Cup finals

The other names submitted to FIFA on a stand-by basis were:

Anderson (Leicester)	Henderson (Portsmouth)
Binning (Queen of the South)	McMillan (Airdrie)
Combe (Hibernian)	Mathers (Partick)
Copland (Raith)	Wilson (Portsmouth)

The minuscule travelling party did not attract much adverse publicity at the time. After all, this was all a new experience for Scotland – even though England were sending seventeen players. More controversial was the composition of the squad. There was only one goalkeeper and no recognised centre-forward. It seemed that the selectors, chaired by Mr T Reid of Partick Thistle, had plucked a group of the most inexperienced footballers they could find and then shoved them off to do their best in the World Cup. The thirteen players had amassed only sixty-three previous caps between them. Over a quarter of these had been earned by Bobby Evans, but he was unfit. In other words, the team virtually picked itself.

What made the make-up of the squad so extraordinary was the long list of experienced names passed over. Lawrie Reilly was recovering from pleurisy and Bobby Johnstone had to pull out of the original squad through injury. But several players were axed permanently following the defeat of England, which seems to have had the same broom-sweeping effect on the Scottish selectors as Hungary's earlier demolition at Wembley had had on England's. Some indication both of the low esteem in which the World Cup was held and of the under-strength nature of the squad could be seen in the decision of Glasgow Rangers to embark on a tour of North America, thereby ruling out any Ibrox player from appearing in Switzerland. For good measure, the SFA omitted to include any training kit for their players, who had to train in whatever gear they happened to have brought with them.

Wednesday, 16 June 1954
AUSTRIA v SCOTLAND   Zurich 25,000

Scotland could hardly have found themselves in a tougher section. If anybody was going to wrest the Jules Rimet Trophy off the Uruguayans, the obvious candidates were Hungary or Austria. The Austrians had, in fact, faced the Hungarians in a warm-up match, and been a trifle unfortunate to go down 0-1. Their ominous domination of Scotland was firmly inscribed in the record books. Austria had been the first country to defeat Scotland outside Britain – in 1931 – and also the first 'foreigners' to win at Hampden – in 1950. Of five previous meetings, Scotland had yet to register a victory, and the most recent encounter – in Vienna in 1951 – had seen the Scots trounced 0-4.

Austria had only contested one previous World Cup, when their earlier great team had reached the 1934 semi-finals, there to be knocked out by the hosts and eventual winners, Italy. Some of their current players were widely known, and feared, in Britain – foremost amongst them being their roaming pivot, Ocwirk, and his fellow half-backs Happel and Hanappi. The muscular Happel, in fact, had been selected by FIFA for a 'Rest of Europe' team which had played at Wembley the previous autumn. If Scotland had a glimmer of hope it lay with a hint that the Austrians were now a few years past their best and were possibly a waning force. But few Scotsmen were likely to take comfort from that suggestion. Whichever way you looked at it, the match bore all the signs of pitching men against boys. Scotland were set fair for a good hiding.

The team which Andy Beattie was asked to field was ridiculously inexperienced when compared to their opponents. No fewer than six of the Scottish team had made their international debuts in the warm-up matches against Norway and Finland, and two more – McKenzie and Ormond – during the British qualifiers.

Beattie couldn't manufacture either instant teamwork or experience, but he could instil enthusiasm and aggression, both of which Scotland unleashed from the start. During the first, fast, fifteen minutes the Austrians were hustled out of their elegant stride, disconcerted by a collective physical challenge distinctly alien to them. During this period

B

both McKenzie and Mochan fired over – the latter from no more than six yards.

Fred Martin of Aberdeen was probably the most surprised goalkeeper in the world to find himself playing in the World Cup finals, but he was assuredly gaining confidence that his goal was not to be overrun. Scotland were giving every bit as good as they got, and when Mochan by-passed Happel only to be crunched in an Austrian sandwich he must have felt aggrieved at winning merely an indirect free kick from the Belgian referee. Even more so when, shortly afterwards, the Austrians contrived to score a classic goal. Probst slipped the ball out to Alfred Koerner, raced for the return, and shot clinically past the sprawling Martin from a sharp angle.

Such a morale-crushing goal could reasonably be expected to open the Austrian flood gates. Instead it was Scotland who came back to seize the initiative and apply mounting pressure to their opponents. Neil Mochan took the eye as he roamed across the Austrian defence in search of the tiniest gaps. At half-time Scotland could feel harshly treated by the scoreline, and afterwards set out with even greater gusto to redress it. Austria were unable to string more than a couple of passes together in the face of tigerish Scottish tackling, though three minutes into the half Schleger was put clear by Probst yet shot well wide. Overall, Martin was much less overworked than Schmied; the Scottish half-back line of Docherty, Davidson and Cowie were doing everything expected of them and more; and the Austrians were increasingly resorting to the other side of their character which regrettably comes to the fore when faced with adversity. As time went by, their concentration switched from playing the ball to playing the man.

These questionable methods seemed to be effective, for despite their second-half offensive the Scots rarely got close enough to the Austrian keeper to notice the colour of his eyes. Once Ormond's header and Mochan's drop-shot had passed over Schmied's crossbar, Scotland were left rueing their missed first-half chances. The game was in its closing moments when Mochan turned on a threepenny bit, forced his shot through a jungle of limbs and watched horror-struck as Schmied leapt across his goal to gather the ball at the second attempt right on the goal-line.

Scotland had been as close as that – not to a draw, but to forcing the lunacy of thirty minutes' extra time. The performance in defeat, however, brought widespread approval. Had Scotland won – which with hindsight did not seem in the least fanciful – it would have ranked as a momentous victory. They were now in the mood to take on Uruguay.

AUSTRIA (1)1   SCOTLAND (0)0
   Probst

AUSTRIA: Schmied, Hanappi, Happel, Barschandt, Ocwirk, Koller, R Koerner, Schleger, Dienst, Probst, A Koerner.

SCOTLAND: F Martin (Aberdeen), W Cunningham (Preston, capt.), J Aird (Burnley), T Docherty (Preston), J Davidson (Partick), D Cowie (Dundee), J McKenzie (Partick), W Fernie (Celtic), N Mochan (Celtic), A Brown (Blackpool), W Ormond (Hibs).

Saturday, 19 June 1954
URUGUAY v SCOTLAND   Basle 34,000

Uruguay. The mere name in 1954 had a debilitating effect on European ears, much as 'Brazil' would have for later generations. If it seemed that Uruguay were invincible, it was precisely because they *were* invincible. They had entered the World Cup twice before – in 1930 and 1950 – and won it both times. They had yet to sample their first defeat, and were now bidding to win the Jules Rimet Trophy for a record third time, which, if successful, would entitle them to keep it outright. What was particularly impressive about these double world champions was how they could compete, and dominate, at the highest level when forced to pick players from a country less populous than Scotland. It was food for thought.

The one aspect assumed to be in Scotland's favour was that both Uruguay's previous triumphs had been in South America. This was their first experience of the World Cup in Europe, and their first experience of playing Scotland. But from watching Uruguay dismiss Czechoslovakia 2-0 in their first match, it did not seem they were too discomfited by operating in a foreign environment.

Such were the deficiencies in organisation of the 1954 World Cup finals that Scotland were virtually out of the competition after only one match. To avoid returning home immediately after their second, Scotland obviously needed to beat the world champions – thereby joining them on two points at the end of the scheduled programme. But in the days when goal average and goal difference were futuristic concepts to FIFA, tied teams had to resort to a play-off. Assuming Austria beat Czechoslovakia to head the group, Scotland would need to defeat Uruguay *twice* in order to join Austria in the quarter-finals.

This was liable to be an insuperable obstacle for Scotland. Odds on their survival – shortened by their fighting display against Austria – lengthened again when Andy Beattie announced hours before the match that he would be relinquishing 'control' of the team at the final whistle, no matter what the outcome. It was presumed that he had had a major difference of opinion with the selectors who – once Cunningham's X-rayed shoulder had been cleared – nominated an unchanged Scottish team. It would be the first occasion in memory that Scotland had fielded an unchanged eleven for consecutive matches – but there was scarcely any alternative.

The weather in Basle gave a suitable impression of that in the Sahara. The pale blue shirts of the Uruguayans seemed fully acclimatised: the heavy shirts and boots of the Scots did not. Still, once Scotland had dutifully stood erect to verse after verse of the Uruguayan national anthem, they set about their opponents as they had left off against Austria, winning their share of the ball and making good use of it. In the early minutes both Brown and Mochan saw fleeting opportunities come their way.

Scotland, once again, tried to employ man-for-man marking. For their part, Uruguay performed the 'bolt' system of defence – as had Austria before them. The right-back played as central defender, with the left-back supporting him. The wing-halves did the job of the full-backs – marking the wingers – leaving the nominal centre-half to do, and go, as he pleased. This role – performed for Austria by Ocwirk – was allocated by Uruguay to Varella.

The system may have been the same as Austria's, but Scotland hadn't budgeted for the speed of Uruguay's wingers. In the seventeenth minute Fernie's pass went astray, Abbadie skipped contemptuously round Aird, and crossed for Uruguay's other winger, Borges, to put his team one up. Scotland still played confidently, and still found openings for themselves. But on the half-hour Miguez, Uruguay's central attacker, capitalised on Docherty's wayward pass to demonstrate how goals should be taken.

A two-goal half-time deficit did not really do justice to Scotland's positive contribution. Perhaps the kilted pipers who entertained the crowd hoped to inspire the Scots. But from the restart Scotland were in for an unpleasant surprise. Uruguay simply changed up a gear – or two. They freed themselves from the shackles of Scotland's man-for-man marking by finding space before the ball was passed, and Abbadie and Borges began to treat Aird and Cunningham like the international novices they were. The Uruguayan wingers went on the rampage. Three minutes into the half Docherty's slack pass when Scotland looked threatening again led to a goal. Borges raced past the static Cunningham, homed in on Martin, and finished off with yet another mighty shot.

To Scotland's disquiet, Uruguay now turned on the power. It was murder in the sun. Aird and Cunningham were turned inside out by wingers who went on to score seemingly as they pleased. Miguez claimed his second merely to prevent their monopolising the scorecard. The crowd cruelly whistled and hooted at the Scots' inability to resist. Ninety minutes is a long time in football. After the Austria match Scotland's international standing had probably never been higher: now, never lower. Amidst the carnage Scotland still managed to create, and miss, opportunities of their own, but the real lessons were all being learned at the other end. In truth, it could have been even worse than it was.

URUGUAY (2)7   SCOTLAND (0)0
   Borges 3, Abbadie 2, Miguez 2

URUGUAY: Maspoli, Santamaria, Martinez, Andrade, Varella, Cruz, Abbadie, Ambrois, Miguez, Schiaffino, Borges.

SCOTLAND: F Martin (Aberdeen), W Cunningham (Preston, capt.), J Aird (Burnley) T Docherty (Preston), J Davidson (Partick), D Cowie (Dundee), J McKenzie (Partick), W Fernie (Celtic), N Mochan (Celtic), A Brown (Blackpool), W Ormond (Hibs).

Not surprisingly, it was a dispirited Scotland squad which came home. The memory of one close result was obliterated by the ensuing disaster, which showed just how much Scotland had to learn in world terms. Having overcome one British team, Uruguay completed the double, knocking out England in the quarter-finals 4-2. In the semis Uruguay came unstuck (after extra time) against the Hungarians in a match which should have graced the final. Austria fell at the same stage to West Germany, who went on to inflict Hungary's first defeat in over thirty matches in the final. Austria found partial compensation in the third/fourth place play-off. There they met Uruguay in the match they were not asked to play in Group 3. It was the Austrians, somewhat unexpectedly, who won 3-1.

Group 3 – final positions

	P	W	D	L	F	A	PTS
URUGUAY	2	2	0	0	9	0	4
AUSTRIA	2	2	0	0	6	0	4
Czechoslovakia	2	0	0	2	0	7	0
Scotland	2	0	0	2	0	8	0

Scotland appearances and goal-scorers:
World Cup qualifying rounds and final competition 1954

	A	G		A	G
Brown A	4	2	Johnstone R	2	1
Cowie D	4	–	Martin F	2	–
McKenzie J	4	–	Mochan N	2	–
Cox S*	3	–	Young G*	2	–
Evans R*	3	–	Aitken G*	1	–
Farm G	3	–	Fleming C	1	2
Ormond W	3	–	Haughney M	1	–
Aird J	2	–	Liddell W*	1	–
Brennan F	2	–	McPhail J*	1	–
Cunningham W	2	–	Reilly L*	1	1
Davidson J	2	–	Telfer W	1	–
Docherty T	2	–	Waddell W*	1	–
Fernie W	2	–	Watson J	1	–
Henderson J	2	1	own-goals		1
			caps	55	8 goals

27 players

Scottish League	35
English League	20
	55

*Appeared in 1950 World Cup

Tommy Docherty was a member of Scotland's World Cup squad in both 1954 and 1958. He was later to become Scotland team manager in 1971.

CHAPTER 3

The 1958 World Cup

It was with the 1958 World Cup, held in Sweden, that the competition finally came of age. Previous tournaments had all been disfigured by the non-participation – for whatever reason – of some of the world's strongest footballing nations. These handicaps did not mar the 1958 finals – nor any of those thereafter.

Improved reorganisation, it must be said, was also responsible for scrapping the system of patronage which entitled British clubs to one-eighth of the sixteen final places available. Although there existed an argument based on sentiment – why should the founding fathers of soccer have to fight each other to qualify? – there were less flattering realities to be considered. Nothing had happened in the World Cups of 1950 and 1954 to suggest that Britain *deserved* two teams in the finals. And for this unflattering reappraisal of British football Scotland were not exactly without blame – as instanced by their insensitive non-attendance in Brazil, followed by the debacle against Uruguay.

Not that the SFA mourned the passing of the British qualifying zone. They had never approved of interference in the Home Internationals in this fashion. From now on the four British teams would take their chances, being thrown into the wider European lottery. The end result might see all four make the trip to Sweden – or maybe none at all. When the draw was announced, Scotland found themselves grouped with Spain and Switzerland, with only one team to qualify.

Scotland's international progress since the 1954 World Cup was, at best, cause for concern. Sixteen internationals were played prior to the 1958 qualifiers – only six won. The only notable scalp taken was that of deteriorating Austria, for whom defeat in Switzerland was handsomely avenged 4-1 in Vienna. Against this stood some significant defeats: worst of them being a 7-2 hiding by England. Hungary recorded two victories over Scotland in the space of six months, including an impressive 4-2 win at Hampden. In Scotland's final international before World Cup commitments resumed they went down 1-2 at Wembley.

The Qualifying Rounds

Wednesday, 8 May 1957
SCOTLAND v SPAIN   Hampden 89,000

In the mid and late 'fifties every British fan was familiar with Spanish football, though Spain's great reputation at that time lay less with her international team than with the aura which surrounded her leading club sides – Barcelona and, above all, Real Madrid. Real had won the first ever European Cup, in 1956, and had just eliminated Manchester United from the semi-finals in 1957. Centre-forward di Stefano and outside-left Gento were two of the greatest names in club, Spanish, and European football (di Stefano, an Argentine by birth, was eligible – according to FIFA statutes at the time – to play for the country in which he resided). As for Barcelona, they were already en route to winning the first European Fairs Cup competition. Five of the Spanish side at Hampden were drawn from Barcelona, among them goalkeeper Ramallets – still around after frustrating England in Brazil in 1950 – and Hungarian-born inside-forward Kubala.

Strange to say, Spain had no pedigree in the World Cup. They had finished fourth in 1950, having disposed of England, but had failed to qualify in 1954. They had never before faced Scotland, but – in what was likely to be a critical setback – had already been held 2-2 in Madrid by the third team in the group, Switzerland. Notwithstanding, Spain were still justifiable favourites to qualify.

For Scotland, three years had elapsed since the nightmare of Uruguay. Naturally, the present side was different in almost every respect. Only Tommy Docherty of the current team had played in the 1954 World Cup finals, though 'Corky' Young had returned to lend his massive experience to the Scottish defence, having switched in 1955 from right-back to centre-half. He had already announced his retirement from international football with effect from the return match in Spain later in the month. This was to be his Hampden swan-song, eleven years after he had first pulled on the navy shirt of Scotland.

The regular goalkeeper since 1955 was Liverpool's Tommy Younger, now winning his thirteenth consecutive cap. All eyes, however, were on the forward line where Blackpool's Jackie Mudie switched from inside-forward to centre-forward. Only John Charles had scored more English First Division goals the previous season. What Mudie lacked in physique would hopefully be compensated for by the inclusion alongside him of Rangers' burly Sam Baird. Clearly the selectors for once were not being panicked into mass changes: nine of the side beaten at Wembley in April retained their places. One of the unfortunate two was Lawrie Reilly, who never recaptured his place and thereby missed by one game the distinction of appearing in three World Cups.

Twenty-four hours of rain had turned Hampden into a habitat for ducks, not the footballers of sunny Spain. Even in aquatic conditions nothing could detract from the skills of Gento, out on the left touchline – nothing, that is, until the inexperienced Caldow slowly but surely took his measure. The first goal, midway through the half, fell to Scotland. Shots in rapid succession by Sam Baird and Gordon Smith had produced a corner, which Mudie headed first on to the crossbar before wisely aiming the rebound beneath it.

Scottish joy was soon replaced by much shaking of heads. Gonzales' inconsequential pass was followed by Kubala's inconsequential shot and Younger's inconsequential attempt to save. 1-1. Play grew fiercer by the minute. Gento was felled inside the box by Young, who had no chance of winning the ball. No penalty. Then an indirect free kick to Scotland inside the Spanish penalty area needed three attempts before it was satisfactorily taken, Tommy Ring thumping the ball over the bar. With four first-half minutes remaining Scotland regained the lead. Ring set off in pursuit of Docherty's pass and was impeded by Olivilla. Hewie's penalty seemed to pass straight through Ramallets' body.

Either side of the interval play became more appropriate to the proceedings in a bull-ring, none of which prevented Mudie, immediately upon the resumption, heading against the bar. Spain desperately sought a second equaliser, which they secured after fifty minutes. A delightful backheel by di Stefano and shot from Gento elicited a fine save from Younger – but Suarez nipped in to poach the rebound.

Now Scotland surged forward with the Hampden roar pounding in their ears. On the left Ring teased and tantalised Olivilla. With twenty minutes to play wee Bobby Collins slipped the ball through the slime to Mudie who blasted home from the edge of the box. Ramallets stood stationary as if auditioning for Madame Tussaud's. Scotland had their tails up now, and eleven minutes from time scored the best goal of the match – unblemished in manufacture or execution. McColl put Collins clear on the right, a sweeping series of passes found Mudie, who casually and contemptuously stuck the ball away for his hat-trick. It was a goal of genuine quality scored by a fine-looking team.

SCOTLAND (2)4   SPAIN (1)2
    Mudie 3, Hewie (pen)   Kubala, Suarez

SCOTLAND: T Younger (Liverpool), E Caldow (Rangers), J Hewie (Charlton), I McColl (Rangers), G Young (Rangers, capt.), T Docherty (Preston), G Smith (Hibs), R Collins (Celtic), J Mudie (Blackpool), S Baird (Rangers), T Ring (Clyde).

SPAIN: Ramallets, Olivilla, Garay, Verges, Campanal, Zarraga, Gonzales, Kubala, di Stefano, Suarez, Gento.

Sunday, 19 May 1957
SWITZERLAND v SCOTLAND   Basle 49,000

In the World Cups of the 'fifties and 'sixties competing nations saw nothing wrong with cramming in fixtures in as short a period as possible. Today, it is uncommon to find a country playing two World Cup qualifiers inside a month. In 1957 Scotland completed their first three in the space of nineteen days. They set off fresh from their sparkling Hampden victory on a week's tour of the Continent. World Cup eliminators would be contested in Basle and Madrid, with a friendly in West Germany in between.

Switzerland had already taken a point off Spain, who were now in desperate straits following the loss of two more at Hampden. A Scottish win in Basle would put Scotland three points out in front, with one foot propping open the door to Sweden. Whether or not they achieved this victory depended in large measure on the mood of their hosts, historically – like their Central European neighbours Austria and Hungary – one of the most fluctuating of continental sides. At their best the Swiss were acclaimed tactical innovators: at their worst – not surprising with part-timers – one of Europe's weaker units.

When Tommy Docherty stepped out into the St Jakob's Stadium, he could have been forgiven haunting memories of the last time he did so. But now the opponents were Switzerland, not Uruguay; and the weather filthy, not scorching. Hopefully, Docherty was not too sensitive about the colours he was wearing, for it appeared that the Scotland team were resorting to optical skullduggery. The match was being transmitted on Eurovision (the second half live to Scotland), and in those days of black and white pictures the Swiss strip of red and white was not easily distinguishable from the Scots' blue and white. Switzerland requested that Scotland change their shorts, but no others were available. The hosts then provided a set of their own – bright orange – not the most agreeable complement to navy shirts and scarlet socks!

There had been no need, or cause, to make changes to the Scotland eleven, but if the players had hopes of providing football as dazzling as their appearance, the Swiss had other ideas. Scotland were a goal behind after just twelve minutes. Caldow had tried to bring it about earlier, but his two suicidal back-passes had been retrieved. Now, Vonlanthen despatched the ball to Meier, whose fast, low, return pass was thrashed past Younger from fifteen yards.

The goal was no more than Switzerland deserved. The home side did not appear inconvenienced by the chilly, heavy atmosphere or the sodden pitch, and for most of the opening half were in unquestioned control of the match. Meier, Ballaman and Schneiter slowed the pace of the game to their wishes, assisted by the sight of their opponents regularly being dumped on their backsides from unsure footing, and encouraged by Younger fumbling almost everything that came his way. Docherty stood out as the one Scot most capable of resisting the home side.

The change in Scotland's fortunes began twelve minutes from half-time. It owed everything to a corner awarded in error and Mudie's massive header which flashed past the groping Parlier. It was as well that the Scottish viewing public had not been privy to the first-half performance, for they would not have been comforted. The second period was little better, except that the Swiss had now run out of steam – the clinging pitch having its effects on part-time legs. Even so, the Scottish attack – Mudie excepted – was singularly bereft of penetration. The team was left to rejoice at one flash of inspiration nineteen minutes from time. Collins dived to meet Smith's corner and flicked the ball beyond Parlier to wedge in the far stanchion.

There was still time for Collins' defenders to attempt hara-kiri, as when McColl's back-pass was clutched by Younger down at the far post with inches to spare. Switzerland couldn't pull the game back, fluffing the chances which came their way. With the final whistle Scotland possessed a three-point lead at the halfway stage in their group, but the Scottish press were not in the mood for congratulations: 'Some Scottish players probably realised that they will never again play so badly and be on a winning side'.

SWITZERLAND (1)1   SCOTLAND (1)2
    Vonlanthen   Mudie, Collins

SWITZERLAND: Parlier, Kernen, Koch, Grobety, Frosio, Schneiter, Antenen, Ballaman, Vonlanthen, Meier, Riva.

SCOTLAND: T Younger (Liverpool), E Caldow (Rangers), J Hewie (Charlton), I McColl (Rangers), G Young (Rangers, capt.), T Docherty (Preston), G Smith (Hibs), R Collins (Celtic), J Mudie (Blackpool), S Baird (Rangers), T Ring (Clyde).

Sunday, 26 May 1957
SPAIN v SCOTLAND   Madrid 90,000

From Basle the Scottish party made the short journey to Stuttgart where they produced one of the finest results in their history, winning 3-1 against the reigning world champions West Germany. With two continental victories achieved in quick succession – whatever the contrast in the performances – it was an understandably buoyant Scottish squad which descended on Madrid.

As their group record showed, Scotland were so near to qualifying – yet so far.

	P	W	D	L	F	A	PTS
Scotland	2	2	0	0	6	3	4
Switzerland	2	0	1	1	3	4	1
Spain	2	0	1	1	4	6	1

Two points from their final two matches would guarantee a place in Sweden, and a draw now would eliminate Spain. To qualify themselves Spain needed to beat Scotland, and then pray that Switzerland avoided defeat at Hampden before entertaining Spain for the final match of the group.

As the Scottish party settled down in a mountain retreat at Escorial, twenty miles outside Madrid, there were just a couple of team positions to be sorted out. George Young had hoped to bow out of international football in the Chamartin Stadium, but he had been omitted in favour of Bobby Evans in Stuttgart, and now Evans retained his place amid much bickering and recriminations. The only other change from Basle was at right-half where Hearts' workhorse Dave Mackay made his debut in circumstances as testing as he could find anywhere in the world. For their part, Spain partially restructured the defence beaten four times at Hampden. It was the start of a passionate week for the inhabitants of the Spanish capital. Four days later the city would host the second European Cup Final (and would celebrate the trophy's retention by Real Madrid).

It may have been over-confidence (having beaten the World Cup holders, why worry about Spain?), but from the kick-off there was only one side ever likely to win, and that side wasn't Scotland. It seemed, once again, that putting on two impressive performances in a row was beyond them. Even the slippery pitch was in their favour: Scotland were the most unpopular of visitors, for wherever they played of late they brought torrential rain with them. Once play began, the ball was propelled towards

Younger as if it contained iron filings and his goal magnets. Di Stefano was his usual immaculate self, and Kubala – quiet at Hampden – turned on his skills with a vengeance.

During the opening spell only Younger prevented a rout, but he was beaten after thirteen minutes by a goal of brilliance – the move culminating in Mateos' unstoppable shot. Perversely, the minutes that followed were the only ones throughout the match in which Scotland made any impact. Had Mudie's looping header finished in the net, rather than produced a flying save from Ramallets, who knows what the outcome might have been? The question was purely academic, for shortly afterwards Kubala ran on to a through pass to put the outcome beyond Scotland's reach.

From then on it was a matter of Scotland saving not the game, but their dignity. The Chamartin Stadium's seats, banked high above the pitch, were filled with frenzied Spaniards morbidly ecstatic at the public execution being played out before their eyes. Captain Docherty did his best to close ranks, Younger was on top of his game, but these were but minor inconveniences to Spain's unstoppable momentum. Twelve minutes into the second half a goalmouth scramble led to Basora thundering the loose ball past Younger.

The match had drifted beyond Scotland long before then. Mackay was out of his depth, Garay patrolled Mudie as a lion might manoeuvre a wounded zebra, Ring was totally eclipsed by Segarra, and Gordon Smith would never play for his country again. The one moment of Scottish heat was generated by Baird, who retaliated after Gensana's foul. The pair swung insults, fists and boots until separated by English referee Mr R Leafe, who took Baird's name.

Eleven minutes from the end of Scotland's evening of embarrassment, Smith pulled a goal back with a header from Ring's cross. This act of effrontery to Spanish superiority was later cancelled out by Basora taking a flying hack at the ball and enjoying the sight of it rolling obligingly past Younger. The goalkeeper was due his one moment of frailty: his teammates had been specialising in them. Over ninety minutes Scotland had got off lightly, and this realisation was not lost on the *Scotsman*: 'Spain played with Scotland as a cat would a mouse, to win much more convincingly than the margin would indicate'.

SPAIN (2)4   SCOTLAND (0)1
  Mateos, Kubala, Basora 2   Smith

SPAIN: Ramallets, Quincoces, Segarra, Gensana, Garay, Verges, Basora, Kubala, di Stefano, Mateos, Gento.

SCOTLAND: T Younger (Liverpool), E Caldow (Rangers), J Hewie (Charlton), D Mackay (Hearts), R Evans (Celtic), T Docherty (Preston, capt.), G Smith (Hibs), R Collins (Celtic), J Mudie (Blackpool), S Baird (Rangers), T Ring (Clyde).

Wednesday, 6 November 1957
SCOTLAND v SWITZERLAND   Hampden 57,000

Scotland were probably glad of a six-month respite before tackling their last, and decisive, World Cup qualifier. The situation was straightforward. If Scotland beat the Swiss they would head the group. If the game was drawn, but Spain won in Switzerland later in the month, a play-off would be required on neutral territory. After the Madrid experience even the most patriotic Scot did not relish the prospect of a third meeting with Spain. As for Switzerland, if they could beat the Scots and Spanish in turn, it would be they who went to Sweden. In short, both Scotland and their opponents desperately needed to win, and that simple fact was bound to turn the game into a cracker.

The Scots may have been unaware of it, and in any case they wouldn't have given a damn, but they were probably the only nation on earth rooting for a Scottish victory. Real Madrid's retention of the European Cup meant they were fast becoming the most talked about and romanticised of European club sides. With the greatest footballing show on earth about to take place, neutral football lovers the world over were hoping that di Stefano and Gento – not to mention Kubala, Suarez and others – would be there where they belonged, onstage at the World Cup finals.

There were four changes to the Scottish team. The previous month they had achieved the dreariest of draws in Belfast, which did not augur well for Hampden. Falkirk's Alec Parker came in to partner Caldow at full-back. The inconsistency of Willie Fernie was preferred to the inexperience of Dave Mackay. Fernie could seemingly play in any position he chose. His previous caps had been at inside-forward or out on the wing: now his role was as wing-half. Alec Scott of Rangers returned in place of the struggling Gordon Smith. Archie Robertson stood in for Sam Baird, giving the left side of attack an all-Clyde look. Switzerland, surprisingly, lined up with nine of the side which had fallen away in Basle. It might have been eight, thanks to confused travel arrangements which nearly left key forward Vonlanthen – who played in the Italian league – stranded.

If the attacking nature of the match was predictable, the all-round impressiveness of the Swiss was not. They had looked skilful, if short on stamina, in Basle. Clad in all-orange, they looked no less adroit at Hampden. Ballaman was in a class by himself, the two wingers each had the beating of their respective full-backs, and the side's creative play was fluid and penetrating. None the less, it was Scotland who opened the scoring on twenty-nine minutes. For once, the Swiss defence was exposed as Docherty left Robertson free to side-foot the ball under Parlier's dive.

Switzerland did not have long to ruminate on their disappointment. Docherty's passing was again a critical factor, only this time for the wrong reason. Riva cut out a slackly-played ball and accelerated goalwards. He evaded one tackle on merit, another when Evans stumbled, but retained his composure to equalise.

From the Swiss perspective it was unfortunate their defence was occasionally brittle. It was spreadeagled when, seven minutes into the second half, Fernie – the most influential Scot on view – drilled in a fast, low centre swept home by Mudie. On the experience of Basle, it might have been expected that Switzerland would now capitulate. Not a bit of it. Mudie's goal signalled a prolonged Swiss offensive of such intensity that the *Glasgow Herald* was moved to write: 'Midway in the second half Switzerland had Scotland in a state of disintegration, the defence panic-stricken, and the forwards disillusioned and devoid of ideas'.

The outcome of the match turned on a hotly-debated spell of end-to-end activity. The Swiss had reduced the home defence to rubble with their repeated interchanging of positions. Chiesa surged past Docherty and Evans, Younger took the venom out of the shot, and Parker raced back to clear off the line. With Hampden still agog with relief, Scotland swept upfield. The Swiss had anticipated Collins' through pass and moved out en bloc. Scott was so palpably offside that when the ball was played he hesitated himself, and only put the ball into the net as a gesture – assuming play would be brought back.

When the referee – Mr Leafe of England, who had officiated during Scotland's defeat in Madrid – allowed the goal to stand Switzerland were justifiably incensed. Mr Leafe had seemingly eliminated Switzerland from the World Cup – but they weren't out yet. With ten minutes left Riva nodded down a corner which Younger might have claimed and Vonlanthen lashed the ball inside a post. Hampden then held its breath as Chiesa broke clear yet again, but was thwarted by Parker's desperate tackle. At the end officials of both sides were in agreement – Switzerland had been desperately unfortunate – but they were out, and Scotland were through.

SCOTLAND (1)3	SWITZERLAND (1)2
Robertson, Mudie, Scott	Riva, Vonlanthen

SCOTLAND: T Younger (Liverpool), A Parker (Falkirk), E Caldow (Rangers), W Fernie (Celtic), R Evans (Celtic), T Docherty (Preston, capt.), A Scott (Rangers), R Collins (Celtic), J Mudie (Blackpool), A Robertson (Clyde), T Ring (Clyde).

SWITZERLAND: Parlier, Kernen, Morf, Grobety, Koch, Schneiter, Chiesa, Ballaman, Meier, Vonlanthen, Riva.

World Cup Qualifying Group 9:

	P	W	D	L	F	A	PTS
SCOTLAND	4	3	0	1	10	9	6
Spain	4	2	1	1	12	8	5
Switzerland	4	0	1	3	6	11	1

Other group results

Spain v Switzerland	2-2
Switzerland v Spain	1-4

World Cup Finals – SWEDEN – June 1958

So Scotland had qualified – none too convincingly, to be sure – but qualified none the less. Yet Scotland's was part of a wider British assault on Sweden. If the detractors of the British game hoped that putting an end to the British qualifying zone would see fewer than two representatives from these islands competing in Sweden, they were in for a shock. England had made sure of their place in May 1957 – at the expense of Denmark and the Republic of Ireland. Following Scotland's success it was Northern Ireland's turn, remarkably defeating Italy in Belfast in January 1958 to head their own group and register as the third British team in Sweden. Wales had not been so fortunate – Czechoslovakia pushing them into second place – but in the space of a climactic couple of days in early February 1958 the fortunes of all four countries were turned topsy-turvy.

Politics was, as usual, interfering with sport somewhere or other. In the Asia-Africa zone of the World Cup qualifying campaign no country would agree to play Israel. FIFA would not permit Israel to appear in Sweden, however, without first beating somebody to get there. In the search for suitable opponents all the runners-up in the European sections were involved in a lottery for the right to meet Israel. Wales' name was drawn. Her footballers won 2-0 in Tel Aviv, and by the same score in Cardiff on 5 February 1958, so that the unlikely name of Wales was pencilled in as the Asian-African representatives in Sweden. This meant that a quarter of the places available were filled by British teams, an achievement which justifiably delighted our soccer coaches and administrators. The whole of Britain was excited at the prospects ahead, but the day after Wales' qualification disaster struck.

The Munich air-crash of 6 February 1958 did more than destroy Manchester United's outstanding young team. It claimed the lives of four England players and ended the career of Northern Ireland's centre-half Jackie Blanchflower. Wales and Scotland lost no players, but were disrupted at managerial level. Jimmy Murphy, who doubled as Manchester United's second-in-command and Welsh team manager, had to devote the bulk of his energies to Old Trafford, inevitably to the detriment of Wales. The club's manager, Matt Busby, had a month earlier agreed to take charge of the Scotland squad in Sweden. Alas, his injuries proved too severe.

Scottish pride had taken a battering following the events of 1950 and 1954. Even so, Scotland had prepared for the Swedish tournament with no improvement in thoroughness or professionalism. Since 1954 team selection – especially of the forward line – had been subject to an unending series of musical chairs. Now, as the finals approached, no successor to Matt Busby was appointed. This meant that Scotland participated as the only team without a manager in Sweden, a situation that was unlikely to instil confidence.

Nor was a 4-0 trouncing at Hampden by a hastily reassembled, post-Munich England team. Much of the blame was heaped on skipper Tommy Docherty, who was dropped for the duration of the World Cup. In their final preparations, having belatedly decided to adopt a short-passing style throughout the forthcoming tournament, Scotland drew with post-Revolution Hungary at Hampden, before moving on to Poland a week before the gloves came off. This time Scotland scraped through 2-1, but it was scarcely a performance to remember.

Geographical seeding would operate for the 1958 World Cup finals, a product of the sixteen finalists being neatly arranged into four regions: Britain, Western Europe, Eastern Europe, and South and Central America. One country from each region would appear in each pool. In Switzerland, Scotland had found themselves in a powerful section. They could not grumble this time, being included with Yugoslavia, Paraguay and France – none of whom had any kind of tradition in the World Cup, none of whom had a habit of beating Scotland, and none of whom seemed likely to prevent Scotland's progress to the quarter-finals. The crazy experiment in 1954 – of playing only two group matches – was thankfully abandoned. Scotland would meet all three of their rivals, doubtless preferring them to England's – Brazil, the Soviet Union and Austria.

The Scotland squad, mercifully raised to the permitted twenty-two, was:

Name	Position	Club	Age	Caps	Goals
Tommy Younger	goalkeeper	Liverpool	28	21	–
Bill Brown	goalkeeper	Dundee	26	–	–
Eric Caldow	full-back	Rangers	24	10	–
Alec Parker	full-back	Everton	22	14	–
John Hewie	full-back	Charlton	29	11	1
Harry Haddock*	full-back	Clyde	32	6	–
Eddie Turnbull	wing-half	Hibernian	35	5	–
Tommy Docherty*	wing-half	Preston	30	22	1
Ian McColl*	wing-half	Rangers	31	14	–
Doug Cowie	wing-half	Dundee	32	18	–
Dave Mackay	wing-half	Hearts	23	1	–
Bobby Evans	centre-half	Celtic	30	34	–
Graham Leggat	winger	Aberdeen	24	5	2
Tommy Ewing*	winger	Partick	21	2	–
Alec Scott*	winger	Rangers	21	5	2
Stuart Imlach	winger	Nottingham Forest	26	2	–
Archie Robertson	inside-forward	Clyde	28	4	2
Sam Baird*	inside-forward	Rangers	28	7	1
Jimmy Murray	inside-forward	Hearts	25	3	–
Bobby Collins	inside-forward	Celtic	27	19	6
Johnny Coyle*	inside-forward	Clyde	27	–	–
Jackie Mudie	centre-forward	Blackpool	28	14	8
		Averages	27.1	9.9	

*Players who would not appear in the 1958 World Cup finals

The managerless Scottish party was led by trainer Dawson Walker. Though fully-manned it did contain some unusual features. Tommy Younger was announced as captain, the first goalkeeper to skipper Scotland since Third Lanark's Brownlie held that honour at the time of the First World War. Bobby Evans was listed as the only centre-half, and Jackie Mudie, despite his lack of inches and deep-lying mode of play, the only centre-forward. Scotland were evidently expecting to rely heavily on the three of them.

The Scottish selectors' frequent chopping and changing of the side over the years was once again reflected in the remarkably low average number of caps per man – less than ten. This figure was even lower than that for the England squad, which had had to be completely rebuilt following the Munich air-crash.

Sunday, 8 June 1958
YUGOSLAVIA v SCOTLAND   Vasteraas 9,500

The Scottish party set up residence in Eskiltuna, within easy access of their three World Cup venues in eastern Sweden. The team selected to play Yugoslavia was identical to that which had just faced Hungary and Poland, and contained five players unused in the qualifying rounds. Former captain Tommy Docherty, after a splendid run, had lost his edge. The other wing-halves – McColl, Mackay and Fernie – were also left out, so that both the No 4 and No 6 shirts had found replacements. Eddie Turnbull was enjoying a remarkable recall to international honours eight years after his previous cap, and ten years after his first. His fellow wing-half was the experienced campaigner from 1954, Dundee's Doug Cowie. A fresh pair of wingers had been located in Aberdeen's Graham Leggat and Nottingham Forest's diminutive Stuart Imlach. It was hoped that both would increase the ammunition to Mudie, who had had such an excellent series in the qualifiers. Partnering non-stop Bobby Collins at inside-forward was the Hearts' player Jimmy Murray. Leggat, Imlach and Murray had all won their first caps during the previous two months.

Scotland could take encouragement from their past record against Yugoslavia. The countries had met twice in recent years, drawing 2-2 in Belgrade in 1955, Scotland winning 2-0 at Hampden a year later. Whether Yugoslavia's recent 5-0 crushing of England said more about Yugoslavia or their opponents remained to be seen, although Yugoslavia now fielded ten of that side. The indications were that their national eleven were less formidable than their leading club, Red Star Belgrade, who had reached the semi-final of the European Cup in 1957 and the quarter-final (whence knocked out by Manchester United) in 1958. Neither Yugoslavia nor Scotland could claim to be in form: Yugoslavia had won only four of their last nine matches; Scotland, only two from seven. Nevertheless, Yugoslavia looked to be the strongest of Scotland's opponents. A win here – or even a draw – was not going to harm Scotland's prospects.

In the event it was a fast, if undistinguished, match of the kind which commentators are apt to say was 'of two halves'. Yugoslavia started off treating Scotland as they had England (Scotland were wearing England's white shirts) and were ahead after just six minutes. Veselinovic had already broken through, to shoot apologetically, when he bamboozled Cowie on the right, presenting Petakovic with time and space. Younger appeared to be slow reacting to the shot, and Caldow, lunging back, only narrowly failed to clear.

Yugoslavia seemed entirely in control. Caldow belted a shot from Milutinovic off the line, and the woodwork also came to Scotland's rescue. Scotland could be grateful that their opponents' finishing did not seem to match their build-up, but they were also being let down by their new boys. Imlach, Leggat and Murray were struggling to make their presence felt, though Imlach did have the excuse of a painful blow on the knee sustained in the first minute. Scotland managed only two real chances before the interval: Murray, put clear, shot wide; and Collins intercepted a back-pass. As he lunged for the decisive touch he could only prod the ball against the advancing Beara.

Perhaps some scathing insults were exchanged in the Scotland dressing room during the break. The second half saw much greater physical resolve. Within six minutes the game had been thrown open. Petakovic's shot came back off Younger's post, and taking advantage of that let-off Scotland equalised. Caldow's free kick to Turnbull was directed back to the far post. Beara and Krstic confused one another and Murray headed through the keeper's hands.

Now Yugoslavia's earlier skills were flattering to deceive. Scotland were in territorial command of the game till the end. The admirable Evans policed one end, while at the other Mudie and Collins inflicted repeated wounds on a defence marshalled by the evergreen Zebec, who had played (at outside-left) for the Rest of Europe against Britain as long ago as 1946. The perky Yugoslav wing-half, Boskov, so prominent in the first half, was outshone by Turnbull in the second.

As Yugoslavia watched the initiative slipping from them the match became no spectacle for the squeamish. Collins would afterwards complain of a couple of teeth loosened by Sekularac, and some other 'tackles' were not designed to take prisoners. Yet for all the Scottish improvement it was Yugoslavia who came nearest to scoring the winning goal: Veselinovic's thunderous drive left a dent in an upright, and his delicate lob cleared Younger – but also his crossbar. Caldow earned his wages when his despairing lunge took the ball off Milutinovic's toe in shooting stride.

Scotland were unable to translate their second-half possession into clear chances. The nearest they came was when Beara, under pressure from

Mudie, dropped a cross. The ball bounced into the net but the Swiss referee dubiously penalised Mudie for a foul.

Scotland had avoided defeat in the World Cup finals for the first time, with the promise of even better things to come.

YUGOSLAVIA (1)1   SCOTLAND (0)1
    Petakovic   Murray

YUGOSLAVIA: Beara, Sijakovic, Crnkovic, Krstic, Zebec, Boskov, Petakovic, Veselinovic, Milutinovic, Sekularac, Rajkov.

SCOTLAND: T Younger (Liverpool, capt.), E Caldow (Rangers), J Hewie (Charlton), E Turnbull (Hibs), R Evans (Celtic), D Cowie (Dundee), G Leggat (Aberdeen), J Murray (Hearts), J Mudie (Blackpool), R Collins (Celtic), S Imlach (Nott'm F).

Wednesday, 11 June 1958
PARAGUAY v SCOTLAND   Norrkoping 12,000

Paraguay were the unknown quantity in Group 2. They were certainly unknown as far as Scotland were concerned. On the one hand, any country of one and a half million people which could deprive Uruguay of a place in the World Cup finals had to be taken seriously. On the other, Paraguay had just been walloped 7-3 by France. (Strangely, they had at one stage led 3-2: perhaps the northern air had sapped their stamina.) If Scotland could defeat Paraguay, which the Scottish press insisted was a formality, there was a healthy chance of making the quarter-finals for the first time.

The selectors, chaired by Mr Waters of St Mirren, made three changes necessitated by injury. Imlach's knee was still swollen, so in came the brilliant-or-awful individualist Willie Fernie for his second World Cup finals. At full-back, Alec Parker (now of Everton) replaced John Hewie, while goal-scoring hero Jimmy Murray had his place taken by Archie Robertson.

It was a sunny evening in Norrkoping, reminding the Paraguayans of home. They lined up – a short, stocky set of players – in broad-striped shirts, with Scotland permitted to return to their traditional navy. If Scotland, eyeing the French result, expected Paraguay to serve as a punchbag they were given notice of contrary intent as early as the third minute. Mudie had already shot narrowly wide when Paraguay carved through the Scottish defence. Parker failed to clear and allowed Aguero a shot which seemed to pass through the advancing Younger's legs. For the second time, Scotland would need to force their way back into a match having lost an early goal.

The first quarter of the game proved embarrassing. Scotland were quite unprepared for the South Americans' fleetness of foot and wholehearted – sometimes excessive – determination. The Scottish half-back line, composed entirely of over-thirties, had not been exposed by Yugoslavia's slower style. But their current opponents, with an average age of only twenty-three, were treating them with the disrespect which youthful hooligans might employ on ageing school janitors.

Encouragingly, Paraguay looked anything but secure at the back. Mudie and Collins put in testing shots, and Echague blocked Robertson's mis-hit effort on the goal-line. At last, midway through the first half, Scotland equalised when Leggat's angled drive was parried by a flashing limb, only to rebound to the lurking Mudie. Collins then nearly put Scotland in front, but shot too high.

Back on terms, the last thing Scotland needed was to lose another goal before half-time. Younger's save from Romero seemed to have averted that fate, but with a minute to go Paraguay were back in front, following another burst of rapid man-to-man passing. Parker's feeble challenge did not impede Aguero, who imitated his first goal when cutting in to score his second. Younger half-saved, but had to watch helplessly as the ball squeezed inside a post. The match was not yet semi-completed, but Younger and Parker must have known it was not their day.

From Paraguay's point of view, they now had only to hold out for a further forty-five minutes to record a notable victory. They were not too fussy how they achieved this. Immediately, Lezcano scythed down danger-man Mudie. The Blackpool forward was taken from the field for repairs and was never the same threat when he returned. Shots passed over at either end, but the fists were more accurate when Evans and Aguero took a mutual dislike. With Fernie and Robertson ill-equipped for a physical battle, and Mudie half-crippled, it was difficult to anticipate a second Scottish equaliser. Leggat, playing with an as-yet-undiagnosed broken wrist, came nearest when shooting into the side-netting.

With fifteen minutes left, Paraguay increased their lead. Younger claimed a high ball, lost it, and Paraguay's outstanding player – Parodi – jubilantly scored. Younger hung his head, then lifted it again as, within a minute, Collins leant into a twenty-yard drive which beat Aguila's right hand. 3-2. As the statutory ninety minutes expired Scotland thought they'd found an equaliser, but Mudie and Fernie had point-blank shots charged down with the goalkeeper sprawled on the floor and the goal gaping.

Afterwards the blame was heaped on Younger and Parker. Someone might have mentioned the Paraguayans' speed.

PARAGUAY (2)3   SCOTLAND (1)2
     Aguero 2, Parodi   Mudie, Collins

PARAGUAY: Aguila, Arevalo, Echague, Villalba, Lezcano, Achucarro, Aguero, Parodi, Romero, Re, Amarilla.

SCOTLAND: T Younger (Liverpool, capt.), A Parker (Everton), E Caldow (Rangers), E Turnbull (Hibs), R Evans (Celtic), D Cowie (Dundee), G Leggat (Aberdeen), R Collins (Celtic), J Mudie (Blackpool), A Robertson (Clyde), W Fernie (Celtic).

Sunday, 15 June 1958
FRANCE v SCOTLAND   Orebro 13,500

While Scotland were eating humble pie against Paraguay, Yugoslavia were going to the top of Group 2 – a late goal defeating France 3-2. With one match to play the group looked like this:

	P	W	D	L	F	A	PTS
Yugoslavia	2	1	1	0	4	3	3
France	2	1	0	1	9	6	2
Paraguay	2	1	0	1	6	9	2
Scotland	2	0	1	1	3	4	1

To reach the quarter-finals Scotland had a tough schedule. They needed to beat France, but that would only give them the right to meet either Yugoslavia or Paraguay for a second time, in a play-off decider. For their part, France could not afford to play for a draw for fear of having to partake in a play-off themselves. The prospect of two attacking teams promised an exciting match.

Notwithstanding France's later achievements in Sweden they went into the competition as one of its genuine no-hopers. They had never made any impact in past World Cups, and their pre-Sweden form was so wretched that the win over Paraguay was their first victory of any kind for many months. Further, France's all-time record against Scotland was abysmal, the Scots claiming five wins out of six.

Yet as the Scottish players pondered their own inability to *create* seven chances against Paraguay, let alone *take* seven, they might have had an insight into France's success. The French might not appear to have much of a team, but they did have some exceptional players – especially in attack. Raymond Kopa played in the same Real Madrid forward line as di Stefano and Gento, and had helped the Spanish club to win the European Cup for the third time on the eve of the World Cup finals. Just Fontaine, the swarthy, Moroccan-born, inside-forward went into the World Cup as a footballing nobody, but would leave it a footballing legend. To set things rolling he had notched a hat-trick against Paraguay, followed by a pair against Yugoslavia.

Now was the time for Scotland to make changes. Tommy Younger's one miserable match out of two dozen found him dropped and relieved of the captaincy. His place went to Dundee's Bill Brown (understudy throughout the Younger era); the captaincy – not before time – to Bobby Evans. Parker was shown out of the door as quickly as he was shown in – Hewie returning. Dave Mackay took Cowie's place in the engine room; Murray returned for the wrist-damaged Leggat; and Sam Baird replaced Robertson. Mudie and one or two others played despite not being fully fit.

In the leafy setting of Orebro, and with Scotland again wearing white, France's attacking flair was soon confirmed. Less than two minutes had elapsed before Brown was called upon to produce his first memorable save of the game, from winger Wiesnieski. Further breathtaking French moves ended with one shot into the side-netting, and Brown thwarting Fontaine. It came as a surprise to no-one when, after twenty minutes, the French scored. A mesmerising French move saw Fontaine dance round Hewie and turn the ball back into the path of the irrepressible Kopa, who volleyed past Brown.

Long shots by Turnbull and Baird did not threaten an equaliser, but Lerond's moment of rashness in the 29th minute did. Abbas gathered Mackay's distant shot and Mudie advanced to challenge, only to be brusquely manhandled by the French defender. The French went berserk at the penalty decision. Responsibility for taking it was entrusted to Scotland's South African left-back John Hewie, but his kick smacked against a post and rebounded into play, whereupon a frightful brawl ensued. Hewie was perceived to be on the ground with his feet up in the air, surrounded by galled Frenchmen, with Scottish reinforcements steaming to the rescue. Every one of Scotland's matches had now involved the improper use of fists and feet, not a distinction of which to be proud.

Following the example of Paraguay, France scored a second, killer, goal on the stroke of half-time. It followed a further spell of French pressure, after Abbas had saved well from Collins at the other end. Almost inevitably the scorer was Just Fontaine, latching on to a long ball and racing past Evans and Hewie before beating Brown as the keeper came off his line. Six goals in two and a half matches. Not bad.

Scotland were to be remembered for two aspects of their play during the 1958 World Cup finals. The first was the violence which attended all their matches; the second, the admirable way in which they always came back at their opponents in the second half. For fifteen minutes France were pushed back in defence, during which time the clearly-struggling Mudie missed with an inviting opportunity to reduce the deficit. The likes of Fontaine, however, could not easily be suppressed. His snap-shot was pushed on to the bar by Brown – a critical save, because with twenty-five minutes remaining Scotland scored. Baird collected Murray's pass, wriggled-free, and shot splendidly past Abbas and in off a post.

One could sense a glimmer of hope. Abbas swooped to snatch the ball off Mudie's foot, but still the flashes of magic belonged to France. Brown repeatedly came to the rescue, never more spectacularly than when he once again made good use of his crossbar to keep out Piantoni's fierce free kick. When all was said and done, Scotland could have few complaints.

FRANCE (2)2   SCOTLAND (0)1
    Kopa, Fontaine   Baird

FRANCE: Abbas, Kaelbel, Lerond, Penverne, Jonquet, Marcel, Wiesnieski, Fontaine, Kopa, Piantoni, Vincent.

SCOTLAND: W Brown (Dundee), E Caldow (Rangers), J Hewie (Charlton), E Turnbull (Hibs), R Evans (Celtic, capt.), D Mackay (Hearts), R Collins (Celtic), J Murray (Hearts), J Mudie (Blackpool), S Baird (Rangers), S Imlach (Nott'm F).

So Scotland were out, once again bottom of their group, still without a win in the finals of the World Cup, and with a total of four defeats stacked against them. The three other British teams needed play-offs to determine their fate. England went out, but Wales and Northern Ireland – to the immense pleasure and surprise of both – reached the quarter-finals before returning home. The Irish were put out 4-0 by France, who emerged as the revelation of the tournament, alongside Brazil its winners. In finishing third, France amassed twenty-three goals from six matches, with Just Fontaine scoring thirteen – an all-time record. If only he had played for Scotland.

Group 2 – final positions

	P	W	D	L	F	A	PTS
FRANCE	3	2	0	1	11	7	4
YUGOSLAVIA	3	1	2	0	7	6	4
Paraguay	3	1	1	1	9	12	3
Scotland	3	0	1	2	4	6	1

Scotland appearances and goal-scorers:
World Cup qualifying rounds and final competition 1958

	A	G		A	G	
Caldow E	7	–	Fernie W*	2	–	
Collins R	7	2	Imlach S	2	–	
Mudie J	7	6	Leggat G	2	–	
Younger T	6	–	Mackay D	2	–	
Evans R*†	5	–	McColl I	2	–	
Hewie J	5	1	Murray J	2	1	
Baird S	4	1	Parker A	2	–	
Docherty T*	4	–	Robertson A	2	1	
Ring T	4	–	Young G*†	2	–	
Smith G	3	1	Brown W	1	–	
Turnbull E	3	–	Scott A	1	1	
Cowie D*	2	–	caps	77	14	goals
23 players						

Scottish League	52
English League	25
	77

*Appeared in 1954 World Cup
†Appeared in 1950 World Cup

Her Majesty the Queen meets Willie Ormond and Kenny Dalglish at a Glasgow Select match. Willie was the Scotland team manager in the 1974 World Cup Finals held in Germany. Kenny has played in the 1974, 78, 82 and 86 campaigns.

Danny McGrain keeps his eye on the ball. The popular Celtic player represented Scotland in the World Cups of 1974, 78 and 82.

CHAPTER 4

The 1962 World Cup

Scotland had been unable to illuminate the World Cups of Switzerland and Sweden. If they hoped to do better in 1962 they would have to do so in South America – in Chile. To reach the finals, Scotland would need to dispose of Czechoslovakia and the Republic of Ireland in Group 8 – three of the four qualifying matches to be played in the space of twelve days in May 1961.

Scotland's international results in the three years since Sweden were more a source of dejection than celebration. 1959 had seen an encouraging victory over West Germany; 1960 depressing defeats by Poland (at Hampden), Austria and ... Turkey! Worst of all, at Wembley in April 1961, Scotland disintegrated. The team fell apart, lost 9-3, and recorded their heaviest defeat in history. The World Cup qualifiers were a mere three weeks away, a state of affairs unlikely to add to the confidence of the new, nominal, manager Ian McColl. He had been a reliable servant of Rangers and Scotland, having played in World Cup qualifiers against Spain and Switzerland in 1957. He had stepped from player to international manager with no previous administrative or managerial experience at all. The butler had turned overnight into Lord of the Manor: less a case of *Jim'll Fix It* than inexcusable naïveté on the part of the SFA. McColl was still only 34, and combined his restricted responsibilities for Scotland with running his own garage business. Now, in the wake of the Wembley holocaust, he had some heads to lift.

Eight years previously, England's 6-3 defeat by Hungary had spelled the end of six international careers. Scotland's numbing result at English hands resulted in no comparable persecution. Only two players, one of them keeper Frank Haffey, would never be given the chance to make amends for their country. Three other players would be temporarily 'rested': the others had to pick themselves up and pull themselves together – quickly.

By coincidence, England were responsible in another sense for murmurings of discontent north of the border. Players in the English Football League were no longer restricted financially by the indignity of the 'maximum wage'. Their income was, from now on, negotiable, and England captain Johnny Haynes (of Fulham) had become British football's first £100 a week player. This wage revolution had the effect of making senior players in Scotland – where the maximum wage was retained – listen wistfully to the talk of 'big money' being earned by their colleagues down south. Several Scottish players whose contracts with their clubs had expired appeared less willing to sign new ones, in the hope of receiving lucrative invitations from England. What with a crushing recent defeat and financially unsettled players, it was not an auspicious time for Scotland to be concentrating on the World Cup.

The Qualifying Rounds

Wednesday, 3 May 1961
SCOTLAND v REPUBLIC OF IRELAND   Hampden 47,000

This was Scotland's first-ever meeting with the Irish Republic. Even taking account of the debacle against England, the Scots would have justifiably expected to win. The Irish had been paired with England in the qualifying stages of the previous, 1958, World Cup, losing 1-5 at Wembley, drawing 1-1 in Dublin. The Irish team, managed by Johnny Carey, all earned their living in the English League. It contained players of proven quality, not least full-back Noel Cantwell and winger Johnny Giles – both then of Manchester United – and uncompromising Sunderland centre-half Charlie Hurley.

The Scottish side, of course, was all-change from that of Sweden. Only Eric Caldow remained. Lawrie Leslie of Airdrie returned to keep goal in place of the disgraced Frank Haffey, while Bobby Shearer retained his place to win his second cap, alongside Ibrox club-mate Caldow. No-one could foresee it, but the half-back trio now lining up for the first time would establish themselves as one of the most glittering ever assembled. With Dave Mackay due to play for Spurs in the FA Cup Final the following Saturday, his place went to a Celtic player winning his first cap – Paddy Crerand. His partners were comparative veterans – both claiming second caps – Celtic's Billy McNeill and Rangers' Jim Baxter.

The forward line had to be patched up, for asked to take a 'rest' after the Wembley shambles were Denis Law and Ian St John. Their replacements were Ralph Brand of Rangers coming out for his second international, and David Herd of Arsenal (the solitary Anglo) for his fourth. The three forward players who kept their places were the wingers John McLeod of Hibernian and Davie Wilson of Rangers – the fifth player from Ibrox – plus Pat Quinn of Motherwell. The team as a whole was notably youthful.

Scotland's early pressure on a bright sunny evening paid off after fourteen minutes. Caldow's free kick was headed out by Hurley, but only as far as Brand, who killed the ball and drove it back hard inside Dwyer's right post. The lead was nearly sacrificed when Cummins' free kick was misjudged by a tense-looking Leslie and pushed, not over, but on to the face of the bar.

A second, and hopefully decisive, Scottish goal was secured in the closing minutes of the half. A sweet move involving Crerand, Herd and Brand culminated in the last-named beating Dwyer comprehensively with a fierce shot. There was still time before the intermission for Herd – who was enjoying a memorable duel with Hurley – to connect firmly with Wilson's cross. Dwyer, with admirable agility, turned the header against a post.

A three-goal half-time lead would have been a mountain for any team to climb. Two, and the opposition was still just about within catching distance. Ireland evidently felt battle to be worth resuming, for they re-commenced the more impressive team, fired up once a goal had been pulled back after fifty-one minutes. Giles escaped from Baxter – who would commit several unseemly fouls on this, his eloquent first Hampden appearance – to cross beyond the far post. Arsenal's Haverty was giving Shearer a tough time: now the Irish winger was unattended to shoot undeniably past Leslie.

Ireland had snatched the initiative and threatened to retain it. They might have done so but for a magnificent Scotland goal on the counter-attack: the score stood at 2-1 for only eight minutes before a silky-smooth Scottish build-up, involving almost half the team, ended with an unstoppable drive by the thick-set David Herd.

The game appeared safe again. Brand seemed determined to register a memorable hat-trick, and came near when his shot struck the advancing Dwyer to loop over the bar. The Irish continued to display neat touches, but a scoreline a mite harsh was forced on them in the last minute. Davie Wilson's header elicited yet another fine save from Dwyer, but the ball squirmed from his hands and Herd was in the right spot for the tap-in.

It was a sound enough victory, but learned discussion afterwards dwelt less on the score than on savouring the exciting potential shown by the wing-halves, Crerand and Baxter. The partnership was, and would continue to be, so successful that it would survive unbroken for eleven consecutive matches, until November 1962.

SCOTLAND (2)4   REPUBLIC OF IRELAND (0)1
   Brand 2, Herd 2   Haverty

SCOTLAND: L Leslie (Airdrie), R Shearer (Rangers), E Caldow (Rangers, capt.), P Crerand (Celtic), W McNeill (Celtic), J Baxter (Rangers), J McLeod (Hibs), P Quinn (Motherwell), D Herd (Arsenal), R Brand (Rangers), D Wilson (Rangers).

REPUBLIC OF IRELAND: Dwyer, McNally, Cantwell, McEvoy, Hurley, Saward, Giles, Fogarty, Curtis, Cummins, Haverty.

Sunday, 7 May 1961
REPUBLIC OF IRELAND v SCOTLAND   Dublin 40,000

Various aches and pains were given only four days to disperse before Scotland turned out for the return match in Dublin. It was the first occasion that Scotland had played a full international in that fair city since 1913. The hope was to collect another two points, giving them a lead of four over the Czechs – who had yet to commence their programme – to exert maximum pressure on them. Victory would not be a formality: apart from the creditable show the Irish had put on at Hampden, of nineteen games at Dalymount Park since the formation of the Republic they had lost but four.

Scotland had hoped to send out an unchanged team, but David Herd was taken unwell at the last minute, enabling Alex Young of Everton – soon to become a Goodison legend – to reclaim the No 9 shirt. Ireland were less inclined to keep the same side, bringing in four new faces. Among them was Leeds' Fitzgerald at centre-forward, who had had the experience of playing for Sparta Rotterdam against Rangers in the European Cup the previous year.

The ground was hard, the wind was high, and the game was a mess. Scotland played into the gale to begin with, yet almost found the break-through coming as early as the third minute when Brand appeared to be pulled down in the box from behind. The referee, a portly, elderly Belgian by the name of Grandain – who put one immediately in mind of Agatha Christie's distinguished detective, Hercule Poirot – on this occasion saw nothing illegal. Nor did he sixty seconds later when Scotland took the lead. Brand's challenge was too much for the combined attentions of Dwyer and Hurley, and his head-flick across goal was nodded into the empty net from close range by Alex Young. Brand himself was arguably offside: Young manifestly so – as the linesman's raised flag confirmed. Irish shirts buzzed dementedly around the Belgian detective, but he took no notice of them or his colleague and allowed the goal.

On the quarter-hour Scotland appeared to make the game safe. Again the goal was dubious, but this time the Irish contributed to their own downfall. Out of harm's way on the touchline Kelly made a clumsy effort to shield the ball from Davie Wilson. The two players jockeyed for position as if engaged in a time-wasting exercise at the corner flag during injury time. For reasons best known to Kelly he declined to thump the ball into touch and eventually found it spirited away by Wilson – though it already appeared to have gone out of play. Kelly was suitably red-faced when Wilson bore down on Dwyer, forced him to vacate his charge and squared for Young to notch his second 'open' goal.

Scottish-Irish relations were further estranged when Cummins took a swipe at Crerand, who exceeded the 'eye for an eye' principle and proceeded to put the boot in. Monsieur Grandain contented himself with the mildest of admonitions. The more legitimate activity of the half saw chances fall at either end – none taken. Fitzgerald's shot-on-the-run whizzed over Leslie's bar; while Fagan's direct hit left the courageous goalkeeper gulping in air and requiring attention. Scotland, with Crerand in a class of his own, were sorely treated by the Irish goalpost which kept out Wilson's shot.

The second half was more dreary than the first, Dalymount Park rarely witnessing such a yawn-inducing spectacle. The conditions were largely responsible. Crerand and Baxter successfully spoiled the attempted Irish resurrection. On the hour, however, Haverty seemed to be in the clear till dispossessed by McNeill's expertly-timed tackle. At the other end, Scotland frittered away what openings came their way.

It was all too much for the terraces. Boos and slow handclaps resounded round the stadium. Feelings were expressed clearly when twice the ball landed in the crowd, and twice replacements had to be called for when it wasn't returned. That the referee was not an Irishman was amply demonstrated near the end when McNeill up-ended Fitzgerald within the penalty area and was relieved to see Ireland awarded their free kick five yards outside it.

The game was dead long before Brand's final fling five minutes from time, screwing the ball past Dwyer from a tight angle.

REPUBLIC OF IRELAND (0)0   SCOTLAND (2)3
                                                      Young 2, Brand

REPUBLIC OF IRELAND: Dwyer, Kelly, Cantwell, McEvoy, Hurley, Meagan, Fagan, Giles, Fitzgerald, Cummins, Haverty.

SCOTLAND: L Leslie (Airdrie), R Shearer (Rangers), P Crerand (Celtic), E Caldow (Rangers, capt.), W McNeill (Celtic), J Baxter (Rangers), J McLeod (Hibs), P Quinn (Motherwell), A Young (Everton), R Brand (Rangers), D Wilson (Rangers).

Sunday, 14 May 1961
CZECHOSLOVAKIA v SCOTLAND   Bratislava 48,000

A week later Scotland turned out in Bratislava for the last in this exhausting spell of World Cup matches. Only the visit of the Czechs to Hampden in September would remain. Over the next twenty years Scotland and Czechoslovakia would come to know one another rather well – but all this lay in the future. The Czechs had an undistinguished record in the World Cup, if one looked beyond their appearance in the 1934 final when they were beaten 2-1 after extra time by the questionable tactics of the hosts, Italy. More recently, they had been included in Scotland's group in Switzerland, but on account of FIFA's mischievous organisation the two countries were not asked to play one another. Czechoslovakia lost a total of seven goals to Austria and Uruguay: Scotland, eight. In Sweden four years later, the Czechs had been eliminated after sustaining two defeats by Northern Ireland – the second in a play-off. So, while the Czechs could be expected to present a sterner test than the gentlemen of Dublin, they seemed nothing out of the ordinary. Ominously, however, in the first-ever European Nations Cup, completed in 1960, the Czechs had survived a 0-2 defeat in Dublin to claim third place. Was that a valid or illusory guide to their worth?

Whatever the overall strength of the current Czech side, it could boast two of Europe's outstanding half-backs, Josef Masopust, now aged thirty, and the stocky Pluskal. It was a perfect opportunity to see how Crerand and Baxter would fare by comparison. What Scotland were soon to learn was that the Czechs also possessed flying wingers, who tormented the Scottish full-backs from the first whistle. It would have been a cool, pleasant evening except for the heat generated by Pospichal and Masek, who gave Caldow and Shearer a roasting.

Czechoslovakia wanted an early goal and their wish was Pospichal's command. In the seventh minute Baxter allowed Scherer time and space to carry the ball deep into the Scottish danger area. Scherer had earlier thumped the ball against Leslie's arm: now he passed out to Pospichal and the winger's venomous shot from the edge of the area flew low inside Leslie's left post. Five minutes later the dazzling Czechs scored again, and this time Baxter was even more culpable. His untidy challenge on Kadraba was worth half a penalty; his elbow coming into contact with the ball another half. The Austrian referee, Herr Steiner, knew his fractions, and Kvasnak scored from the spot.

Scotland's cause seemed lost almost before it had begun. The Czechs were stronger and faster in all departments. It was all too frustrating to bear for poor Crerand. He was now experiencing the agony following the ecstasy of his earlier performances. In Dublin he was magical, in Bratislava mundane. He and Baxter were being given the lesson of their lives. Ten minutes before the break Crerand's inclination to retaliate – as instanced in Dublin – was given a second airing. He and Kvasnak indulged in a bout of lawlessness and the referee pointed dramatically to the stand. Play was held up for two minutes, partly due to recalcitrance on the part of the offenders, partly because the referee was unknowingly pointing in the opposite direction to the dressing rooms.

When all was restored the twenty players remaining carried on where they had left off, Czechoslovakia attacking, Scotland running round in circles. Scottish penetration was non-existent. There had been two changes to the forward line: Alex Young's two goals in Dublin were sufficient justification for him to be dropped from the international team for five years. In the short-term, David Herd returned. Perhaps the Scottish selectors operated in five-year cycles, for Ian McMillan of Rangers – who claimed the inside-right position ahead of Pat Quinn and brought the Ibrox representation up to six – had been in the international wilderness for five seasons. For both Herd and McMillan the sentence for the team's woeful performance in Bratislava would be international banishment, not for five years, but for eternity.

Herd, at least, showed some self-respect. Two minutes before the break his solo run and shot at goal was a rare gesture of defiance. His disappointment at seeing Schroiff save was turned to anguish when the goalkeeper's long punt downfield was fastened on by Kadraba, who sped through a flimsy McNeill challenge to score a dramatic goal from twenty yards.

The Scottish changing room at half-time must have resembled a mortuary – inappropriate to the benign weather and the picturesque Slovan Stadium surrounded by tall, dignified cypress trees. The Czechs' style of play – slow, methodical build-up until they reached the penalty area, followed by lightning explosions of speed – simply could not be contained, let alone countered. The second half was straightforward shooting practice for the Czechs, every Scottish pass derisively cheered by the home crowd. Herd was injured and spent the last quarter of the match receiving treatment or hobbling on one leg. The left side of the Scottish defence was ruthlessly exposed. Baxter could not defend as well as he could attack, and Caldow was overrun. Five minutes from the end of a nightmarish Scottish performance Pospichal hammered home number four. Scotland licked their wounds, but Czechoslovakia had looked good – really good.

CZECHOSLOVAKIA (3)4   SCOTLAND (0)0
    Pospichal 2, Kvasnak (pen), Kadraba

CZECHOSLOVAKIA: Schroiff, Safranek, Tichy, Pluskal, Popluhar, Masopust, Pospichal, Scherer, Kadraba, Kvasnak, Masek.

SCOTLAND: L Leslie (Airdrie), R Shearer (Rangers), E Caldow (Rangers, capt.), P Crerand (Celtic), W McNeill (Celtic), J Baxter (Rangers), J McLeod (Hibs), I McMillan (Rangers), D Herd (Arsenal), R Brand (Rangers), D Wilson (Rangers).

Tuesday, 26 September 1961
SCOTLAND v CZECHOSLOVAKIA   Hampden 52,000

There must have been mixed feelings in the Scottish camp at the thought of the Czechs' return match at Hampden: eagerness, from the desire to exact revenge; apprehension, at the thought of a second drubbing. The Scottish selectors plied the knife ruthlessly: Leslie, Shearer, McLeod, McMillan and Herd would not play international football again. Brand was dropped – temporarily, and Quinn could not win back his place, despite the pair of them heading the list of Scottish goalscorers in the new season.

    There was a recall in goal for Bill Brown, now of Tottenham, and for Celtic full-back Duncan McKay. The half-back trio, despite its mauling in Bratislava, was retained. Four new attacking faces were brought in to accompany the solitary survivor from the forward line, Davie Wilson. Alec Scott replaced John McLeod, and there was a summons for three central forwards who had first played together two years previously – John White of Tottenham, Ian St John of Liverpool, and Denis Law, now of Torino.

    This attacking combination was selected mindful of the possibility that the Czechs might come to defend. A draw would leave them needing just three points from their matches with Ireland to qualify. Certainly, they did stiffen their defence, making three changes. These included the return of the outstanding full-backs Bomba and Novak, the Czech captain, now earning his 65th cap.

The weather was not kind, given the importance of the match. A vicious wind gurgled its way round Hampden, marginally benefiting the Czechs in the first half. In each of Group 8's matches to date an early goal had been scored, and the pattern was maintained when in the sixth minute a back-heel from Masopust, a lay-back from Kadraba and a fierce shot from Kvasnak high to Brown's left put the visitors in front. It was a truly incisive goal and the white-clad Czechs danced a ghostly tango in delight.

Czechoslovakia, like all East European teams, had been scathingly dismissed as dour, one-paced, unimaginative. The stereotype had its source in political propaganda, not footballing analysis, and was shown to be hopelessly misplaced. The Czech forwards constantly switched position, and the whole side bristled with imagination and power. Not for one moment had they come to defend. Now, a goal behind, the calibre of the Scottish team was held up for inspection.

The Scots could not compete with their opponents' imagination but they could, and did, combat Czech power. The game surged from end to end. One moment Brown was leaping at the feet of Scherer; the next, shots from Scott and will-o'-the-wisp John White were charged down in front of Schroiff.

On twenty-one minutes the Scots were level. White's cross was headed up and back by Law. The ball fell to St John whose header might have been saved, but Schroiff, caught in two minds about staying on his line, allowed the ball to creep under his body. The goal was less than spectacular, but it was all Scotland needed to restore their confidence. Now they powered forward, though the Czechs continued to threaten a goal every time they broke out of defence. One slide-rule pass from Scherer enabled Kadraba a shot which Brown turned behind.

Either side of the interval Scotland pressed, only to lose a dreadful goal six minutes into the second half. Popluhar's belted clearance found Scherer, who to his disbelief was permitted to stroll forty yards into the Scottish box without molestation and beat Brown with ease. It was the sort of goal to have the victims tugging at their hair.

With the wind at their backs and the Hampden roar all around them, Scotland dug up the resources for a spell of frenzied attacking. St John gave the giant Popluhar a mighty struggle, and Denis Law was at his magnificent best, a constant thorn in the Czech rump. After sixty-two minutes he equalised, hammering White's cross into the net. Hampden was now a cauldron, Scotland mercilessly turning the screw against a cool, calm defence which refused to panic. Falling rain could not dampen the atmosphere. St John was felled but won an indirect free kick, not a penalty. Wilson collided with Schroiff and was crudely flattened by Kvasnak. Czechoslovakia seemed as impressive when forced to defend as when on the attack, but seven minutes before the end of a memorable match Scotland took the lead. White made his third goal of the game, engineering the move which culminated in Denis Law swerving clear of two tackles, keeping his balance on a soaking pitch, and rifling the ball past the helpless Schroiff at the far post.

In view of the quality of the opposition, the win was a testament to Scottish football. Denis Law had enjoyed his finest hour. If Czechoslovakia dropped a point to the Irish the following month, Scotland would qualify for Chile. To no-one's surprise Czechoslovakia won 3-1 in Dublin, 7-1 in Prague, and would now meet Scotland for the third and decisive time – in a play-off.

SCOTLAND (1)3	CZECHOSLOVAKIA (1)2
St John, Law 2	Kvasnak, Scherer

SCOTLAND: W Brown (Spurs), D McKay (Celtic), E Caldow (Rangers, capt.), P Crerand (Celtic), W McNeill (Celtic), J Baxter (Rangers), A Scott (Rangers), J White (Spurs), I St John (Liverpool), D Law (Torino), D Wilson (Rangers).

CZECHOSLOVAKIA: Schroiff, Bomba, Novak, Bubernik, Popluhar, Masopust, Pospichal, Scherer, Kadraba, Kvasnak, Masek.

Wednesday, 29 November 1961
CZECHOSLOVAKIA v SCOTLAND   Brussels 6,000

Following Czechoslovakia's twin victories over Ireland, they and the Scots were locked together on six points. Goal average, as such, didn't count – otherwise the Czechs would have been through with something to spare. The only occasion on which the goal columns would take effect would be in the event of the play-off being drawn – after extra time. Then the team with the superior goal average at the conclusion of the scheduled group matches would progress. In other words, Scotland had to win: Czechoslovakia needed only to draw.

The SFA tried to pull a fast one, when asked to suggest a neutral venue. 'Wembley' they replied, perhaps hoping the Czechs were unaware that Scotland played there every other season. The Czechs were not taken in, declined the suggestion, and Brussels was agreed upon as the place where the fifteenth of the sixteen final places in Chile would be settled.

In the interim Scotland had taken pleasing victories against Northern Ireland (6-1) and Wales (2-0), but the wingers Wilson and Scott were now unfit and ruled out. So was goalkeeper Bill Brown. He was replaced by Eddie Connachan of Dunfermline, while the two incoming wingers were Ralph Brand (no longer used in that position by Rangers) and Dundee's Hugh Robertson. It was Connachan's and Robertson's first (and last) cap. The two other additions to the side which beat the Czechs were right-back Alec Hamilton and centre-half Ian Ure – both from a Dundee team on its way to the Scottish championship. The average age of the Scotland eleven was a youthful twenty-three.

Three of the Czechs' four team-changes were in defence, Hledik becoming the third right-back to face Scotland in as many matches. As before, the bulk of the players came from the Czech league champions – the Army team, Dukla Prague.

There were no more than 6,000 spectators – including a contingent of Scottish soldiers – in the Heysel Stadium to watch a game which, with so much at stake, could euphemistically be described as 'hard'. The Czechs showed perfectly clearly that they were equipped for all contingencies. If they needed to play, they could play: if they needed to kick, they required no lessons from anyone.

For once, the game did not have any early goal in store. Danger-man Law's performance at Hampden guaranteed that he was shackled so tightly as to make breathing difficult. Half-time was only ten minutes away when the deadlock was broken. And it was Scotland who broke it, having already created chances at regular intervals. St John was fouled by Popluhar – not for the first time. Baxter took the free kick and St John, spurting forward, headed past the stranded Schroiff.

Now the Czechs had to attack. The game grew rougher, too rough for the lightweight John White, whose skills on a heavy pitch were rendered even less effective against the iron men of the 'Red' army. Ian Ure emerged as equally ferric, stamping himself with his conspicuous fair hair as Scotland's most visible source of resistance. St John splendidly led the front line despite the lack of service from his tightly-marked wingers. Early in the second half he found room for a shot, but the ball flew straight at Schroiff.

The rain-sodden minutes were slowly consumed, but there were still twenty of them left when the Czechs drew level. Intense pressure led to a sequence of corners conceded by a backs-to-the-wall Scottish defence. From the fifth, Hledik emerged to plant a header past Connachan. The goal was a near-replica of St John's, and had an astonishing sequel. Less than a minute later Scotland were awarded a disputed free kick. Brand flighted the ball for St John – stung by Czech plagiarism – to side-foot into the net.

It was, or ought to have been, a killer goal. Czechoslovakia had to start all over again. Had they the heart to emulate the Scots at Hampden and come from behind twice? There were eight minutes remaining when Scotland learned the answer. Kvasnak's shot ricocheted around the penalty area. When it was partially cleared Scherer slammed it back without fuss. 2-2.

Scotland were still admirably giving their all. In the last seconds of normal time Law drove inches too high, and in the first minutes of extra time the ill-treated White summoned the energy to whack the ball from twenty yards against the junction of post and bar. White's near-miss would provide Scotland with an agonising 'if only', for Czechoslovakia were now firing on all cylinders. It surprised none of the neutrals when, within four minutes, Popischal volleyed past Connachan, nor when on the stroke of half-time Kvasnak hammered a shot from all of twenty-two yards in off the bar. The second period of extra time was superfluous.

Scotland had done themselves proud. They had been a sickeningly-short eight minutes from Chile. But looking back, there was a sense of fairness about the outcome. Ian McColl was honest enough to say: 'Even when we were ahead twice we were never in command in the same way we had been at Hampden while we were behind'. *The Times* confessed: 'The Czechs came out like thoroughbreds when it really mattered ... The best side won, and won worthily'. It was *The Times*, too, which offered, by implication, the finest praise for Scotland and the most astute prophecy: 'Czechoslovakia will take some stopping in Chile'.

CZECHOSLOVAKIA (0)2 *4*   SCOTLAND (1)2 *2* (after extra time)
   Hledik, Scherer, Pospichal, Kvasnak   St John 2

CZECHOSLOVAKIA: Schroiff, Hledik, Tichy, Pluskal, Popluhar, Masopust, Pospichal, Scherer, Kvasnak, Kucera, Jelinek.

SCOTLAND: E Connachan (Dunfermline), A Hamilton (Dundee), E Caldow (Rangers, capt.), P Crerand (Celtic), I Ure (Dundee), J Baxter (Rangers), R Brand (Rangers), J White (Spurs), I St John (Liverpool), D Law (Torino), H Robertson (Dundee).

Czechoslovakia did indeed take some stopping in Chile. They forced a draw with defending champions Brazil in qualifying from the first round. In the quarter-finals Brazil eliminated England 3-1, while the Czechs overcame Hungary, then Yugoslavia in the semis to find themselves facing Brazil again, this time in the World Cup Final. The Czechs took the lead, too, before eventually going down 1-3. Measured by these standards, Scotland's exclusion became easier to bear.

World Cup Qualifying Group 8:

	P	W	D	L	F	A	PTS
CZECHOSLOVAKIA	4	3	0	1	16	5	6
Scotland	4	3	0	1	10	7	6
Republic of Ireland	4	0	0	4	3	17	0

Czechoslovakia qualified after play-off with Scotland

Other group results

Rep of Ireland v Czechoslovakia 1-3
Czechoslovakia v Rep of Ireland 7-1

Scotland appearances and goal-scorers:
World Cup qualifying rounds 1962

	A	G		A	G
Baxter J	5	–	St John I	2	3
Caldow E*	5	–	White J	2	–
Crerand P	5	–	Brown W*	1	–
Brand R	4	3	Connachan E	1	–
McNeill W	4	–	Hamilton A	1	–
Wilson D	4	–	McKay D	1	–
Leslie L	3	–	McMillan I	1	–
McLeod J	3	–	Robertson H	1	–
Shearer R	3	–	Scott A*	1	–
Herd D	2	2	Ure I	1	–
Law D	2	2	Young A	1	2
Quinn P	2	–	caps	55	12 goals

23 players

Scottish League	45
English League	8
Italian League	2
	55

*Appeared in 1958 World Cup

Denis Law registers his delight in scoring against Ireland in a 1972 match. Denis played for Scotland in the World Cup campaigns of 1962, 66, 70 and 74. He scored 5 goals and played in 11 matches, including qualifying rounds.

CHAPTER 5

The 1966 World Cup

The 1966 World Cup finals were to be staged in England. For that reason above all others, it was imperative for Scotland to qualify. Never before or since would any of the British teams stand so favourable a chance of performing well in, or even winning, the Jules Rimet Trophy. Wembley, of course, was a second home to Scotland's international footballers. They played there bi-annually. And the half-dozen other stadiums to be utilised were also familiar territory to all those Scottish players who earned their living in the English League.

Scotland had come so close to qualifying for Chile that there was understandably some apprehension about the identity of the opposition this time around. They were allocated to the same group as Finland, Poland and Italy, with just one to qualify. Italy, the seeded team, were probably happier with the draw than Scotland.

Irrespective of the close fights given to Czechoslovakia, Scotland's international performances between 1961 and 1964 gave no real grounds for optimism – with one dazzling exception. In 1962 Scotland lost at home to Uruguay, then in 1963 put five results together which simply did not make sense – except perhaps to a psychiatrist. In April they won praiseworthily at Wembley; in May equally impressively in a match abandoned against Austria at Hampden. In June Scotland went on a ten-day excursion to Norway, the Irish Republic, and Spain. They slumped to a 3-4 defeat in Bergen, against one of the weakest sides in the world; followed this up by losing 0-1 in Dublin (permitting the Irish some consolation for their two recent World Cup defeats at Scottish hands); and then, unbelievably, walloped Spain 6-2 in Madrid. To this day that scoreline probably ranks as the most impressive Scotland have ever achieved outside Britain.

It was a pity that Ian McColl could not watch his side gain 'competitive' experience, for alone of British teams Scotland declined to enter the 1964 European Nations Cup. The general led his troops into the new World Cup campaign just a couple of weeks after they had slipped to a 2-3 defeat in Cardiff.

The Qualifying Rounds

Wednesday, 21 October 1964
SCOTLAND v FINLAND   Hampden 55,000

The Scotland team which had failed so honourably against Czechoslovakia was not to be lightly discarded. Of the players who carried Scotland so near in the 1961 series, nine were still turning out for their country in 1964 and beyond. Three of them – Alec Hamilton in defence, Jim Baxter in midfield, and Denis Law (now with Manchester United) up front – were in the line-up to face Finland at Hampden. Temporarily keeping goal was Campbell Forsyth of Kilmarnock. Enjoying a run at left-back was Jim Kennedy of Celtic. Paddy Crerand still had some international mileage in him, but for this match his position went to another of Scotland's crop of outstanding wing-halves, John Greig of Rangers. No 8 was Davie Gibson of Leicester; No 9 Stevie Chalmers of Celtic – winning his second cap. So was No 7, Jimmy Johnstone, while No 11 was none other than Alec Scott, now with Everton, but about to take part in his third World Cup.

There was one debutant, centre-half Jackie McGrory of Kilmarnock. The 'Killies' dual representation was a tribute to the team which had finished second in the league the previous two years and which was just six months from taking the Scottish title. Irrespective of the wealth of experience available to the selectors, for the present match six players turned out with no more than four caps to their names.

As for the Finns, they were far and away the weakest team in the group, and no slip-ups could be permitted. The best that could be said of them was that they had recently taken the Scandinavian championship for the first time in fifty-six years – although they had managed to lose to Norway even in claiming that honour! Scotland had faced Finland only once, when they had scraped through 2-1 in Helsinki as their final warm-up before the 1954 World Cup finals. There was just one professional in the Finnish side, Peltonen, who played for Hamburg in the West German Bundesliga. The side was handicapped by the unavailability of both first-choice wingers, in that the supply to 6'3" centre-forward Tolsa was likely to be even more meagre than otherwise.

The frailty of the Finnish opposition was fully demonstrated after just two minutes, thanks to a goal of comical proportions. Scott took a corner, Halme failed to gather, and Law swung a hopeful foot. The ball looped gently goalwards where two line-bound defenders were perfectly positioned to clear. They didn't.

It is a common failing among professional footballers that they are frequently unable to summon maximum effort against third-rate opponents. Scotland were almost taught a painful lesson in the eleventh minute, when Tolsa's hook-shot produced an acrobatic save from Forsyth. But in the main the Finnish goal endured siege conditions. Halme had to leap at Law's feet, Rinne came perilously close to putting through his own net, and Chalmers fired wide from close in.

As further Scottish goals refused to arrive, one could sense the Finns growing in confidence. Scotland abruptly ended such notions in the final seven minutes of the half, when Gibson's cross was headed home by the unmarked Chalmers. Shortly afterwards Law was presented with a gaping goal but hit the bar. His frustration was soon eased when Gibson, with Scott's assistance, worked his way down the left and unleashed a shot which Halme didn't seem to expect.

The game was therefore won at half-time, but there followed an opportunity for Scotland to display a killer streak and stack up a mountain of goals. The opportunity was passed by. The Scottish players absorbed themselves in exhibition play, content to tickle the opposition rather than murder them. Baxter became casual beyond belief, and Denis Law, with a glorious opportunity, attempted to score with a backheel. Scotland had their faces slapped for their impertinence twenty minutes from time when Peltonen's swerving shot from nowhere appeared to present no insurmountable danger. But charity had extended even to Forsyth, who obligingly helped the ball into the far corner of his goal. It wasn't cheers which greeted the Scottish players as they trooped off, but whistles.

SCOTLAND (3)3   FINLAND (0)1
  Law, Chalmers, Gibson   Peltonen

SCOTLAND: C Forsyth (Kilmarnock), A Hamilton (Dundee), J Kennedy (Celtic), J Greig (Rangers), J McGrory (Kilmarnock), J Baxter (Rangers), J Johnstone (Celtic), D Gibson (Leicester), S Chalmers (Celtic), D Law (Man U., capt.), A Scott (Everton).

FINLAND: Halme, Makippa, Kautonen, Holmquist, Rinne, Valtonen, Jarvi, Peltonen, Tolsa, Syrjavaara, Hyvarinen.

Sunday, 23 May 1965
POLAND v SCOTLAND   Chorzow 76,000

The first hurdle, small though it was, had been successfully cleared. Now the Scottish Goldilocks was about to tackle the medium-sized bowl in the shape of Poland. Seven months had passed between times, during which the Scots played Northern Ireland (3-2) and England (2-2) in the Home Internationals, and Spain in a 'friendly'. Spain avoided a repeat humiliation of the 6-2 spanking two years previously by forcing a rough, tough goalless draw. Behind the scenes, however, trouble was brewing, and ten days before the Poland match Ian McColl was asked to resign – in other words was sacked. Stepping into the breach on a caretaker basis was Celtic's new manager, Jock Stein, who agreed to administer Scotland's immediate World Cup programme, until a long-term successor to McColl could be appointed.

The chopping and changing of the Scottish team was as feverish as ever. Only three of the team which beat Finland were chosen to play in Chorzow – Hamilton, Greig and Law (the European Footballer of the Year). Of the other eight, Forsyth, Kennedy and Gibson had hung up their international boots. Bill Brown was back to keep goal, seven years after he had first performed that honour. A more than able replacement for Eric Caldow at left-back had been unearthed in Chelsea's Eddie McCreadie. Crerand (now on Manchester United's books) borrowed Baxter's shirt, with Billy McNeill again performing the stopper role. Wee veteran Bobby Collins, now a driving force with Leeds, was back for his last international, having first played for Scotland back in 1950! Willie Henderson of Rangers returned on the right wing; Celtic's John Hughes claimed his second cap on the left; while the search for a genuine centre-forward alighted for the moment on Neil Martin of Hibernian, winning his first cap.

Poland were another of those East European sides who were difficult to assess. After the experiences of Czechoslovakia, no way would Poland be under-estimated. Past results were even: Scotland winning 2-1 in Warsaw in 1958; losing 2-3 at Hampden two years later. Still, Northern Ireland had beaten Poland 2-0 home and away in the first round of the 1964 European Nations Cup (both matches being played in 1962), so unless Poland had improved dramatically since then, Scotland could reasonably expect some reward from their trip.

The weather was worse than foul. The Slaski Stadium in the heart of Poland's coalmining belt suffered a climatic interpretation of Dante's *Inferno*. The driving rain instantly turned Poland's white shirts to an insipid grey. Undaunted, it was the hosts who showed the early superiority, surging through the puddles like power-driven swans. In the first minute Pohl's shot skidded off Brown's chest but thankfully McNeill was on hand to rescue. Scotland seemed content to contain, and their 4-3-3 formation with Collins, Crerand and Law in midfield seemed designed with that intent. During this first period Poland looked strong and fast, the only danger to their own goal coming when McCreadie moved up to force a sharp save from the previously idle Szymkowiak.

0-0 at half-time did not displease Scotland. 1-0 to Poland, five minutes later, did. The exciting Lentner escaped the attention of Greig and Hamilton to fire past Brown. There was now no profit in Scotland's defensive outlook. Law, in any case, was not productive in the middle of the field, away from his favourite haunt – the goalmouth. Now he pushed forward to lead the attack as Scotland strove to save the game. He had been top goalscorer in the English First Division the previous season, and his country could use a flash of his genius now.

With Martin and Hughes also switching positions in an attempt to seek greater penetration, the change in Scotland's fortunes was spectacular. The previous one-way traffic was abruptly turned around. Law powered in one header from Henderson, who looked more dangerous the longer the game went on, only for Szymkowiak to touch the ball on to the post.

Law did even better next time. In the 76th minute Collins' centre was not effectively cleared. Henderson nodded the ball back in, the goalkeeper strained to reach it, and Law punished his mishandling. 1-1. Scotland now felt confident in looking for a second goal. Henderson optimistically expressed his desire for a penalty, while at the other end Brown reacted quickly to turn away Nieroba's effort. By then there was hardly anybody left in the uncovered stadium to care. Most of the bedraggled spectators had long since left for the warmth of their own homes.

POLAND (0)1   SCOTLAND (0)1
  Lentner   Law

POLAND: Szymkowiak, Szczepanski, Ozlizio, Bazan, Gmoch, Grzegorczyk, Banas, Nieroba, Liberda, Pohl, Lentner.

SCOTLAND: W Brown (Spurs), A Hamilton (Dundee), E McCreadie (Chelsea), J Greig (Rangers), W McNeill (Celtic, capt.), P Crerand (Man U), W Henderson (Rangers), R Collins (Leeds), N Martin (Hibs), D Law (Man U), J Hughes (Celtic).

Thursday, 27 May 1965
FINLAND v SCOTLAND   Helsinki 20,000

The result in Poland could reasonably be adjudged by Scotland as a point gained rather than a point lost, especially as the Italians had also been held to a draw there. The Scottish party travelled from Chorzow to Helsinki where they were due to play the return fixture with Finland. Again, no setbacks could be permitted.

Just two changes were made to the Scottish side by Stein – who had insisted on greater control of team selection. The manager now needed a more attack-orientated formation. Thirty-two year old Bobby Collins made way for Hibernian's Willie Hamilton – the pressing claim for inclusion of the young, abrasive Billy Bremner being overlooked for the time being. There were thus two Hamiltons in the Scottish team – Willie, brought in suddenly, afterwards found himself left out equally suddenly.

The other change was on the left side of attack where John 'Yogi' Hughes, suffering the effects of a heavy head cold, was replaced by Davie Wilson – for whom this would the last of his twenty-two caps. Of the crewcut sporting Finns – looking like a prison outfit – only five of the side beaten at Hampden were picked, making a total of just eight players on the field with previous experience of the opposing team.

There was an immediate setback for Scotland in Helsinki's Olympic Stadium. By the fifth minute they might have been two goals up themselves: instead they were a goal behind. The home team's first attack brought a corner, from which Hyvarinen scored with defenders all around him threshing about wildly. Scotland, playing in white shirts, were further discomfited, as when Nasman saved efficiently from Greig. On sixteen minutes Henderson was tripped by Rinne and was awarded a penalty. Law was entrusted to take it but his shot struck the inside of a post and bounced out.

The play was generally scrappy, with the Finns enjoying their share of what good moments there were. Scotland looked progressively more uneasy, both at their own inability to score and at the prospect of the blond Peltonen, Finland's best player, further embarrassing them. Peltonen, indeed, was harshly challenged inside the Scottish penalty area. All eyes flashed in unison to the referee, but he waved play on. It was left to Crerand and Law to inject any quality into Scotland's play. Crerand tenaciously won the ball in the 37th minute and spread it wide to Law, who turned goal-maker rather than goal-taker. Hamilton cannily allowed Law's cross to pass between his legs for Wilson to score a crisp goal.

Scotland opened the second half with a series of raids. Nasman produced a super-save at the top corner from Hamilton. After fifty minutes Crerand crossed for Law, who tee'd the ball up for Greig to bullet home Scotland's second goal. With the urgency passing from Scotland's play, the game now became dreadfully disjointed. The East German referee blew his whistle frequently and capriciously. Finland were on the receiving end for the rest of the match but Scotland, you might say, were unable to finnish the Finns. The hosts could still have saved the game when a frightful mix-up in front of Brown threatened an equaliser until Law arrived to clear the danger. McNeill also brought off a last-ditch tackle to thwart Hyvarinen.

Stein was pleased with the result, less so with the referee and most of the Scottish forwards. The following month Italy arrived in Helsinki with Scotland listening in for news of an upset. Italy won 2-0.

FINLAND (1)1   SCOTLAND (1)2
  Hyvarinen   Wilson, Greig

FINLAND: Nasman, Kautonen, Makipaa, Holmquist, Rinne, Heinonen, Kumpalampi, Peltonen, Hyvarinen, Ruotsalsainen, Nuoranen.

SCOTLAND: W Brown (Spurs), A Hamilton (Dundee), E McCreadie (Chelsea), P Crerand (Man U), W McNeill (Celtic, capt.), J Greig (Rangers), W Henderson (Rangers), D Law (Man U), N Martin (Hibs), W Hamilton (Hibs), D Wilson (Rangers).

Wednesday, 13 October 1965
SCOTLAND v POLAND   Hampden, 108,000

The new league season did not open auspiciously from Scotland's point of view, the national team succumbing to a 2-3 defeat against Northern Ireland in Belfast just eleven days before the Poles were due to turn out at Hampden. Poland were in even worse spirits. Their unexpected 0-2 reverse in Finland the previous month made qualification nigh-on impossible for them. But Poland, with matches against Scotland and Italy to come, could still be king-maker if not king. Scotland, in terms of results so far, had done everything required of them. With two future matches against Italy to round off the group, it was vital that Scotland put the final seal on Poland's elimination. In other circumstances, the Poles might have been well-satisfied with a draw. Their defeat in Finland meant only a win would keep their flickering hopes still flickering.

Jock Stein had admirably sought to introduce some stability into the Scottish line-up. Eight players were chosen for their third successive World Cup match under his charge. Tottenham's Alan Gilzean had been in and out of the No 9 shirt for two years. Now he pulled it on for the first time in the World Cup. Billy Bremner was at last given another opportunity to show that he could do for his country what he could do for his club. Being provided with his international baptism out on the left touchline was the eighteen-year old Rangers' starlet Willie Johnston. He was given his chance in preference to John Hughes. The Poles made five changes from the Chorzow match.

Scotland began as if the occasion was too much for them. Brown was called upon to move smartly three times in the first five minutes, with Faber out on the left looking particularly menacing. As Scotland steadied the ship, Law was given half a chance by Bremner, and after fourteen minutes McNeill put his team in front. Henderson's corner was bungled by Kornek, under pressure from Gilzean. The keeper slapped the ball towards McNeill who chested it down and hoofed it into the net.

Suitably encouraged, Scotland began to open up with some splendidly incisive football. Young Willie Johnston – who six months previously was playing in the Scotland youth side – regularly caught the eye, giving his full-back a first-half runaround. When Henderson was crash-tackled by Gmoch, the referee incensed the crowd by awarding an indirect free kick instead of a penalty. Then Kornek smothered the ball at Gilzean's feet, and on the half-time whistle the same forward's dangerous header from Johnston's corner brought a springing save from the Polish goalkeeper.

Scotland had their tails up and looked good for more goals. But somebody must have put mogodon in their orange juice. They emerged for the second half to play like zombies. All cohesion went, and they were soon reduced to chasing frantically in the shadows of their reprieved opponents. Poland sported socks with narrow hoops, giving them the appearance of miniature zebras scampering around the grasslands of Hampden. Playing to a 4-2-4 formation with Liberda joining Nieroba in midfield in the second half, the zebras now reduced Scotland to lumbering wildebeest. Crerand and Bremner, vital cogs in the Scottish boiler-room, completely lost the rhythm of the game, and Law dropped back to swop roles with Bremner. Faber's trickery on the left spelled constant danger. Pohl's goalbound shots were intercepted – one by Brown's hands, the other by his knees. Law's despairing 'tackle' on Nieroba appeared a trifle high: it took the Pole on the neck.

The Hampden throngs rubbed their eyes in disbelief at the change in fortunes. Their whistles grew in intensity. Somehow the Scottish goal was spared, so that as the game entered its final phase Scotland still led by McNeill's earlier effort. Hampden chewed through a good number of finger nails, most eyes on watches rather than on the field. Eight minutes to go, seven, six ... Then Alec Hamilton lost possession to Faber. The winger's cross to the far post eluded McCreadie and found Liberda in sweet isolation. He pulled the ball down and blasted it over Brown's shoulder.

1-1. Hampden winced at the realisation of a vital point dropped; the whistles were instantly silenced. Scotland kicked off dejectedly. The ball went out of play. When it returned Sadek propelled himself through a despairing Scottish defence to shoot past Brown. The silence told its own story as the zebras celebrated with an abridged Polka. Somewhere up in the stands the watching Italian spies were not displeased either.

The performance – contrasting the two halves – was as unreal as anything most Scots could remember. The *Glasgow Herald* tried to put its tears into words: 'From a first half of interest and enthusiasm Scotland tumbled to a level of incompetence and a condition of total ruin which were incredible to see ... A bed of nails is like a feather mattress to anyone who watches Scottish teams nowadays'. Not that anyone noticed, but Scotland's first home defeat in the World Cup for eleven years coincided with the first team Scotland had ever fielded in that competition comprising a majority of Anglos. Moreover, Denis Law had seriously damaged his right knee, and would never be quite the same again.

SCOTLAND (1)1	POLAND (0)2
McNeill	Liberda, Sadek

SCOTLAND: W Brown (Spurs), A Hamilton (Dundee), E McCreadie (Chelsea), P Crerand (Man U), W McNeill (Celtic, capt.), J Greig (Rangers), W Henderson (Rangers), W Bremner (Leeds), A Gilzean (Spurs), D Law (Man U), W Johnston (Rangers).

POLAND: Kornek, Szczepanski, Ozlizio, Anczok, Gmoch, Nieroba, Sadek, Szoltyski, Liberda, Pohl, Faber.

Tuesday, 9 November 1965
SCOTLAND v ITALY   Hampden 101,000

Those two late goals had torn Scotland's World Cup hopes into shreds. When Poland went on to lose 6-1 in Italy, some measure of Scotland's task against the 'azzuries' became clear. The group positions were:

	P	W	D	L	F	A	PTS
Italy	4	3	1	0	14	2	7
Poland	6	2	2	2	11	10	6
Scotland	4	2	1	1	7	5	5
Finland	6	1	0	5	5	20	2

Only the two Scotland-Italy fixtures were outstanding. If Scotland could win both they would still qualify. They would need three points to force a play-off. Anything less and it was goodbye to the 1966 World Cup finals.

Jock Stein was not one for panicking, but certain team changes could not be gainsaid. Alec Hamilton's international career was terminated; so was the redoubtable Crerand's. For this most crucial of matches two new caps were awarded, to Ronnie McKinnon of Rangers – when Billy McNeill withdrew with a knee injury – and to Celtic's Bobby Murdoch, taking over from Crerand. John Greig turned makeshift full-back in place of Hamilton. With McCreadie serving a suspension and replaced by Rangers' Davie Provan, the entire Scottish back line was reconstructed.

Jim Baxter had broken his leg a year previously, and following his transfer to Sunderland under the managership of Ian McColl had found it difficult to force his way back into the Scotland team. There could be no more opportune occasion for Slim Jim to display his class. He was irresistibly brought back into the side, and handed the captaincy. Denis Law, for all his intimate knowledge of Italian football and the fact that he was now Scotland's top scorer in history, had run into a lean spell and was left out for just the second time in three years. This permitted Neil Martin (also now on Sunderland's payroll) to return for his final cap. The experience of John Hughes was preferred to the dash of Willie Johnston. All told, only five players were retained from the numbing Polish experience.

The Italians would field some of Europe's most famous players. Italy had won the World Cup twice in the distant past – in 1934 and 1938 – but, strangely, had failed dismally in post-1945 competitions. They had found themselves knocked out in the first round in 1950, 1954 and 1962, and in 1958 had failed even to reach the finals – when Northern Ireland had been their conquerors. This was the first Scottish-Italian meeting for thirty-four years, since Scotland journeyed to a 0-3 defeat in Rome in 1931.

It was the strength and reputation of Italy's strongest clubs which impressed more than any tangible success of the national team. The two Milanese clubs – AC and Internazionale – had carried off the European Cup in 1963, '64 and '65, and six of the current Italian side played in that city, including the renowned Facchetti, Mazzola and Rivera. Facchetti and Henderson would be resuming an old acquaintance: they had faced one another twice the previous season, in the European Cup.

The Italian side was managed by Edmondo Fabbri, who enjoyed the luxury of one complete month free from Italian League distractions in which to prepare with his squad for the task in hand. Given the shape of the group, it surprised no-one to find Italy – one broad hoop encircling their chests – packing seven or eight men immediately in defence; nor that Gilzean and Martin were marked so closely as to border on personal indecency.

Hampden's new floodlights beamed down on ninety minutes of relentless Scottish effort. Without a winger to mark, Provan could venture up the left at will. His shot after sixteen minutes was sliced by Facchetti over his own bar. If most of the play was to be found inside the Italian half, however, the more dangerous moments were happening at the other end. The tall, quick Barison gave Greig a hard time, and the speed of Sandro Mazzola constantly kept McKinnon on his toes. Bremner fought throughout to curb Gianni Rivera. In the midst of Scottish pressure Barison powered in a header to the top corner which had to be nodded out by Greig. For Scotland, Baxter shone like a beacon light, illuminating all his team's inventive moves. The last memory of a stirring first half was of Baxter pile-driving a shot inches wide of Negri's post.

After the break Italy continued to frustrate Scotland, soaking up shots, crosses, headers and lobs like a human sponge. Yet Italy also had their moments. Lodetti's drive beat the thigh-strapped Brown but was thumped clear by Greig, and Mazzola's flick squeezed under the goalkeeper and past a post. Rivera then escaped Bremner to shoot into the side netting. Brown had come nearer than Negri to losing a goal.

Hampden was already emptying as Scotland mustered one final surge. Gilzean's point-blank effort was parried by the goalkeeper. With less than two minutes on the clock, and the Italians content to hump the ball into the crowd, Baxter – who else? – slipped a precision pass through the Italian defence. Greig, who had already distinguished himself with two clearances off his own goal-line, galloped through to crash Baxter's pass low inside Negri's left post.

Hampden went potty. At the end the crowd refused to disperse, demanding an encore. The players returned to acknowledge the cheers and chaired Greig from the pitch. Scotland were, after all, still alive in the World Cup, but the *Glasgow Herald* was in no mood to get carried away: 'Before the blood rushes to one's head it is sobering to recall the pattern of the 88 minutes which went before the goal. There were very few of them in which Scotland looked capable of penetrating a superbly organised Italian defence'.

SCOTLAND (0)1   ITALY (0)0
  Greig

SCOTLAND: W Brown (Spurs), J Greig (Rangers), D Provan (Rangers), R Murdoch (Celtic), R McKinnon (Rangers), J Baxter (Sunderland, capt.), W Henderson (Rangers), W Bremner (Leeds), A Gilzean (Spurs), N Martin (Sunderland), J Hughes (Celtic).

ITALY: Negri, Burgnich, Facchetti, Guarneri, Salvadore, Rosato, Lodetti, Bulgarelli, Mazzola, Rivera, Barison.

Tuesday, 7 December 1965
ITALY v SCOTLAND   Naples 72,000

Greig's life-saver meant that Scotland had achieved the first of two necessary victories over Italy, if a place was to be secured in the England World Cup. The second was likely to be even harder, if only for the fact that it would not take place at Hampden. Scotland would either have to win in Naples to qualify directly, or they would need to draw, and then – in view of their markedly inferior goal figures – beat the Italians in a play-off decider.

The question of which of these objectives to aim for preoccupied Stein during the month in hand. Should he instruct his side to frustrate the Italians and play for a draw, or go for broke in the hope of a shock victory? This decision was eventually made easier by outside considerations. Brown and McNeill were still ruled out through injury. They were joined on the wounded list by Jim Baxter, so influential at Hampden. Then, on the Saturday preceding the match, there was some ill-feeling expressed towards Bill Shankly and Matt Busby – the Scottish managers of Liverpool and Manchester United – for not releasing key players from league engagements. Injuries to certain members of the Scottish squad were sustained that day, none more publicised than that to Denis Law -- though it was doubtful whether he would have been reinstated into the Scottish side.

The Scotland manager found his squad of twenty-two cut down to fifteen fit players – fourteen, when hours before kick-off Willie Henderson ruled himself out. Stein could still have fielded a side recognisable in terms of defence, midfield and attack, but he opted to withdraw Gilzean from the No 9 shirt and hand it to ... Ron Yeats, the Liverpool centre-half. Fears that Yeats would act as a stopgap centre-forward were removed after kick-off, when he took his place alongside McKinnon as a second orthodox stopper. There were no longer any lingering doubts about the type of game Scotland would try to play.

Given the significance of the match, the Scotland team looked alarmingly unwieldy and inexperienced, which could not be excused by the injury situation. Adam Blacklaw had last played in goal for his country two and a half years previously. Now he was summoned to replace the unfit Brown. McCreadie's suspension was served, so he returned to the defence, permitting Greig to move back into midfield. Included in the side were two players who had made their debuts a fortnight earlier in beating Wales 4-1, Charlie Cooke of Dundee and Jim Forrest of Rangers. Forrest and Hughes would be all Scotland had to show for an emasculated attack. If Scotland should lose a goal, goodness knows how they were going to manufacture one themselves in reply. Looking at the team as a whole, only one player – Greig – had earned more than seven caps, an extraordinary state of affairs that did not augur well.

Edmondo Fabbri had made three changes, one of them in goal when bringing in Albertosi for the injured Negri. Barison was dropped, solely on the grounds of his culpability in permitting Greig to advance unattended to score at Hampden.

Naples, and its San Paolo Stadium, was regarded in Italy as something of a soccer outpost, away from the more prosperous and fashionable cities to the north. On a wet, windy night the early minutes passed without alarm for the white-shirted Scots. The visitors succeeded in extracting the sting from the hosts to such an extent that there was little atmosphere in the stadium, whose spectators huddled under a myriad of umbrellas. Scotland methodically funnelled back, attempting to slow the pace of the game, so that there was little positive action to report until the 38th minute. McCreadie shaped to clear Rivera's cross, only to completely miscue the ball, which fell for Pascutti to score from close in. Cushions rained down from the terraces in the unmistakable language of celebration. Poor McCreadie's inexplicable error had effectively put Scotland out of the World Cup, for they were hardly equipped to exert pressure on Italy's formidable defence now that they needed to. Beforehand Italy had looked tense and irritable: now they imposed an iron grip on the game till the end. Scotland, it seemed, could only hope to depart with dignity, for they failed to create a single worthwhile opening throughout the match.

In fact, there were only sixteen minutes remaining when Italy formally made the game safe. Blacklaw collided with a defender in punching out a centre. Before the goalkeeper could recover, Facchetti – all of twenty-five yards distant – flighted the ball back under the crossbar. Blacklaw leapt upwards and back but the ball dipped beyond his groping fingers and into the net.

At the death Rivera's lateral flick was angled home by Mora to complete

Scotland's anti-climactic exit from the 1966 World Cup. Afterwards, Albertosi the goalkeeper was asked what had been his most anxious moment during the match. 'When Yeats dived on me,' he replied. Enough said. Up on the cold, wet terraces of the San Paolo Stadium the night was pierced by constellations of bonfires.

ITALY (1)3   SCOTLAND (0)0
    Pascutti, Facchetti, Mora

ITALY: Albertosi, Burgnich, Facchetti, Rosato, Salvadore, Lodetti, Mora, Bulgarelli, Mazzola, Rivera, Pascutti.

SCOTLAND: A Blacklaw (Burnley), D Provan (Rangers), E McCreadie (Chelsea), R Murdoch (Celtic), R McKinnon (Rangers), J Greig (Rangers, capt.), J Forrest (Rangers), W Bremner (Leeds), R Yeats (Liverpool), C Cooke (Dundee), J Hughes (Celtic).

So the despair of Naples followed the euphoria of Hampden. But Italy's jubilation was also to be transient. Within seven months they were to experience defeat at the hands of North Korea and ignominious elimination from the World Cup finals. Tomatoes and ridicule awaited their return to Rome. Meanwhile Scotland could only look on in frustration as England, playing every match at Wembley and latterly without wingers, lifted the World Cup. How far Scotland would have reached would remain a question without an answer.

World Cup Qualifying Group 8:

		HOME					AWAY					
	P	W	D	L	F	A	W	D	L	F	A	PTS
ITALY	6	3	0	0	15	2	1	1	1	2	1	9
Scotland	6	2	0	1	5	3	1	1	1	3	5	7
Poland	6	1	2	0	8	1	1	0	2	3	9	6
Finland	6	1	0	2	3	4	0	0	3	2	16	2

Other group results

Poland v Italy	0-0
Italy v Finland	6-1
Finland v Italy	0-2
Finland v Poland	2-0
Poland v Finland	7-0
Italy v Poland	6-1

Scotland appearances and goal-scorers:
World Cup qualifying rounds 1966

	A	G		A	G	
Greig J	6	2	Provan D	2	–	
Brown W*†	4	–	Blacklaw A	1	–	
Hamilton A	4	–	Chalmers S	1	1	
Henderson W	4	–	Collins R†	1	–	
Law D*	4	2	Cooke C	1	–	
McCreadie E	4	–	Forrest J	1	–	
Bremner W	3	–	Forsyth C	1	–	
Crerand P*	3	–	Gibson D	1	1	
Hughes J	3	–	Hamilton W	1	–	
Martin N	3	–	Johnston W	1	–	
McNeill W*	3	1	Johnstone J	1	–	
Baxter J*	2	–	Kennedy J	1	–	
Gilzean A	2	–	McGrory J	1	–	
McKinnon R	2	–	Scott A*†	1	–	
Murdoch R	2	–	Wilson D*	1	1	
			Yeats R	1	–	
			caps	66	8	goals

31 players

Scottish League	39
English League	27
	66

*Appeared in 1962 World Cup
†Appeared in 1958 World Cup

'Slim Jim' Baxter (Rangers) played for Scotland in the World Cup
qualifying rounds of 1962 and 66. He made 7 World Cup appearances
in all.

CHAPTER 6

The 1970 World Cup

If Scotland intended to win the World Cup in 1970 they would have to perform far from the familiar climate and conditions of Britain, and travel to Mexico with its hazards of heat and altitude. Not being seeded in their qualifying group, Scotland were also bound to face one of Europe's strongest sides. Too true. Scotland should get the better of Cyprus; they might get the better of Austria; but could they overcome West Germany? The Germans had reached the 1966 World Cup Final, taken England to extra time, and lost because a Russian linesman erroneously believed Hurst's shot off the crossbar bounced behind the goal-line.

There was, as seems distressingly familiar reporting, further cause for despondency in Scotland's international results twixt World Cups. Of thirteen matches played prior to the curtain raiser against Austria in 1968, Scotland won only four. Three of these were against Northern Ireland, Wales and Denmark. The other was at Wembley, Scotland proudly inflicting on the world champions their first defeat since their coronation. Scottish fans lived off the Wembley triumph, sucking it dry of any long-term meaning. It flattered to deceive that all was well with the Scottish team when the truth was more sobering. The previous year defeats had been recorded against England, Holland and Portugal – all at Hampden. And following the Wembley festival Scotland lost at home to the Soviet Union and then to the Irish in Belfast. This string of defeats revealed the overall worth of the Scottish team more accurately than the isolated success at Wembley, which took on all the qualities of an oasis in a prolonged Scottish desert.

Circumstances also rendered the taste of victory at Wembley less sweet. Scotland had agreed to compete for the 1968 European Championships. For the one and only time British access to the quarter-finals was reserved for the winners of the Home International Championships over two successive seasons, 1966-67 and 1967-68. In that context, Scotland's Wembley victory was cancelled out by the defeat in Belfast, and England finished top of the pile.

But what helped make 1967 such a memorable year for Scottish football was that hard on the heels of the Wembley win came Celtic's momentous victory in the European Cup Final. It would surprise no-one that a whole batch of Celtic players would now be included in Scotland's World Cup teams.

Since February 1967 Scotland also had a full-time professional manager, Bobby Brown, who would enjoy greater all-round autonomy than any of his predecessors.

The Qualifying Rounds

Wednesday, 6 November 1968
SCOTLAND v AUSTRIA   Hampden 65,000

Notwithstanding the resurgence of Celtic's fortunes or the depressing national defeats, there was a refreshing continuity about Scotland's team affairs between 1965-68. Baxter may have gone – drifting away before his time – but no fewer than eight players who lined up against Austria had seen active service in the previous World Cup campaign. The three players enjoying their World Cup baptisms were also experienced internationalists. They were all, predictably, on Celtic's payroll. Goalkeeper Ronnie Simpson had made his Scottish debut on the occasion of the 1967 Wembley win at the venerable age of 36. Striker Bobby Lennox had been a Scottish regular for two years, and full-back Tommy Gemmell for even longer.

With West Germany obvious favourites to head Group 7, it was vital that maximum points be taken against Austria and Cyprus. Yet history suggested Scotland would have a struggle on their hands with Austria. The teams had met once previously in the World Cup, when Austria had won 1-0 in Switzerland in 1954. Of nine completed contests since 1931 Scotland had come out on top only once. There was also one 'uncompleted' match, in 1963. When Austrian discipline vanished after seventy-nine minutes with Scotland 4-1 ahead, the referee opted to abandon the game.

Denis Law was the only player still around with active memories of that bloodbath. He had been out of the Scotland side for over a year, the result of a knee operation. Now he was paired in attack for the first time with Charlie Cooke – who had swopped Dundee's blue for Chelsea's. The Celtic pair of Jimmy Johnstone and John Hughes played wide with the function of providing the ammunition. Billy Bremner assumed the captaincy from John Greig, and was now the non-stop motor in midfield in Scotland's 4-2-4 formation.

For Austria, the qualifying situation was already desperate. Although they had disposed of Cyprus 7-1, they had lost their critical home fixture with West Germany 0-2. That setback seemed to rule out the Austrians as likely qualifiers: defeat at Hampden certainly would. Austria, in fact, were performing almost apologetically when compared to their great days in the early 'thirties and early 'fifties. Their thrashing of Cyprus and a victory over Finland were the only successes they had to show for the past two seasons.

The game had an astonishing start. The Austrians scored after just two minutes. Tam Gemmell was caught in possession as he tried to dribble clear of his own goalmouth. The Austrians worked the ball cleverly to Starek who hit a swerving twenty-five yarder past the perplexed Simpson.

If Hampden was stunned, it was soon ecstatic. Five minutes later Lennox won a corner, taken by Cooke, and finished by Law at the far post. Scotland then came close to taking the lead. Cooke raced on to Bremner's pass to crash the ball against the bar.

The rest of the game could hardly live up to that electric opening. With a draw suiting neither side, both went purposefully in search of a second goal. Sometimes too purposefully. There were a number of charged incidents. Starek kicked Hughes in preference to the ball, and was booked – the first of several from either side. But Austria looked much more capable than Scotland anticipated. Starek was a gem in midfield, Hasel held the front line effectively, and some of their touch play was a delight to behold.

Substitutes were at long last permissible in World Cup football. For the second half the Austrians brought on Kogelberger in place of Redl. The Scots, with the wind behind them, began to see more of the ball. The temperature rose. Hughes was 'sandwiched' without gaining a penalty, and both teams had players cautioned.

Law and Cooke, however, were not enjoying the most productive of partnerships, and it looked as if any further goals would stem from an alternative source. With twenty minutes left wee Jimmy Johnstone hit the bar. Bremner dived to head home the rebound, but the effort was cancelled for offside.

Five minutes later Denis Law became the first Scottish player to be substituted in the World Cup – Gilzean deputised – whereupon Scotland immediately scored. Fuchsbichler had made several important interceptions, but now he failed to hold Greig's deceptive cross. In rugby terms, a ruck ensued, amid which scrum-half Bremner forced the ball over the line at the cost of an injured leg.

Austria now resumed their twinkling footwork. Scotland lived dangerously. Gilzean was the next to be booked. Chances fell to the home side to make the game safe, but they weren't taken and many a Scottish fingernail was shortened by the end. Simpson came to the rescue, hurting himself in diving at Kogelberger's boots. The defeat all but eliminated

Austria from contention, but the *Glasgow Herald* gave them their due: 'The entertainment was provided mainly by the Austrians, a well-drilled and skilful side who at times made the Scots look out of their class'.

SCOTLAND (1)2   AUSTRIA (1)1
   Law, Bremner   Starek

SCOTLAND: R Simpson (Celtic), T Gemmell (Celtic), E McCreadie (Chelsea), W Bremner (Leeds, capt.), R McKinnon (Rangers), J Greig (Rangers), J Johnstone (Celtic), C Cooke (Chelsea), J Hughes (Celtic), D Law (Man U) (*sub* A Gilzean, Spurs), R Lennox (Celtic).

AUSTRIA: Fuchsbichler, Gebhardt, Sturmberger, Eigenstiller, Pumm, Starek, Ettmayer, Metzler, Hasil, Siber, Redl (Kogelberger).

Wednesday, 11 December 1968
CYPRUS v SCOTLAND   Nicosia 12,000

Five weeks later the Scotland party jetted to the strife-torn Mediterranean island of Cyprus. They travelled happy enough with two points already secured, but they might have been even happier. West Germany had themselves recently played in the National Stadium in Nicosia. At the end of ninety minutes the Germans, despite constant pressure, had failed to score. A dropped point would have been à godsend to the Scots, but as the dying seconds of injury time ticked away the Germans found the goal they so desperately needed.

If Germany could struggle in Cyprus, so could Scotland. Bobby Brown was evidently aware of this and made changes. Three Celtic players were ruled out by injury on the Saturday – Gemmell, Johnstone and Hughes, and the other two – Lennox and Simpson – were dropped. Time had caught up with the evergreen Celtic goalkeeper. It was time to look ahead. His replacement might have been Bobby Clark, but Aberdeen had conceded eleven goals over the previous fortnight. Instead Birmingham's Jim Herriot won a second cap.

Three other players also came in for their second international appearances: Doug Fraser in place of Gemmell, Tommy McLean of Kilmarnock deputising for Johnstone, and Colin Stein replacing Hughes. The other newcomers were more experienced: Bobby Murdoch became Celtic's sole representative – policing the midfield with Bremner – while Gilzean wore the No 10 shirt previously worn by Law.

It was a journey into the unknown for Scotland. They had never played Cyprus before, nor did they have experience of a pitch which was grassless, based on clay with a gravel overlay, and compelling the wearing of rubber boots. Bremner called correctly and set the opposition to face the setting sun. Fears that Cyprus would obstinately resist on their own pitch (as the Germans had discovered) were removed within three minutes when Gilzean powered home McCreadie's cross. Cypriot spirits were further dampened when Pakkos, their one 'quality' player, was taken off injured.

Scotland, playing in white, threatened to score with every attack against the assortment of amateurs. Murdoch flashed home No 2 in the 23rd minute from way outside the box. Gilzean had the frustration of having one effort disallowed before he notched his own second. Five minutes from the interval Stein's drive was deflected past Alkiviades by a hapless defender, and there was still time for another Stein cross-shot to be helped home by an obliging Cypriot defence. By half-time Herriot had only touched the ball twice.

Second-half rain dampened Scotland's attacking frenzy and turned the playing surface into a concoction that resembled mortar. McNeill replaced McKinnon and headed a corner just too high. Near the end the hobbling Stein gave way to Lennox but there were no more goals. The hundreds of British servicemen in the ground were satisfied with the first half; bored with the second. Cyprus's sum achievement over ninety minutes was a solitary corner.

CYPRUS (0)0   SCOTLAND (5)5

Gilzean 2, Murdoch, Stein 2

CYPRUS: Alkiviades, Iacovou, Theodorou, Koureas, Panayiotou, Michaeil, Eftimiades, Crystalis, Asprou, Pakkos (Markos), Stylianou.

SCOTLAND: J Herriot (Birmingham), D Fraser (WBA), E McCreadie (Chelsea), W Bremner (Leeds, capt.), R McKinnon (Rangers) (*sub* W McNeill, Celtic), J Greig (Rangers), T McLean (Kilmarnock), R Murdoch (Celtic), C Stein (Rangers) (*sub* R Lennox, Celtic), A Gilzean (Spurs), C Cooke (Chelsea).

Wednesday, 16 April 1969
SCOTLAND v WEST GERMANY   Hampden 90,000

So far so good, but now came the real test. Scotland needed to beat a West German team which included six members of the 1966 World Cup Final eleven. The German team was brimming with world-class players – Schnellinger, Vogts, Beckenbauer, Schulz, Haller, and young Gerd Müller. The mere prospect was enough to make the mouth water.

West Germany's record in the World Cup was awesome. They had first competed in 1954 when they had confounded all predictions to beat the Hungarians in the final. In 1958 they had finished fourth; had been quarter-finalists in 1962; and finalists in 1966. The Germans had never lost a World Cup qualifying match in their history.

Nevertheless, Germany were (and are) curiously vulnerable against the weakest sides: only an injury-time goal had secured victory in Cyprus; and failure to win in Albania had seen the Germans eliminated from the first phase of the 1968 European Championships. Furthermore, the Germans had a poor track record against British sides. They had so far failed to record a victory against Scotland, had beaten England for the first time in June 1968, and in the past year had twice been held to 1-1 draws by spirited Welsh outfits.

Scotland's team showed a further five changes from that in Nicosia, although man-for-man it was still an experienced looking unit. The only real talking point was the return of fourteen-stone Liverpool goalkeeper Tommy Lawrence to replace Herriot, out with an injured hand. Lawrence's solitary previous cap had been earned six years back. Bobby Brown had hoped to field two wingers, but an injury to Hughes meant a recall for Bobby Lennox. Law and Gilzean provided a dual spearhead of potentially devastating aerial power.

Looking back over the previous three World Cups, Scotland had always managed a famous home win over their principal challengers – Spain in 1958, Czechoslovakia in 1962, and Italy in 1966. They sorely needed to extend that sequence, for otherwise the odds would be heavily stacked in favour of the Germans.

The pattern of the ninety minutes was soon established. The well-oiled German machine funnelled back as Scottish zest threatened to drive the visitors into the Clyde. On a cloudless evening Schnellinger stuck tight to Gilzean, Schulz swept up at the back, and Beckenbauer patrolled here, there and everywhere to keep his side on an even keel.

It was not a night for second-raters: there was excellence wherever the eye looked. Bremner and Murdoch relentlessly pushed Scotland forward from midfield, and Law and Gilzean both had headers on target. At the other end Müller had the ball in the net, but it had earlier passed out of play. Then the overworked Wolter pushed out a cross towards Johnstone. It only needed a clean return strike, but Johnstone's half-hit shot trundled towards goal and was hacked away.

In the 39th minute, with Germany generally backpedalling but still liable to streak upfield with lightning speed, Beckenbauer was fouled outside the Scottish penalty area. He pushed the free kick to Müller, who shielded and twisted in one moment, squeezed past McKinnon and Greig and found space to shoot wide of Lawrence. It was a goal of stunning virtuosity: and to rub salt in the wound, Wolter made an improbable save from Murdoch on the half-time whistle.

For some reason the Germans sent out a new keeper for the second half, but Scotland derived no advantage, for young Sepp Maier proved even more resilient than his predecessor. It must have been especially galling to Scotland that, even as their pressure intensified, the Germans never seemed to be breaking sweat, and even their goalmouth clearances seemed to find a free team-mate.

The Scottish wingers were perhaps the least penetrating of the home players, with the effect that Law and Gilzean were less able to employ their heading ability than was the intention. Murdoch came through the middle to plant a massive shot that speared inches the wrong side of Maier's post. The Hampden gasps of anguish hung in the air like the wail of the banshee. Shortly afterwards Lennox was pulled off in favour of the tricky skills of Charlie Cooke. The Germans responded by bringing on Lorenz for Overath.

If anything, the last ten minutes saw Germany breaking free of the Scottish stranglehold, but after eighty-eight minutes all was back in the melting pot. Scotland's substitution finally paid off. Cooke sold a dummy and stroked the ball into the path of the on-rushing Bobby Murdoch. The Celtic midfielder strode past Patzke to send a blinding shot into the far top corner of the net. Maier was forced to concede defeat and Hampden exploded with relief. It would have exploded a second time, but Bremner's last-gasp effort was headed off the line by – needless to say – Beckenbauer. The Germans' earlier composure was suddenly replaced by a desire to be rid of the ball, which spent more time on the terraces than on the pitch as the final seconds ticked away. Bobby Murdoch was justifiably the toast of Hampden.

SCOTLAND (0)1   WEST GERMANY (1)1
  Murdoch   Müller

SCOTLAND: T Lawrence (Liverpool), T Gemmell (Celtic), E McCreadie (Chelsea), W Murdoch (Celtic), R McKinnon (Rangers), J Greig (Rangers), J Johnstone (Celtic), W Bremner (Leeds, capt.), D Law (Man U), A Gilzean (Spurs), R Lennox (Celtic) (*sub* C Cooke, Chelsea).

WEST GERMANY: Wolter (Maier), Schnellinger, Vogts, Beckenbauer, Schulz, Patzke, Deerfel, Haller, Müller, Overath (Lorenz), Held.

Saturday, 17 May 1969
SCOTLAND v CYPRUS   Hampden 39,000

The euphoria was understandable: the celebrations lasted long into the night. The cold light of reality, however, told that Murdoch's sterling effort was unlikely to prove sufficient. Germany had come for the draw and had achieved it. The programme was now half-complete. Both Scotland and Germany had five points from three games, but the Germans could now look forward to three home fixtures. Already it was clear that Scotland would need some improbable results in Hamburg and Vienna come next autumn.

The first task was to dispose of Cyprus. Scotland had an undistinguished preparation. The three Home Internationals were crammed into a week at the beginning of May. A spectacular 5-3 win in Wrexham was followed by an abject 1-1 draw with the Irish at Hampden. The series concluded with Scotland being walloped 4-1 at Wembley, hardly the ideal confidence-raiser for the Cyprus match a week later.

The Scotland eleven showed further changes. Liverpool were not prepared to release Tommy Lawrence from their league fixture (English league clubs were obliged to release players for the England national team, but not for Scotland, Wales or Northern Ireland). Jim Herriot kept goal. Eddie McCreadie turned out for what transpired was his last international. Bobby Murdoch had been showing signs of battle weariness during the British Championships and was omitted from the midfield in favour of Charlie Cooke. A jinking, twisting young winger from Leeds United, Eddie Gray, brought into the side against England, retained his place. On the other touchline it was Rangers' Willie Henderson's turn for a few games at the expense of Jimmy Johnstone.   The Cypriots made a number of changes themselves, and had had the morale-booster of having scored a goal – despite losing 1-2 at home to Austria.

When Scotland failed to score within the first five minutes they became fidgety. Cyprus began to look composed, even cheeky. It was new-boy Gray who settled the nerves on the quarter-hour with a sizzling run and shot into the far corner. Billy McNeill, with precious few defensive responsibilities to fulfil, then moved upfield to take Greig's throw-in and belt the ball past Alkiviades for number two.

It was now that Colin Stein got into the act. It is doubtful whether he knew, going into the match, that no Scotland player this century had scored more than four goals in one game, and that the last person to achieve that feat was Hughie Gallacher in 1929. In the 28th minute Stein headed in Cooke's corner, and he was on his way.

Cyprus brought on two fresh pairs of legs for the second half, in their endeavour to keep the score respectable. It was slightly less respectable four minutes later when Stein intercepted a slack back-pass and dribbled the ball around the goalkeeper before slotting home. Ten minutes later the score was less respectable still, as Henderson hared down the right to set up the ball for ... Colin Stein.

Stein had his hat-trick, and there were thirty minutes left for him to inflict further damage on the Cypriot defence. On sixty-seven minutes he did just that: Alkiviades pushed away Gray's attempt, leaving Stein to thrash home at the near post.

Meanwhile Jim Herriot got bored. So did the Scotland substitutes, for none of them was invited to join in the party. Gilzean set up Henderson for the seventh goal, and with fourteen minutes left Scotland were awarded a penalty. Stein had equalled Gallacher's record, now was his chance to overtake it. Instead, responsibility for the kick was entrusted to the team's authorised penalty-taker, Tommy Gemmell. Why demean the cherished records held by the legendary heroes of old?

Scotland felt smug enough afterwards to look at the accumulated goals column with satisfaction. They had equalled their World Cup record of eight goals, established against Northern Ireland in 1949. More importantly, should there be any necessity for a play-off with West Germany, Scotland looked like having the better goal difference – in which case they would only need to draw with the Germans, not beat them. Scotland should have known better. Four days later Cyprus played in Germany and lost – 12-0. The Germans thereby overhauled Scottish goal difference. But things were looking up for Cyprus. In Nicosia they had earned one corner: at Hampden they managed two.

SCOTLAND (3)8   CYPRUS (0)0
    E Gray, McNeill, Stein 4,
    Henderson,
    Gemmell (pen)

SCOTLAND: J Herriot (Birmingham), E McCreadie (Chelsea), T Gemmell (Celtic), W Bremner (Leeds, capt.), W McNeill (Celtic), J Greig (Rangers), W Henderson (Rangers), C Cooke (Chelsea), C Stein (Rangers), A Gilzean (Spurs), E Gray (Leeds).

CYPRUS: Alkiviades, Mertakis, Savakis (Fokk), Stephanis (Constantas), Koureas, Sotirakis, Panikos, Marcou, Crystalis, Mellis, Stylianou.

Wednesday, 22nd October 1969
WEST GERMANY v SCOTLAND   Hamburg 72,000

The crunch came the following October with a visit to the Volkspark Stadium in Hamburg. In the interim the Germans had managed another critical win: 1-0 at home to Austria, and now Scottish backs were well and truly to the wall. This was the Germans' last fixture: the Scots had to travel to Vienna a fortnight later. The respective positions were:

	P	W	D	L	F	A	PTS
West Germany	5	4	1	0	17	1	9
Scotland	4	3	1	0	16	2	7

Defeat in Hamburg would put Scotland out, and they could not really even afford to draw. True, that would keep them alive for the moment, but they would then need outright victories over Austria and in the German play-off to reach Mexico. Four years previously, when faced with a similar dilemma, Jock Stein had taken a vital decision: go for a draw rather than a win in Italy. Bobby Brown now had the same choice to confront, but his conclusion differed. The devil take the hindmost: Scotland would go all out to win in Hamburg. That would leave them needing only a draw in Vienna to secure qualification.

It was a familiar looking side which Brown entrusted with the task of gaining an immortal victory – with one notable exception. Hibernian's Peter Cormack picked up a rare cap, bringing his hard-running attributes to bolster Bremner and Gray in midfield. There would have been a second unfamiliar face, Hugh Curran of Wolves, to lead the attack in place of Colin Stein. The Rangers striker was going through a lean spell in the new season, but Curran went down with flu on match day and Stein unexpectedly kept his place. His past scoring record for Scotland was exceptional, ten goals from six games, and only once had he failed to find the net. Another of his goals would be invaluable in Hamburg.

With the Germans employing two central strikers, Uwe Seeler and Gerd Müller, it was sensible for Brown to match them with twin central defenders, McKinnon and McNeill. Greig switched to right-back to partner Gemmell. Given the importance of the match, which was shown live on Scottish television, key Scottish League matches were postponed. The English League was less co-operative, but it was the Germans who suffered most at the hands of 'foreign' leagues. Helmut Haller arrived late from Juventus, and AC Milan simply refused to release world-class defender Karl-Heinz Schnellinger for the big match.

Scotland could not have dreamt of a more sensational opening. A weaving run by Eddie Gray after just three minutes ended with a shot-cum-centre which Maier, straining upwards, couldn't hold. Jimmy Johnstone, the smallest player on the field, could hardly believe it as the ball dropped sweetly for him to bang Scotland in front.

Brown's team showed no inclination to fall back and protect their lead, making the Germans look almost mundane as they played some of the most controlled football anyone could remember. Bremner fought for everything in midfield, while Gray and Johnstone teased and tormented the German full-backs. For half an hour Herriot barely touched the ball, although Beckenbauer's flicked free-kick did set up Haller to crash an almighty shot against the keeper's right post. Undeterred, Scotland had chances of their own to make it 2-0, none better than when Gilzean hoisted the ball over Maier's crossbar.

In the 38th minute the Germans equalised. McNeill's inattentive back-pass cost an unnecessary and expensive corner. The flighted ball eluded Herriot and bobbed about in a scrummage before Fichtel lashed it home. The Scots' immediate riposte was to force Maier into a flying save from Gray.

The game was already one to be savoured, and it increasingly became one unsuitable for faint hearts. The Germans were fired up from the start of the second half. Johnstone spent as much time on his bottom as on his feet. Yet twice within minutes Scotland came close to retaking the lead. Gemmell, wide on the left, clipped the bar, before Bremner crashed a ferocious shot squarely against the same length of timber.

By this stage the number of bookings exceeded goals, but on the hour the game exploded. Seeler, the German captain making his 62nd appearance, headed a free kick to Müller who mercilessly hooked past Herriot. But German celebrations were strangled in mid-cheer when Gilzean rose almost nonchalantly to nod McKinnon's cross past Maier.

Scotland sensed blood and proceeded to force the Germans back towards their own goal. Müller and Overath were added to the list of bookings, and Stein saw his best effort of the night headed out by Vogts. It seemed as though Scotland would leave with a famous, if probably futile, draw when the Germans pulled out their master punch. The fleet-footed Libuda had given Gemmell a trying time throughout. There were less than ten minutes left when Haller's diagonal pass out of defence found Libuda out on the right. The winger set off as if propelled by fear and evaded Gemmell yet again to score a supreme goal. The Scottish players collapsed where they stood. It was bad enough to lose when they scarcely deserved to, but ignominy was to follow. The frustrated Gemmell swung a criminal kick at Haller and was ordered off. Scotland could not save the game with eleven men, let alone ten, and made a tearful farewell.

WEST GERMANY (1)3　　　　　SCOTLAND (1)2
　　Fichtel, Müller, Libuda　　　　　Johnstone, Gilzean

WEST GERMANY: Maier, Höttges, Vogts, Beckenbauer, Schulz, Fichtel, Libuda, Seeler, Müller, Overath, Haller.

SCOTLAND: J Herriot (Birmingham), J Greig (Rangers), T Gemmell (Celtic), W Bremner (Leeds, capt.), R McKinnon (Rangers), W McNeill (Celtic), J Johnstone (Celtic), P Cormack (Hibs), A Gilzean (Spurs), E Gray (Leeds), C Stein (Rangers).

Wednesday, 5 November 1969
AUSTRIA v SCOTLAND　　　　　　　　　　　　　　Vienna 11,000

So Scotland, once again, had been beaten in the vital away fixture against the group's toughest opposition. In that respect defeat in Hamburg simply accorded with those in Spain (1958), Czechoslovakia (1962) and Italy (1966). Yet this time there was honour in defeat. Seldom had Scotland played better and lost, but Reinhard Libuda would go on to destroy other teams in Mexico.

Whatever moral honours went to Scotland, they were out of the World Cup. Their visit to Vienna two weeks later was utterly meaningless, an aggravation which they could easily have done without. All the match could offer, apart from pride, was an opportunity to experiment, and Brown made six team changes. Aberdeen's Ernie McGarr won a second, and final, cap. Strangely he would be the fourth goalkeeper Scotland had called upon in six World Cup matches. The persistent failing to find a settled keeper over the years cannot have helped continuity or confidence in the Scottish defence.

At left-back Manchester United's Frances Burns made his one and only international appearance in place of the suspended Gemmell. Also making his delayed debut was Wolves' Hugh Curran, as Colin Stein stepped down. With Cormack injured there was a recall for Bobby Murdoch, for what turned out to be his last game for Scotland. There was no longer any need for a second orthodox centre-half, so Billy McNeill gave way in defence to Hibernian's Pat Stanton. Only three Austrian players remained from the side beaten at Hampden twelve long months before.

After the champagne, the beer. In Vienna Scotland were as dreadful as they had been impressive in Hamburg. The pitch was wet, the crowd small, and Curran didn't get a kick. Scotland fell behind after fourteen minutes, when Redl climbed above Burns to head home Parits' centre.

Scotland were finished from that moment. Greig became the most unpopular man in the Prater Stadium when he crudely crunched the scorer, who needed lengthy treatment. A half-hearted shot from Cooke was the only effort on goal Scotland could muster throughout the first half. They went off fortunate to be only one goal in arrears.

It was not that Scotland were apathetic: they were simply bad. The tackling was as fierce and committed as in a cup-tie, but it could not prevent Austria increasing their lead after fifty-three minutes. Geyer, wide on the right, lost and regained possession three times as he forced his way past clumsy challenges. Eventually the ball ran to Redl who finished off the messiest of goals.

With a two-goal lead under their belts, Austria sat back as Scotland pressed unimaginatively forward. Colin Stein substituted for Curran, and Leeds' Peter Lorimer became the third Scottish player to win a first cap when he took over from Cooke. Nothing transpired which either substitute would remember with favour. For Scotland, the 1970 World Cup was well and truly over.

AUSTRIA (1)2   SCOTLAND (0)0
   Redl 2

AUSTRIA: Harraither, Wallner, Sturmberger, Schmidradner, Fak, Geyer, Hof, Parits, Kaiser, Ettmayer, Redl.

SCOTLAND; E McGarr (Aberdeen), J Greig (Rangers), F Burns (Man U), R Murdoch (Celtic), R McKinnon (Rangers), P Stanton (Hibs), C Cooke (Chelsea) (*sub* P Lorimer, Leeds), W Bremner (Leeds, capt.), A Gilzean (Spurs), H Curran (Wolves) (*sub* C Stein, Rangers), E Gray (Leeds).

The jinx which had haunted German football in the shape of British teams had first been laid to rest in 1968, with a win over England at Hanover. Following the tense victory over Scotland in Hamburg, the Germans with proper sense of balance duly eliminated England, by the same score – 3-2 – from the quarter-finals in Mexico. The exhaustion imposed by that extra-time marathon, as much as anything else, was responsible for the Germans falling at the next hurdle – to the Italians – also after extra time. Italy, in turn, lost the Final to the magnificent Brazil.

World Cup Qualifying Group 7:

		HOME					AWAY				
	P	W	D	L	F	A	W	D	L	F	A	PTS
WEST GERMANY	6	3	0	0	16	2	2	1	0	4	1	11
Scotland	6	2	1	0	11	2	1	0	2	7	5	7
Austria	6	2	0	1	9	3	1	0	2	3	4	6
Cyprus	6	0	0	3	1	8	0	0	3	1	27	0

Other group results

Austria v Cyprus	7-1
Austria v West Germany	0-2
Cyprus v West Germany	0-1
West Germany v Cyprus	12-0
Cyprus v Austria	1-2
West Germany v Austria	1-0

Scotland appearances and goal-scorers:
World Cup qualifying rounds 1970

	A	G		A	G
Bremner W*	6	1	Law D*†	2	1
Gilzean A*	6(1)	3	Burns F	1	–
Greig J*	6	–	Cormack P	1	–
Cooke C*	5(1)	–	Curran H	1	–
McKinnon R*	5	–	Fraser D	1	–
Gemmell T	4	1	Henderson W*	1	1
McCreadie E*	4	–	Hughes J*	1	–
Stein C	4(1)	6	Lawrence T	1	–
Gray E	3	1	Lorimer P	1(1)	–
Herriot J	3	–	McGarr E	1	–
Johnstone J*	3	1	McLean T	1	–
Lennox R	3(1)	–	Stanton P	1	–
McNeill W*†	3(1)	1	Simpson R	1	–
Murdoch R*	3	2	caps	72	18 goals
27 players					

Scottish League	38
English League	34
	72

Bracket signifies appearance was as a substitute
*Appeared in 1966 World Cup
†Appeared in 1962 World Cup

Billy Bremner attended by Zairinho of Brazil in an international match between the two countries. Billy was to play for his country in the World Cup campaigns of 1966, 1970 and 1974.

The 1974 World Cup

The qualifying draw for the 1974 World Cup – the finals of which would be staged in West Germany – pitched Scotland into a welcome three-team group. Even more welcome was the identity of the other two teams: Denmark and Czechoslovakia. There was no need to fear either of them, and for the first time since qualifying in 1958 Scotland could claim a genuinely kind draw.

They needed it. Taken overall, Scotland's form since being eliminated from the previous World Cup caused even the most enthusiastic supporter to dig deep for excuses. Twenty-one internationals had been played: only seven won; only fourteen goals scored. Scotland had failed to survive the first phase of the 1972 European Championships – their opponents being Denmark, Portugal and Belgium. Scotland had, almost predictably, won their three home games: equally predictably, lost their three away ties.

And there lay the nub. Scotland's performances continued to invite firm diagnosis of schizophrenia. At Hampden, Scotland feared no-one. Away from Hampden, no-one feared Scotland. In between the 5-0 thrashing of Cyprus in 1968 and the coming trip to Denmark, Scotland had played eleven internationals overseas. They hadn't won any of them. There could be no better time than the present to break that depressing sequence.

To be sure, Scotland's fortunes seemed to be looking up following the galvanising effects of Tommy Docherty's appointment as team manager in the autumn of 1971, which gave him complete control over team and selection matters. Only three of the first ten matches under Docherty's stewardship had been lost.

Nor was anyone likely to disregard the second notable achievement of a Scottish club side. Celtic had won the European Cup in 1967: now Rangers had captured the Cup-Winners Cup in May 1972. Provided something could be done about that appalling away record, Scottish qualification for West Germany seemed within reach.

The Qualifying Rounds

Wednesday, 18 October 1972
DENMARK v SCOTLAND   Copenhagen 31,000

Tommy Docherty's reign as Scotland manager certainly stirred things up. Unhampered by having to consult with a selection committee, he rung the changes and brought Scottish international football into the modern world. The post-Docherty era could never be as undistinguished as pre-Docherty. He did not flinch from overturning preconceived notions. Docherty's experience of management outside Scotland and outside Britain gave him a wider vision. He wanted the strongest possible Scottish team, and that meant the willing inclusion of 'Anglos'. Almost inconceivably, in Copenhagen there was only one Celtic face in the starting line-up, and none from Rangers – the European Cup-Winners Cup holders.

There had been a marked continuity in Scotland's World Cup players during the 1966 and 1970 campaigns. Twelve of those who took part in 1970 had also appeared in 1966. Docherty was now building afresh. Peter Lorimer and the team captain, Billy Bremner, were the only survivors from 1970. Aberdeen's Bobby Clark had been more or less regular goalkeeper for over a year. In front of him was Old Trafford sweeper Martin Buchan, partnering Sheffield United's Eddie Colquhoun in the centre of defence. Full-backs John Brownlie of Hibernian and Alex Forsyth of Partick completed the defence. Arsenal's George Graham contested midfield with Bremner. The wingers were Peter Lorimer and Willie Morgan; the central strikers, Lou Macari and Jimmy Bone – the Norwich player claiming his one and only cap.

Scotland had won four out of five past clashes with Denmark, although that solitary 0-1 defeat had occurred in Copenhagen as recently as June 1971. Docherty knew his team needed a win. He also could not escape the fact of Scotland's traditional failings abroad. Docherty told the press: 'The game is becoming too academic. The ball is being treated too gently. I want it hit hard'.

His players – kitted in white to assist the requirements of black and white television – perceived little distinction between ball and man: Danish footballers were not treated too gently either. Docherty had no interest in witnessing sporadic brilliance from his players, preferring them to exhibit cold, clinical professionalism.

Despite being 'softened up', the part amateur, part expatriate Danish team must have entertained early hopes of a repeat win in the Idraetspark

Stadium, for up to the seventeenth minute all of Scotland's goal attempts had been confined to long-range pot-shots.

This Danish accomplishment counted for little when the likes of Peter Lorimer were in the opposing side. It was his venomous drive which, despite being turned for a corner, opened the lock. Taking the kick himself, Lorimer drove the ball waist-high across goal where Lou Macari stole in at the near post and stooped to head home. Capitalising on the breakthrough, George Graham strolled through the middle two minutes later to shoot against Therkildsen's legs. Bone was in the right place to hit back the loose ball: 2-0.

Such a score was just the tonic, and to keep the speedy Danes quiet Buchan crash-tackled Henning Jensen and found himself entered into the little black book of Mr Bakramov – the Russian referee who in the 1966 World Cup Final had been the linesman who decided Geoff Hurst's shot off the bar *did* cross the goal-line.

The sprightly, red-shirted Danish team hit back before the half-hour to cut Scotland's lead. Eigil Nielsen cleared Forsyth's tackle and bore down on Clark, only to be floored by the full-back's second attempt twenty-two yards out. Laudrup marched up to thump the free kick high to Clark's right. The keeper got a touch but couldn't save. Scotland reacted with a series of intimidatory challenges on their opponents, and Bremner effectively slowed up the dangerous Eigil Nielsen. More worthily, Lorimer's 45th-minute ground shot threatened to snap a post at the base.

The first half had been hard going. The second period was equally dour, with Scotland succeeding in keeping the Danes at arm's length. Bremner became the most imposing player on the pitch. After sixty minutes Graham almost restored Scotland's two-goal margin when he hammered Brownlie's centre against bar and post.

Four minutes later, Bone was replaced by fellow-debutant Joe Harper – which doubled the Aberdeen representation. Harper was the Scottish First Division's top scorer last season and this. With ten minutes remaining the wee man took Macari's backheel to stroke the most casual of goals and make the game safe for Scotland.

Harper was clearly in the mood. Within three minutes his jinking run culminated in a shot against the post. Lorimer lobbed the rebound on to Morgan's head for Scotland's fourth. Macari was then pulled off and a young man called Kenny Dalglish experienced his first taste of World Cup football.

Scotland might have had five or six by the end. But over ninety minutes the win had been harder, and less attractive, than the scoreline suggested.

None the less, a new-look national team had recorded Scotland's first victory outside Britain for four long years.

DENMARK (1)1   SCOTLAND (2)4
    Laudrup   Macari, Bone, Harper, Morgan

DENMARK: Therkildsen, T Nielsen, M Jensen, Roentved, Ahlberg, Bjoernmose, J Hansen (B Jensen), Laudrup, Olsen, H Jenson, E Nielsen.

SCOTLAND: R Clark (Aberdeen), J Brownlie (Hibs), A Forsyth (Partick), W Bremner (Leeds, capt.), E Colquhoun (Sheff U), M Buchan (Man U), P Lorimer (Leeds), L Macari (Celtic) (*sub* K Dalglish, Celtic), J Bone (Norwich) (*sub* J Harper, Aberdeen), G Graham (Arsenal), W Morgan (Man U).

Wednesday, 15 November 1972
SCOTLAND v DENMARK   Hampden 47,000

Strategically, Scotland set about qualifying for the 1974 World Cup as they had that of 1962. Then, as now, they and Czechoslovakia were joined by a weaker third country – the Irish Republic in 1962, Denmark now. Then, as now, Scotland chose their first two matches to be against the 'third' team. The two games between Czechoslovakia and that other country would follow, leaving the Scots and Czechs to round up the group with their own dual confrontation. Following the example of 1962 Scotland hoped to have four points in the vault before the Czechs commenced their programme, putting maximum pressure on their East European rivals.

And so, four weeks after returning from Copenhagen, Scotland sought to finish off the Danish challenge. Docherty made four changes: the Danes six – capitalising on the availability of a couple of expatriate players not released for the earlier match. The Leeds influence on the Scottish team was steadily being extended. Added to Bremner and Lorimer was the Elland Road goalkeeper, David Harvey. Born in England of Scottish parents, Harvey was turning out for his first international. (There might have been four Leeds players on display, save for an injury to Eddie Gray which caused him to withdraw from the squad.) The only other change in defence was the recall of Willie Donachie in place of Forsyth.

Bremner and Graham continued in midfield; Lorimer and Morgan wide on the flanks. Joe Harper and Kenny Dalglish, both brought on in Copenhagen, lined up from the start – Dalglish gaining his opportunity when Macari called off. Traditionalists would have been mortified by the overall composition of the Scottish team. Only three players were from

A Scotland squad of the 70's gathered at Largs. Back row (left to right) – Donachie, Parlane, Hay, Holton, Forsyth, Johnstone, Jardine. Middle row Dalglish, McGrain, McAllister, McCloy, Hunter, Stanton, Duncan. Front row – Morgan, Stein, Graham, Hartford, Bremner, Macari, Doyle, Schaedler.

north of the border: the rest were all Anglos – the most ever included in a Scottish World Cup fixture.

Any Scottish nerves disappeared from the second minute when they took a brisk lead. Lorimer, as with Scotland's opener in Denmark, won a corner which he took himself. The ball was cleared towards the opposite corner flag, and when Colquhoun finally despatched it back into the goalmouth, Kenny Dalglish was on hand to score his first international goal.

Spurred on by Bremner and Graham, the game was Scotland's for the taking. Lorimer and Morgan each came desperately close to adding to the score, and the Manchester United winger proved a constant irritation to the prickly Danes. The visitors had clearly been unsettled by some of the fierce Scottish 'tackles' in Copenhagen, for their current eleven included its share of hit-men. But after Jensen had failed to squeeze the ball past Harvey, and Jansen had kneed an inviting equaliser wide of the post, Danish scoring opportunities evaporated.

Scotland sealed the result, sensibly, by repeating the lesson of the first half and scoring immediately play resumed. A substitute goalkeeper, Hildebrandt, awaited the Scots, but he could do nothing as Lorimer collected Graham's cross to the far post, held off a challenge, and whacked the ball into goal.

Denmark rarely threatened after that, and the game died as an effective contest. The rest of the second half produced its share of Scottish shots, and more than its share of Danish pass-backs. Denmark seemed concerned only to avoid losing a third goal. Harper, providing a Laurel and Hardy spectacle against the giant Munk Jensen, failed to impose himself legitimately and was booked for taking out his frustration on the substitute goalkeeper. Immediately afterwards Dalglish came off, allowing a sixth and final cap to Coventry's Willie Carr. The referee made a note of two Danish names: Laudrup, who came on as a substitute, and Munk Jensen for an unsporting assault on Lorimer. The Leeds winger did not appreciate the attention he was receiving. In the 84th minute Roentved hacked him once too often, Lorimer swung an angry fist, and both were shown the way to the changing rooms. No sooner had they departed the stage than Carr was fouled, Morgan took the penalty, and the ball sailed over the bar.

If the scoreline in Copenhagen somewhat flattered Scotland, that at Hampden did not do justice to their all-round superiority. But afterwards the foe turned friend. Could Denmark do Scotland a favour the following spring and avoid two defeats from Czechoslovakia? Three World Cups previously the Republic of Ireland had been unable to assist Scotland in this way, losing twice to the Czechs. But in May 1973 came the marvellous news: the Danes had drawn 1-1 in Copenhagen. The Czechs' immediate 6-0 revenge in the return match could not rectify the damage. Scotland were poised to qualify.

SCOTLAND (1)2   DENMARK (0)0
    Dalglish, Lorimer

SCOTLAND: D Harvey (Leeds), J Brownlie (Hibs), W Donachie (Man C), W Bremner (Leeds, capt.), E Colquhoun (Sheff U), M Buchan (Man U), P Lorimer (Leeds), K Dalglish (Celtic) (*sub* W Carr, Coventry), J Harper (Aberdeen), G Graham (Arsenal), W Morgan (Man U).

DENMARK: Therkildsen (Hildebrandt), Ahlberg, J Hansen, M Jensen, Roentved, Bjerre, Olsen, Michaelson, B Jansen, Christianssen (Laudrup), Le Fevre.

Wednesday, 26 September 1973
SCOTLAND v CZECHOSLOVAKIA   Hampden 100,000

It was to be ten months before Scotland embarked on the second phase of their qualifying campaign. Those ten months were pretty near disastrous from the point of view of building on the momentum generated by Tommy Docherty. Within weeks of the second victory over Denmark he had turned his back on SFA bronze in favour of Old Trafford gold. Docherty's successor presented a complete contrast: where the Doc was loud, Willie Ormond was quiet; where Docherty had managed some of Europe's powerful clubs, Ormond had come straight from the provincial pastures of St Johnstone. Of Scotland's first six games under the new manager's direction five were lost – the first, and worst, of them by the margin of 5-0 when England crushed the Scots on 14 February to 'celebrate' the centenary of the Scottish FA. Rarely had a 'St Valentine's Day Massacre' had such painful memories for Scotland. Before the season was through, first Northern Ireland, then Brazil, also came and saw and conquered at Hampden.

If the national stadium was proving an unhappy hunting ground for Scotland of late, they at least had the consolation that, come the World Cup, it would likely revert to being a veritable fortress to visiting teams. Only England (twice in the 1950s) and Poland had ever won there in fifteen World Cup eliminators. The rare but vital Scottish away win in Denmark, followed by the Czechs' failure there, meant that Scotland could lose 20-0 in Bratislava and not care a fig – provided they beat the Czechs at Hampden beforehand. Scotland were just two points away from certain qualification, and the Czechs, pale reflections of their 1962 team, had only recently halted a sequence of nine games without a win. Their 6-0 victory over Denmark would be left as a meaningless statistic unless they could avoid defeat at Hampden.

There were no current Czechs with active memories of previous Scottish–Czech World Cup skirmishes a dozen years back. But there was one Scot – the inimitable Denis Law. He was thirty-three years old now, and in his second stint with Manchester City. Docherty had begun the process of his international resurrection, and now it would be consummated by Ormond. The legendary Law stepped back into the side for his fourth World Cup, twelve years to the day since he carved his own niche in immortality by scoring twice during the Czechs' previous visit to Hampden.

Ormond had built a completely fresh team from that inherited from Docherty. Only Bremner, Dalglish and Morgan remained, though some of the omitted faces would later be recalled. Celtic's Alistair Hunter came back for a rare appearance in goal. The full-backs were Sandy Jardine and Danny McGrain. They flanked Manchester United's young giant Jim Holton and the first of two debutants – the Scottish Football Writers' Player of 1973, George Connelly. The second international baptism was for Coventry's flying winger, Tommy Hutchison. Bremner would police midfield with Celtic's tough-tackling Davie Hay.

For those unable to obtain tickets, the match was transmitted live on TV. Battle was as hard and uncompromising whether viewed from terrace or sofa. Scotland attacked: Czechoslovakia defended. Dalglish and Hutchison were instantly provided with a worm's-eye view of the turf, and Law announced his return to international duty with a horrendous foul on Bendl. Samek clattered Bremner and was booked; the crowd chanted 'Animals', and Bremner whacked Kuna so fiercely that the Czech schemer was forced to limp off, replaced by Dobias. The game was not yet twenty minutes old.

Efforts by Bremner, Jardine and Morgan promised a goal before Ally Hunter, after thirty-three minutes, sent a wave of despair through the stadium. Adamec's clearance upfield, interrupting a raging Scottish attack, had no obvious constructive intent: nor did Nehoda's swipe at the ball out on the right. But Hunter flapped and flopped, and flipped the ball inside a post. Silence.

Scottish tears took only seven minutes to dry. The omnipresent Law won a corner which big Jim Holton powered into the net after outjumping the entire Czech defence – goalkeeper included.

Not subdued, the Czechs looked more impressive after the break.

Pivarnik rolled the ball along Hunter's crossbar. Bremner continued to invite Czech displeasure, and Panenka became the second player booked for crunching the Scottish captain. Ormond recognised the need for greater firepower, and in the 64th minute replaced the subtleties of Dalglish with the brute strength of Leeds' reserve striker, Joe Jordan, for what was hoped would be a make or break substitution. Jordan almost made his mark with a bullet header which flew too high, but Scottish adrenalin was now in full flow. With fifteen minutes left Bremner received Morgan's touched free kick to thump leather on wood. The ball ran along the goal-line, past the opposite post, from where Morgan finally chipped it back into the enemy nerve centre. This time Jordan's header was straight and true. Pandemonium.

Now the pattern changed. Czechoslovakia brought on Capkovic for Panenka and piled men forward. But Scotland were not to be denied and gained a famous victory. Hutchison, Jordan and Law were the talk of the land. Scotland had become the first European team to qualify for West Germany, and the singing lasted long.

SCOTLAND (1)2	CZECHOSLOVAKIA (1)1
Holton, Jordan	Nehoda

SCOTLAND: A Hunter (Celtic), S Jardine (Rangers), D McGrain (Celtic), W Bremner (Leeds, capt.), J Holton (Man U), G Connelly (Celtic), D Hay (Celtic), D Law (Man C), W Morgan (Man U), K Dalglish (Celtic) (*sub* J Jordan, Leeds), T Hutchison (Coventry).

CZECHOSLOVAKIA: Viktor, Pivarnik, Samek, Zlocha, Bendl, Bicovsky, Adamec, Kuna (Dobias), Nehoda, Stratil, Panenka (Capkovic).

Wednesday, 17 October 1973
CZECHOSLOVAKIA v SCOTLAND   Bratislava 10,000

So Scotland were back in the World Cup finals, having gained revenge for that crushing night in Brussels in 1961, when the Czechs had won a bruising play-off. In 1973 the Czechs had hoped that a draw at Hampden would set them up for victory, and qualification, in Bratislava. It was not to be. The present match was about as meaningless as a bikini in Siberia.

The principal Scottish casualty from the unforgettable Hampden triumph was Ally Hunter, who would not sample international football again. In his stead, Harvey returned. Injuries compelled Ormond to make other changes. Holton, Hutchison and Bremner were all unfit. The last-named had an ankle injury which there was no sense in aggravating.

Bremner's withdrawal was eagerly seized upon by the Czech press to imply cowardice. Kuna had not played again following Bremner's 'attentions' at Hampden. The talk was of revenge if the Scottish captain played. Instead, Davie Hay was handed the honour of skippering his country for the first time. The two centre-backs were both newcomers: John Blackley of Hibernian gaining a first cap; Rangers' Tom Forsyth a second.

The Czechs still retained a sizeable nucleus of players from the 1970 team which lost to England in Mexico: Viktor in goal, Hagar, Pollak, Vesely and Capkovic. Three others – Adamec, Kuna and Dobias – from that 1970 side had played at Hampden, though not now in the Telhalne Stadium.

To describe the game as tedious is to be generous. Scotland had every incentive to avoid unnecessary cautions, and their tactics seemed to be no more threatening than to retain possession wherever possible. This they achieved without due distress until the seventeenth minute, when Nehoda carried the ball up to and past Forsyth, who challenged untidily and handled into the bargain. Nehoda, having manufactured the penalty, was given the privilege of scoring from it.

The Scots showed no great enthusiasm to make good the deficit; Czechoslovakia even less to increase it, or exact gratuitous retribution on their opponents. After an hour Ormond pulled off Law and awarded a first cap to Hearts' striker Donald Ford, Scotland's leading scorer in the new season. Ford it was who came nearest to squaring the issue. In the last minute his shot from a tight angle cannoned to safety off Viktor's head. At the end a storm of contemptuous whistling enveloped the ground.

The Scottish players looked none too distressed at losing, but later listened in to extraordinary news. At Wembley Poland had knocked England out of the World Cup. Some Scots were disappointed, others ecstatic, but their own achievement was now all the more laudable. Scotland would be the only British team competing in West Germany.

CZECHOSLOVAKIA (1)1   SCOTLAND (0)0
  Nehoda (pen)

CZECHOSLOVAKIA: Viktor, Pivarnik, Samek, Dvorak, Hagara, Bicovsky, Pollak, Gajdusek, Vesely (Klement), Nehoda, Capkovic (Panenka).

SCOTLAND: D Harvey (Leeds), S Jardine (Rangers), D McGrain (Celtic), T Forsyth (Rangers), J Blackley (Hibs), D Hay (Celtic, capt.), W Morgan (Man U), J Jordan (Leeds), D Law (Man C) (*sub* D Ford, Hearts), K Dalglish (Celtic), T Hutchison (Coventry).

World Cup Qualifying Group 8:

	P	W	D	L	F	A	PTS
SCOTLAND	4	3	0	1	8	3	6
Czechoslovakia	4	2	1	1	9	3	5
Denmark	4	0	1	3	2	13	1

Other group results

Denmark v Czechoslovakia   1-1

Czechoslovakia v Denmark   6-0

World Cup Finals – WEST GERMANY – *June/July 1974*

Scottish euphoria at qualifying for the first time in sixteen years was understandable; their current prospects realistically encouraging. The team included players of real quality. Moreover, Scottish sides invariably performed better when talked of in the language of understatement rather than overstatement. Willie Ormond, fortunately, was not one for shooting his mouth off.

The eagerly awaited draw was not especially kind. Joining Scotland in Group 2 would be defending world champions Brazil. The anticipated difficulty in beating them was offset by the expected ease with which Scotland should dispose of Zaire. Allowing for over-simplification, this probably meant that Scotland would be fighting for the second qualifying place with Yugoslavia, whom they would meet last.

Scotland's form in the build-up to the finals was as inconsistent as one might expect. Which was the real Scotland, the one that beat England at Hampden, or the one that lost to Northern Ireland in the same stadium? En route to West Germany the team stopped off for final 'friendlies' against Belgium and Norway. Scotland impressed in neither match, the first lost, the second laboriously won. In fact these warm-up matches were notable more for their off-the-field revelries than any on-field sparkle. Jimmy Johnstone, having the previous month nearly been swept out to sea on a rowing boat at Largs, was involved in Oslo with Billy Bremner in an 'incident' in a student bar. Both players came near – perhaps very near – to being sent home in disgrace. Team morale was more substantially dampened by failure to settle lucrative commercial contracts.

Willie Ormond was not officially required to name his twenty-two man squad until the obligatory eight days before the tournament commenced. He saw no reason to delay, announcing his list almost a month before the gloves came off. The full party, as they lined up against Zaire, was as follows:

Name	Position	Club	Age	Caps	Goals
David Harvey	goalkeeper	Leeds United	26	7	–
Jim Stewart*	goalkeeper	Kilmarnock	20	–	–
Thompson Allan†	goalkeeper	Dundee	26	2	–
Sandy Jardine	full-back	Rangers	25	16	1
Danny McGrain	full-back	Celtic	24	12	–
Willie Donachie*	full-back	Manchester C	22	11	–
Erich Schaedler†	full-back	Hibernian	24	1	–
Jim Holton	central defence	Manchester U	23	11	2
John Blackley	central defence	Hibernian	24	3	–
Martin Buchan	central defence	Manchester U	25	13	–
Gordon McQueen*	central defence	Leeds United	21	1	–
Billy Bremner	midfield	Leeds United	32	47	2
David Hay	midfield	Celtic	26	24	–
Peter Cormack†	midfield	Liverpool	27	8	–
Tommy Hutchison	midfield	Coventry	26	8	–
Jimmy Johnstone*	winger	Celtic	29	22	2
Willie Morgan	winger	Manchester U	28	19	1
Peter Lorimer	winger/forward	Leeds United	25	13	3
Kenny Dalglish	forward	Celtic	23	19	5
Joe Jordan	forward	Leeds United	22	11	3
Donald Ford†	forward	Hearts	29	3	–
Denis Law	forward	Manchester C	34	54	30
		Averages	25.9	13.9	

*Players who would not appear in the 1974 World Cup finals.
†Players who would not appear in the 1974 World Cup finals, nor play for Scotland again.

The Scotland squad, with Peter Cormack brought in at the last moment for Newcastle's Jimmy Smith, was on the young side and, compared for example with the English squad in 1970, notably inexperienced in international football. There were on average fewer than fourteen caps per man, a consequence of recent Scottish managers' tendencies to bring in their own men, abandon those of their predecessors, yet still indulge in hasty sackings. Only two members of the pool, Bremner and Law, had earned more than two dozen caps. There was also some doubt about the extent of Law's likely contribution in West Germany. It was certainly a sign of changing times that only one player from Glasgow Rangers was nominated in the twenty-two, whereas there were five from Leeds United, and another five from the two Manchester clubs.

Friday, 14 June 1974
ZAIRE v SCOTLAND   Dortmund 27,000

The inaugural match of the 1974 World Cup finals enabled the holders, Brazil, to demonstrate their new, no-nonsense style against Yugoslavia. The Scottish party did not care who won, so long as the match was not drawn. Whoever lost would be under severe pressure to qualify. The game, disappointingly for Scotland, ended goalless.

From their base at Erbismuhle in the Taunus mountains near Frankfurt, the Scotland squad prepared for a demolition job the next day against Zaire. When Scotland had last contested the World Cup finals, in 1958, points were all that mattered. But goal difference was now in operation. Even before the first ball was kicked in Group 2 there was speculation that qualification would be reserved for those teams most ruthless against Zaire. In this sense, Scotland were at a disadvantage in meeting them first, when the Africans would have the benefit of surprise. Brazil and Yugoslavia would be watching closely, so as not to be unprepared when their turn came.

Zaire were a totally unknown quantity. Although coached by the ex-Yugoslavian goalkeeper, Vidinic, they had taken no scalps of which to boast. For the task of beating them handsomely Ormond sent out a side which was largely predictable. David Harvey was now the established goalkeeper; Sandy Jardine and Danny McGrain the splendidly paired full-backs. Doubts surrounded only who would partner Jim Holton at the heart of the defence (the answer was John Blackley); whether Denis Law would earn another Indian Summer (he would); and whether there would be room for either Jimmy Johnstone or Tommy Hutchison on the flank (there wouldn't).

The first team to receive a shock were the Scots. Zaire, like the Paraguayans in 1958, were far, far faster than expected. Perhaps they exerted themselves to keep warm: the Africans felt so chilled by the German summer that they wore vests under their yellow shirts, and with their green shorts and brown skins presented an image of tropical humming birds at play. Scotland's methods for softening-up their opponents did not endear them to the German neutrals in the half-empty Westfalen Stadium. Jordan was offering no kid-glove treatment to the acrobatic keeper, Kazadi. The goalkeeper recovered from an early knock to save from Law. Nevertheless it was the humming birds who could so easily have opened the scoring. Kakoko missed his kick, had time for a second, but put his shot against the outside of a post and into the side-netting.

In time, Scotland's superior strength began to pay, and the obvious tactic of directing high crosses to the heads of Jordan and Law against a team clearly uncomfortable when the ball was off the ground increasingly betokened a goal. It came after twenty-seven minutes and was worth the wait. Jordan at the far post headed back McGrain's centre for Lorimer to crash an unstoppable volley past Kazadi.

Scotland's fortunes seemed even rosier six minutes later when they scored again, this time with a goal of lesser quality – and legality. Jordan raced forward to receive Bremner's chipped free kick, possibly from an offside position, and his firm header was fumbled by Kazadi between his knees.

Zaire were far from disheartened. Before the break Kidumi clobbered Bremner and became the latest in a growing list of players cautioned for their dislike of the Scottish captain. Kidumi was then left unmarked to collect N'daye's pass in front of Harvey, only to dally and have the ball blocked by the keeper.

In the second half Scotland ground forward in the apparent expectation that the Africans would tire. They didn't. Kazadi and Lobilo, the capable centre-half, repelled everything the Scots hurled at them. Nine minutes after the turnaround Jordan felled Kilasu and found himself enclosed within an angry black circle. Mayanga nearly punished the Scots in the most painful manner when he climaxed a long diagonal run with a twenty-yard drive which Harvey plunged to turn aside. The floodlights were then extinguished, providing everybody with a four-minute breather. For a while play continued as if by candlelight, but as Zaire took off Mayanga for a fresh forward, Kembo, the lights were restored to full power.

Improved illumination was evidently to the Africans' liking, for during the last twenty minutes they had the audacity to carry the game to Scotland – much to the crowd's delight. Bremner seemed quite content that his players concentrate on preserving a lead, rather than seeking to increase it. Further substitutes arrived: Zaire bringing on a second fresh forward; Scotland giving the long legs of Hutchison a run out, replacing the industry of Dalglish.

Chances continued to fall at both ends. Lorimer came close to scoring with a piledriver turned on to the bar by Kazadi, but in the final minutes N'daye screwed the ball wide from a good position, and then obliged Harvey to touch over a second effort. The final score might easily have been 6-3 to Scotland, but there was no doubt it was they who were the more pleased to hear the final whistle. Scotland had managed their first-ever win in the World Cup finals, but would the margin of victory be sufficient?

Peter Lorimer (Leeds) in action in a Scotland v England match. Peter gained 6 World Cup caps in 1970 and 1974.

ZAIRE (0)0   SCOTLAND (2)2
                                          Lorimer, Jordan

ZAIRE: Kazadi, Mwepu, Mukombo, Bwanga, Lobilo, Kilasu, Manu, Kidumi (Kiwonge), N'daye, Kakoko, Mayanga (Kembo).

SCOTLAND: D Harvey (Leeds), S Jardine (Rangers), D McGrain (Celtic), W Bremner (Leeds, capt.), J Holton (Man U), J Blackley (Hibs), K Dalglish (Celtic) (*sub* T Hutchison, Coventry), D Hay (Celtic), P Lorimer (Leeds), J Jordan (Leeds), D Law (Man C).

Tuesday, 18 June 1974
BRAZIL v SCOTLAND   Frankfurt 62,000

Under normal circumstances registering a first-ever victory in the World Cup finals at the sixth attempt would have been cause for celebration. But there was little evidence of Scottish self-satisfaction, both because of the nature of the opposition and the already crystallising fear that they had not scored enough goals. One way to dispose of these nagging doubts was to beat Brazil: to do so would guarantee qualification and virtually eliminate the country which had won the Jules Rimet Trophy on three of the previous four occasions. Indeed, Brazil's third success, in 1970, meant that they kept the trophy for good. A new 'World Cup' was now being fought for.

But beat Brazil? The mere question was enough to make most Scots break out into goosepimples. Scotland had never before beaten them. They had lost narrowly, 0-1, on two occasions in the past two years, at Rio and Hampden – and had achieved a 1-1 home draw back in 1966. The indications in 1974 were that Brazil were sacrificing some of their prodigious flair in favour of imitating what they saw as excessive European muscularity. This was probably welcome to Scotland, who were better equipped to counter thuggery than magic. In any case, the Brazilian squad was depleted through the retirement of Pele, Gerson and Tostao, and by injury of Clodoaldo – a list of absentees which did Scotland no harm at all. Jairzinzo, Piazza, Paulo Cezar and the moustachioed captain, Rivelino, were the only survivors of the team which had beaten England 1-0 in Mexico.

Willie Ormond made two changes. Denis Law had struggled against the enthusiastic running of Zaire's younger legs, and now, having earned his 56th cap, he was finally pensioned off for the last time. Amazing to think that his international career had extended over sixteen years, commencing immediately after the 1958 World Cup finals. Now, in came Willie Morgan for his first full game for five weeks. The other change was to introduce Martin Buchan in place of John Blackley, which brought the Old Trafford contingent up to three, one short of Leeds'.

Afternoon rain had softened the pitch in Frankfurt, but the match itself was played in evening sunshine in front of Prime Minister Harold Wilson and some 12,000 Scots in the packed Wald Stadium. Wilson would not have appreciated their whistling at 'God Save the Queen' and its substitution by the echoing stanzas of 'Flower of Scotland'. Nor would he have enjoyed the sight of Brazil threatening to drive their opponents into the River Main. Scotland began as if with a major inferiority complex. They were left hanging on in desperation as Brazil rolled the clock back to their golden years. For around twenty-five minutes Scotland were eye-to-eye with humiliation.

The champions had one red-faced moment when keeper Leao slid a goal-kick over his own goal-line. But the danger to Scotland's goal seemed likely to be more substantial when, in the fourteenth minute, a Rivelino 'special' from twenty-five years forced Harvey into a frantic flying save. From the corner, blond full-back Francisco Marinho's acrobatic volley left the crossbar quivering crazily and Harvey wringing his fingers. With Jardine clearing another effort off the line, Scotland were on the rack. The tartan-bedecked Scots fans watched the action through closed fingers.

Gradually, as Brazil failed to land the decisive touch, the Scottish pulse rate dropped. For the last fifteen minutes of the half Harvey was able to breathe easier, and his colleagues began to create moments of danger at the other end. As the tide started to turn Rivelino increasingly exhibited the shadow side of his character, forsaking his extravagant skills for every kind of skullduggery. He entered the referee's book for an unpleasant foul on – who else? – Bremner. At Hampden the previous year he had likewise been prone to incivility, and likewise Scotland were none too distressed: a violent Rivelino could not be a creative Rivelino.

The attitude of both teams in the dressing rooms at half-time was largely shaped by news of the ongoing Yugoslavia-Zaire match. The Yugoslavs were leading 6-0. This meant that if Brazil could keep Scotland at bay for forty-five minutes they would need only to beat Zaire 3-0 (overhauling Scotland's total) to ensure their own qualification.

Upon the resumption Brazil adopted a 'what we have we hold' policy as an increasingly confident Scotland piled forward like a navy tidal wave. Bremner and Hay emerged as international giants as they put Brazil to the sword. Within eleven minutes Leao had to leap to touch over Hay's effort: then Lorimer's bullet free-kick had the crowd roaring. The beat of Brazilian bongos was drowned by the chants of the Scots. Midway through the half came the moment which would haunt Billy Bremner a lifetime. Leao plunged at a loose ball, pushed it against Bremner's shins, and both watched helplessly as it rebounded inches wide of a post.

Scotland's attacks were now being thwarted by any means (though by the end the foul-count was roughly equal for both sides). Yet for all their pressure, Scotland were unable to carve out the one clear-cut chance which would steal the match, and might still have lost when a lightning Brazilian break-out was neutralised only by Harvey's smothering save. Upon the final whistle Brazil were all smiles and handshakes.

BRAZIL (0)0   SCOTLAND (0)0

BRAZIL: Leao, Nelinho, Pereira, M Marinho, F Marinho, Piazza, Rivelino, P Cesar, Jairzinho, Mirandinha, Leivinha (F Cesar).

SCOTLAND: D Harvey (Leeds), S Jardine (Rangers), D McGrain (Celtic), J Holton (Man U), M Buchan (Man U), W Bremner (Leeds, capt.), D Hay (Celtic), K Dalglish (Celtic), W Morgan (Man U), J Jordan (Leeds), P Lorimer (Leeds).

Saturday, 22 June 1974
YUGOSLAVIA v SCOTLAND   Frankfurt 56,000

A win over Brazil would have gone down as Scotland's greatest ever result. Even the draw was worthy of acclaim, except for its likely bearing on the group's outcome. Brazil had come off worse from two goalless draws, but now looked like stepping effortlessly into the last eight. Yugoslavia, having eagerly scrutinised Scotland's failings against Zaire, had taken the punch-drunk Africans apart. The score, 9-0, equalled the record for the World Cup finals. For Scotland to qualify, one of two things had to happen. Either Yugoslavia had to be beaten, or, if the result was a draw, Brazil must secure only a one-goal win over Zaire. The latter prospect was not worth banking on: Scotland had to win.

The Brazilian press admitted that Scotland had overrun Brazil for seventy of the ninety minutes, and had praised Bremner as a 'small giant'. Ormond saw no reason to change such a team, although its sole failing – an inability to carve out inviting chances – did invite suggestions that Kenny Dalglish be replaced. He had looked lacklustre throughout the Home Internationals and the continental tour, not to mention his two World Cup matches to date. Danny McGrain's performances were up to standard, but he had lost over a stone in weight and would shortly learn that he was a diabetic. With hindsight, he might even have wished to be dropped, rather than exert himself to such an extent that his health could be threatened.

Yugoslavia, coached by Miljan Milanovitch, had been the last team to qualify for the finals – needing a play-off before disposing of Spain. They had never before beaten Scotland, though three of the four previous encounters had been drawn. For Yugoslavia, the present match was as good as a home fixture. There were some 40,000 Yugoslavs actually working in Frankfurt, and with their team containing some outstanding players – Buljan and Katalinski in defence, Oblak in midfield, and Dragan Dzajic on the wing – must have felt confident against Scotland.

With one team needing to win, the other to draw, there was never much doubt which goal would be the busier. A German heatwave did not prevent Scotland powering forward as if defeat was unthinkable. Bremner and Hay, both prominent against Brazil, now turned on the performances of their lives. Free kicks interrupted every move – there were more than sixty of them, evenly divided. By the end there were also five bookings, Hay and Jordan from Scotland. The heading ability of the Leeds forward was a frequent talking point in Germany, and the Yugoslavs made sure he was given few opportunities to exercise it. Ormond's team applied constant pressure, but their inability to create, let alone take, any golden scoring chances continued to frustrate their otherwise sterling efforts. Dalglish was once again (by his own admission) struggling to make any impact, and he was inevitably pulled off to make way, yet again, for Tommy Hutchison.

Dalglish later summed up the match: 'The Yugoslavs didn't allow us to play'. McGrain added: 'The match was a dreadful anti-climax for Scots players and fans alike. Despite heavy pressure from the opening whistle we could not find a way through a nine man defensive barrier'. Yet news of Brazil's progress at Gelsenkirchen offered unexpected salvation. They stood 1-0 at half-time. As both matches entered their final ten minutes Scotland were still alive: Brazil were winning only by 2-0, giving them an identical record to that of Scotland.

Then the world caved in. Although Scotland did not know it, Brazil scored a third when Valdomiro's slack shot from the tightest of angles was fumbled into the net by the Zaire goalkeeper. Back at Frankfurt, Yugoslavia surged out of packed defence. Substitute Karasi began the move which was continued by Dzajic jinking down the right. Karasi raced forward, dived for the cross in front of Jardine, and headed devastatingly past Harvey. Scotland were out of the World Cup.

Yet the causes of much subsequent anguish and debate were still to come. Ormond prepared to bring on Jimmy Johnstone but failed to attract the referee's attention as the minutes slipped away. The flying winger, who five years previously had shredded the Red Star Belgrade defence in the

European Cup, dejectedly re-took his seat. One of the greatest wingers in British football would never kick a ball in the World Cup finals.

Then, with only two minutes remaining, Hutchison's twisting run past Buljan produced a fast, low centre across the goalmouth. Lorimer slashed, and the ball flew to Jordan who, though off-balance, hit it cleanly inside a post. With the players still unaware of Brazil's third goal, they thought Scotland were safe by virtue of having scored one extra goal (a goal difference of 3-1 being superior to 2-0).

The heartbreaking news only reached them once they had left the pitch. As in 1958, Scotland had drawn 1-1 with Yugoslavia: and as in 1958, were eliminated while Yugoslavia prospered. The fact that Scotland had been knocked out despite being unbeaten – they were the first country ever to suffer such a cruel fate – prompted much misplaced pleading of bad luck. True, this was as good a team as Scotland had ever assembled. But equally true, the writing had been on the wall way back against Zaire.

YUGOSLAVIA (0)1   SCOTLAND (0)1
  Karasi   Jordan

YUGOSLAVIA: Maric, Buljan, Katalinski, Bogicevic, Hadziabdic, Acimovic, Oblak, Surjak, Petkovic, Bajevic (Karasi), Dzajic.

SCOTLAND: D Harvey (Leeds), S Jardine (Rangers), D McGrain (Celtic), J Holton (Man U), M Buchan (Man U), W Bremner (Leeds, capt.), K Dalglish (Celtic) (*sub* T Hutchison, Coventry), D Hay (Celtic), W Morgan (Man U), J Jordan (Leeds), P Lorimer (Leeds).

A proud yet despondent Scottish party flew home to the deserved reception of thousands of well-wishers. There was a great sense of 'if'. If Scotland had made the second phase, how would they have fared? For though Scotland had found it difficult to win matches, likewise nobody yet had found it easy, or indeed possible, to beat them.

Yugoslavia went out at the next hurdle, bottom of their second phase group. Brazil, so different from the team revered and respected in the past, kicked their way steadily onwards until even they had no answer to the Dutchmen, Cruyff and Neeskens. Brazil eventually finished an unloved fourth, while West Germany took the title, beating Holland 2-1 in the Final.

Group 2 – final positions

	P	W	D	L	F	A	PTS
YUGOSLAVIA	3	1	2	0	10	1	4
BRAZIL	3	1	2	0	3	0	4
Scotland	3	1	2	0	3	1	4
Zaire	3	0	0	3	0	14	0

Scotland's appearances and goal-scorers:
World Cup qualifying rounds and final competition 1974

	A	G		A	G	
Dalglish	7(1)	1	Blackley J	2	–	
Bremner W*†	6	–	Brownlie J	2	–	
Morgan W	6	1	Colquhoun E	2	–	
Harvey D	5	–	Graham G	2	–	
Hay D	5	–	Harper J	2(1)	1	
Jardine S	5	–	Bone J	1	1	
Jordan J	5(1)	3	Carr W	1(1)	–	
Lorimer P*	5	2	Clark R	1	–	
McGrain D	5	–	Connelly G	1	–	
Buchan M	4	–	Donachie W	1	–	
Holton J	4	1	Ford D	1(1)	–	
Hutchison T	4(2)	–	Forsyth A	1	–	
Law D*†‡	3	–	Forsyth T	1	–	
			Hunter A	1	–	
			Macari L	1	1	
			caps	84	11	goals

28 players		
	Scottish League	35
	English League	49
		84

Bracket signifies appearance was as a substitute
*Appeared in 1970 World Cup
†Appeared in 1966 World Cup
‡Appeared in 1962 World Cup

Archie Gemmill resisting a challenge in an international match against Wales. Archie played 9 times for Scotland in the World Cup, in 1978 and 1982. People still talk about the wonderful goal he scored against Holland in Mendoza during the 1978 finals when he tricked man after man before cutely placing the ball behind Longbloed to score one of the most memorable goals of the whole tournament.

CHAPTER 8

The 1978 World Cup

Even allowing for the frustrating circumstances of their elimination, there was no doubting that Scotland's performances throughout the 1974 World Cup programme – both in qualifying rounds and finals – were the finest they had ever turned in. It may or may not have been coincidence, but the 1974 World Cup series was the first in which Scotland drew more players from the English, as opposed to the Scottish, League. In any case, optimism for the future was no longer misplaced or fanciful, and the international standing of the team and its unassuming manager was probably never higher. Docherty and Ormond had brought Scottish international football out of the shadows. With the World Cup and European Championships alternating every two years, Ormond had an early opportunity to gauge the progress of his players in the European tournament.

Alas, disappointment lay in store. Before 1974 was out, Scotland had lost at home to Spain, and that proved an insurmountable setback to Scotland's hopes of reaching the European finals two years later. In fact, the side bore the symptoms of a year-long German hangover, with a 1-5 defeat at the hands of England to prevent any grandiose notions developing. When the new World Cup came around, Scotland had recorded only one victory in six matches away from Hampden – against Denmark. But, encouragingly, the drubbing at Wembley turned out to be the last Scottish defeat before the team embarked on a nine-match unbeaten run.

News that Scotland's opponents in the 1978 World Cup qualifying stages would be Wales and Czechoslovakia (yet again) invited accusations of incest. In the case of Scotland and Wales, British footballers would need to commit fratricide in order to reach the finals. And as for Czechoslovakia this was the third time Scotland had found themselves in the same group. In 1962 the Czechs had had a fine side, too strong for Scotland's. In 1974 the Czechs were poor, and Scotland turned the tables. But now the Czechs were emerging once more from the doldrums of the early 'seventies. In the early stages of the 1976 European Championships they had eliminated England, swept past the Soviet Union and Holland on their way to the Final, and then taken the title in a penalty shoot-out with West Germany. Clearly Czechoslovakia would be much stronger this time round. Scotland had actually been the seeded team when the draw was made, but it didn't look as if they would necessarily benefit.

The Qualifying Rounds

Wednesday, 13 October 1976
CZECHOSLOVAKIA v SCOTLAND   Prague 38,000

Scotland were not allowed to test the temperature of Group 6 with their fingers, but had to plunge in at the deep end. The match in Prague was likely to be the most testing of Scotland's four matches. They had recently used Finland for shooting practice, hitting them for six, and the records showed Scotland unbeaten for nine games, the last five of which had been won. Level-headed Scots were not carried away by this statistic: all five wins had been at Hampden and would count for little in Prague in view of Scotland's time-honoured frailty away from home.

The Czechs needed retentive memories to recall their own team's last defeat – at Wembley – twenty-three matches earlier. There were a handful of players left from the 1973 clashes with Scotland, and Petras, Dobias and the balding Pollak were still around from the 1970 World Cup. The current Czech side was impressive in all departments, had no glaring weaknesses, and was constructed around a formidable centre-half and captain, Ondrus, and a pair of dangerous strikers, Zdenek Nehoda and Marian Masny.

Scotland, needless to say, were largely a rebuilt unit from 1974. Partick's Alan Rough had been introduced in goal at the start of the team's winning Hampden sequence. Danny McGrain was developing into a world-class full-back, now switching to the right where his overlapping attributes were most effective. Willie Donachie partnered him on the left. With Tom Forsyth injured, the central defenders were the Leeds giant Gordon McQueen, who lined up for his first international in over a year, and Martin Buchan who brought his reassuring presence to the back line.

The critical area of Scottish operations seemed to be in midfield. The classic combination in West Germany of Billy Bremner and Davie Hay had had to be replaced. Hay's international career was abruptly ended by injury, and Bremner's 'misbehaviour' had caused him to fall foul of the authorities. This double loss would have been insurmountable had it not been for the discovery of unlikely replacements. Scotland now had a new 'Anglo' midfield comprising QPR's Don Masson, and the Derby pair Bruce Rioch and Archie Gemmill – the new Scotland captain. Up front, Joe Jordan joined the English First Division's leading scorer, Andy Gray, as a dual striking force, abetted by the free role given to Celtic's captain, Kenny Dalglish.

On the Tuesday the Scottish Under-21 side emerged with a goalless draw against the Czech youngsters. The conduct of the seniors the following day was vastly different from that lacklustre, irrelevant affair when Scotland had last played in Czechoslovakia. The present match was uncompromising and remorseless. At regular intervals throughout the first half Scottish names were jotted into referee Michelotti's notebook – McQueen, Gemmill and Buchan.

These transgressions did not imply Scotland had their backs to the wall. Although Dobias' volley was only inches wide in the first minute, from then on Scotland shaded the first half. They contrived fleeting chances to score, as rapid counter-attacks occasionally pierced the home defence. Jordan's header from Rioch's centre brought a sharp save from Vencel, and Rioch's power shooting served to discomfit the Czechs.

Scotland were doubtless looking forward to the interval, the job half done, when Ondrus and Andy Gray expressed a difference of opinion in a manner which displeased Mr Michelotti. In consequence they both reached the changing rooms two minutes ahead of their fellows.

If Ormond's team, deprived of a key striker, were henceforth tempted to fall back on defence, their plans were at once redundant. Czechoslovakia began the second half in a frenzy. From a quickly won corner Nehoda smashed goalwards, Rough blocked, and Panenka cracked the loose ball under the bar.

McQueen had earlier been responsible for Goegh's retirement following a crude challenge. Now he made atonement to the Czechs. The centre-half completely missed a cross and the blond Petras flashed home a diving header. 2-0 after forty-eight minutes.

Czechoslovakia then went on the rampage, the Scottish midfield brushed aside like gossamer. Birmingham's Kenny Burns brought his stiffening qualities to bear in place of Dalglish, and shortly flattened Dobias. Manchester City's Asa Hartford took over from Masson. The Czech full-backs continued to pour forward in support of their forwards. The names of Donachie and Czech sub Jurkemic were added to the referee's black book. The nearest Scotland came to scoring their first-ever World Cup goal in Czechoslovakia in three attempts came sixteen minutes from time. Donachie's cross produced a looping header from Jordan and a flying stop from Vencel. But by the end the European Champions had soundly disposed of the tartan pretenders.

Asa Hartford played for Scotland in the 1978 World Cup finals in Argentina and the 1982 finals in Spain.

CZECHOSLOVAKIA (0)2   SCOTLAND (0)0
Panenka, Petra

CZECHOSLOVAKIA: Vencel, Biros, Ondrus, Capkovic (Jurkemic), Goegh (Kroupa), Dobias, Panenka, Pollak, Masny, Nehoda, Petras.

SCOTLAND: A Rough (Partick), D McGrain (Celtic), W Donachie (Man C), M Buchan (Man U), G McQueen (Leeds), B Rioch (Derby), K Dalglish (Celtic) (*sub* K Burns, Birmingham), D Masson (QPR) (*sub* A Hartford, Man C), J Jordan (Leeds), A Gray (A Villa), A Gemmill (Derby, capt.).

Wednesday, 17 November 1976
SCOTLAND v WALES   Hampden 63,000

Defeat in Prague put Scotland on the precipice. There could be no more failures. Czechoslovakia had staked a considerable moral advantage, and if Scotland should drop a home point to Wales five weeks later it might effectively scuttle Ormond's team's chances. Wales were no longer the Hampden bogey they had been in the late 'forties and early 'fifties. They hadn't won in Scotland on any of their previous twelve visits – not since 1951. In fact they had gone down 1-3 at Hampden only five months earlier in the British Championships. Wales were aware of the danger confronting them, bringing in seven fresh players, and their side looked stronger in every department. In Wales' favour was the confidence acquired from being the only British team to have reached the quarter-finals of the 1976 European Championships – where they were put out by Yugoslavia.

Ormond saw no need for panic changes, but Andy Gray was missing through suspension, Buchan through injury, and Masson likewise – the result of a painful 'collision' with Welsh skipper Terry Yorath in a recent league fixture. Yorath denied dishonourable intent. Masson was replaced by the more abrasive qualities of Kenny Burns, John Blackley stepped in for Buchan, and Eddie Gray – injured before the Prague game – deputised for his Aston Villa namesake. There was no place for Scotland's leading scorer, Joe Harper of Aberdeen.

Welsh manager Mike Smith was frank about his team instructions, which were to attempt to hold Scotland at bay for twenty minutes, by which time – it was hoped – the Hampden crowd would be losing patience. Wales were still five minutes short of Smith's target when Scotland broke through. Rioch sent the overlapping McGrain galloping up the right touchline. Dalglish took a swipe at the full-back's low cross and Ian Evans did the rest: the Welsh defender lunged to intercept but could only perform Dalglish's job for him. The ball lay snugly in the net.

In theory, the goal should have made the game more open, obliging Wales to venture forth from their defensive cocoon. As it happened, Scotland were in no mood to grant Wales any titbits. All the visitors could offer was a hopeful potshot by Evans – desperate to erase his earlier error – which sailed high out of harm's way, and a Yorath effort which sped through a heap of limbs before being pounced upon by Alan Rough.

Apart from these isolated moments of danger, Scotland comfortably controlled the match till the end. The second half witnessed unrelenting Scottish pressure, though one or two players must have been wary about unnecessarily mixing it. A second booking, on top of those handed out in Prague, carried automatic suspension.

Not long after the change-round the admirable McGrain (who rendered poor Leighton James totally impotent, forcing the frustrated winger's early replacement) embarked on a sixty-yard run. The ball seemed attached by invisible elastic, for the full-back lost and regained control time after time. Finally McGrain's enterprise was spoiled by the intervention of Welsh keeper Dai Davies. McGrain landed upside down. 'Penalty' screamed Hampden. The chorus of boos which followed told of the referee's different opinion.

Burns was unpassable; Dalglish unstoppable. The gifted forward, so often maligned, was producing one of his most effective performances for his country. Jordan and McQueen won more than their share of their respective aerial battles. For Wales, Ian Evans found himself in the referee's notebook twice – once as goalscorer, then as villain for yet another angry tackle on Jordan.

Dalglish set up Rioch, but the shot came off a post to nestle in Davies' grateful arms. Asa Hartford took over from Rioch, and shortly afterwards Welsh wood was thumped a second time, this time the crossbar left twanging from Archie Gemmill.

Welsh and Liverpool striker John Toshack had never played at Hampden before, but he almost made his mark with a firm header from Thomas' centre which Rough thrillingly saved. Scottish hearts missed a beat, but soon recovered. Near the end Willie Pettigrew replaced Eddie Gray, and the final whistle sounded on a victory as clear-cut and merited as defeat had been in Prague. The win was all the sweeter because earlier in the day England had gone down 2-0 in Rome, and were staring elimination in the face. On the same night news arrived that Czechoslovakia had been beaten 2-0 in a friendly in West Germany – their first defeat in twenty-five matches. The Czechs had fielded only a makeshift side, and were not due to visit Hampden for another ten months, but had their bubble burst?

SCOTLAND (1)1   WALES (0)0
   Evans (O.G.)

SCOTLAND: A Rough (Partick), D McGrain (Celtic), W Donachie (Man C), J Blackley (Hibs), G McQueen (Leeds), B Rioch (Derby) (*sub* A Hartford, Man C), K Burns (Birmingham), K Dalglish (Celtic), J Jordan (Leeds), A Gemmill (Derby, capt.), E Gray (Leeds) (*sub* W Pettigrew, Motherwell).

WALES: D Davies, Page, J Jones, L Phillips, I Evans, Griffiths, M Thomas, Flynn, Yorath, Toshack, L James (Curtis).

Wednesday, 21 September 1977
SCOTLAND v CZECHOSLOVAKIA   Hampden 85,000

In those ten months Scotland played eight internationals, defeat being reserved for the last two – Brazil in Rio and East Germany in Berlin. There had been laudable victories, too, especially over England at Wembley and Chile in Santiago. No-one could put much store by Scotland's form, which was never other than unpredictable, but Czechoslovakia had, it seemed, lost their way. Their defeat in West Germany had not proved an isolated setback. In March, the Czechs had travelled to Wrexham and been whacked 3-0 – a godsend to the Scots – and also failed to score in three of their next four matches. Wales, however, were now very much alive and the group was completely open – each team having won and lost a match apiece.

History told that Czechoslovakia had been defeated on all their previous visits to Hampden. They could scarcely afford to lose this time, and sensing themselves to be a team in decline, brought in five new faces to the side victorious over Scotland in Prague. The veterans Dobias and Pollak were retained, as were the formidable striking pair of Masny and Nehoda. Crucially, centre-half Ondrus was still suspended.

Guiding Scotland through the second phase of their qualifying programme was a new manager – someone who would in time prove to be the most unfortunate appointment ever made by the SFA. Willie Ormond had been engaged in long-standing contractual difficulties with his employers, which finally drove him back into the apparently more secure world of club management – with Hearts. Jock Stein, when approached by the SFA, preferred to look after Celtic rather than Scotland, so they turned to the man who had masterminded Aberdeen's 1976 League Cup Final triumph. Ormond's predecessor, Tommy Docherty, had been flamboyant: Ormond's successor was even more so. Defeat never entered Ally MacLeod's head. 'It's Argentina or Siberia', he declared.

MacLeod had taken office at the start of the British Championships in the spring, which Scotland won for the second year running. He had no intention of dismantling Ormond's well-established team, giving the side a much-needed and welcome cohesion. The eleven players announced to meet Czechoslovakia were all part of Ormond's schemes – with the exceptions of a recall for Sandy Jardine and for Willie Johnston. The gifted but wayward Johston had been revitalised following a move from Rangers to West Bromwich Albion. He was now back for a run in international colours for the first time in seven years. Johnston was not the only Scotland player to have recently changed clubs: Dalglish had replaced Kevin Keegan at Liverpool, and Bruce Rioch was now dispensing his wares at Everton – also adding the captaincy of Scotland to his responsibilities. The Scottish team comprised representatives of nine different clubs, and McGrain, Jardine, Dalglish and Jordan all savoured pleasant memories of the 1973 Hampden victory over Czechoslovakia.

Given the importance of the match, the Czechs could be forgiven a few grumbles at their travel arrangements. An air strike obliged them to sit up overnight on a train from London to Glasgow: sleeping accommodation was not available. FIFA refused the Czechs' request for a 24-hour postponement. Yet come the match, any lingering effects of train-lag seemed to have dissipated. The Czechs exhibited some slick footwork, but Scotland, spurred on by Rioch, Masson and Hartford in midfield, refused to let their opponents settle. Scotland's high-ball tactics always looked likely to disconcert the more terrestrially-disposed Czechs.

Chances had been unforthcoming to the home side when they took the lead on nineteen minutes. Rioch won a corner. The ball was swung in by Johnston, and McQueen's decoy jump created space behind him. Jordan utilised it, thumping an irresistible header inside the far post. Shades of 1973.

Before this reverse the Czechs had had their moments, and continued to enjoy them afterwards. Goegh flashed at a corner but miscued, and Dvorak's header sailed wide. But ten minutes before half-time Scotland, now thundering forward, engineered a second, and vital, goal. Johnston's cross seemed to have the entire human contents of the Czech penalty area converging upon it. Keeper Michalik was impeded by a colleague as he came to intercept, and was not helped by colliding with the uncompromising shape of Joe Jordan. Another referee another day would have penalised the striker's robustness. This one didn't, and when the ball fell invitingly for Hartford to poke it into an empty net the goal was allowed to stand.

Czechoslovakia brought on substitute Knapp at the start of the second

A characteristic salute from Joe Jordan as he celebrates his World Cup
goal during the 1982 finals. Joe also represented his country in the
1974 and 1978 finals.

half, and Gallis later. Their earlier composure was a thing of the past, and two players from either side were booked by the end. Czech powers of resistance were finally stilled in the 54th minute when the ubiquitous Dalglish put them three behind. McQueen harassed Michalik at a corner. A bout of head tennis ensued, with McQueen, Jardine and Dalglish the participants – the last-named getting the final, decisive nod. Aerial sorties had produced all three Scotland goals.

Hampden had been noisy from the start, and the 'roar' was now one of eminent approval. Its tone was modified temporarily to one of irritation ten minutes from time when Gajdusek's thirty-yard trundler eluded Alan Rough. In these days of goal difference there was no longer any such thing as a 'consolation' goal. Rough's boob might easily prove costly. But at the end the crowd was happy. Cock-a-hoop in fact. 'We want Ally', they sang. And well they might: the side had looked ominously capable. They were also, according to Czech manager Josef Venglos, a trifle too physical.

SCOTLAND (2)3   CZECHOSLOVAKIA (0)1
   Jordan, Hartford, Dalglish   Gajdusek

SCOTLAND: A Rough (Partick), S Jardine (Rangers), D McGrain (Celtic), T Forsyth (Rangers), G McQueen (Leeds), B Rioch (Everton, capt.), K Dalglish (Liverpool), D Masson (QPR), J Jordan (Leeds), A Hartford (Man C), W Johnston (WBA).

CZECHOSLOVAKIA: Michalik, Paurik, Capkovic, Dvorak, Goegh, Dobias (Gallis), Gajdusek, Moder (Knapp), Pollak, Masny, Nehoda.

Wednesday, 12 October 1977
WALES v SCOTLAND   Anfield, Liverpool 51,000

When the draw for Group 6 was first announced the Czechs had some cause for grumbles. This had to do with playing two British teams. The Czechs knew that the four home countries played each other annually, and that most Scottish and Welsh international footballers were familiar with one another through the medium of the English League. These regular meetings meant, in effect, that there was no such thing as an 'away' fixture within the almost incestuous British context. Scotland and Wales each viewed a visit to the other as only marginally less homely than actually playing at home. In essence, while the Czechs had to play two away fixtures, the Scots and Welsh had only one.

Only a Scottish defeat by Wales would leave the Czechs a chance to qualify. Yet the Scots were more likely to pick up points in Wales than almost any place you cared to mention beyond these shores. Scotland were invited to ride down the M6 motorway, not having lost on any of their past six visits to Wales. The Czechs were even more disgruntled when the Welsh FA opted to transfer the fixture to Liverpool, in order to offset drastic crowd restrictions imposed on the Cardiff and Wrexham stadiums. By far the majority of tickets fell into Scottish hands, so that Scotland could enjoy an 'away' match in an environment tantamount to playing at Hampden.

Wales' recent form had been impressive, with a six-match unbeaten run behind them – losing only one goal in the process. But with Wales fielding four players from outside the English First Division (including one, Micky Thomas, straight from Wrexham's reserves), the pundits were unanimous in predicting a Scottish victory.

This was Ally MacLeod's ninth match in charge, and the team was as settled as any in recent memory. Nevertheless, he was now missing two key players through injury. Danny McGrain had succumbed to a mysterious foot ailment, and Rioch had a calf strain. Their replacements were Willie Donachie and Lou Macari, but the team could still boast a total of 245 caps. Don Masson took over the captaincy from the absent Rioch.

It was a night of passion rather than quality. Scotland immediately seized the initiative, winning a profusion of corners. There were appeals for a penalty when Dai Davies brought down Dalglish who had burst clear. The reprieved Welsh keeper then allowed the ball to squeeze like soap through his hands, precipitating much flailing of legs before the danger passed.

Midway through the opening half Wales had recovered from their early inferiority, and half-chances began to come their way. One fell to Peter Sayer, who had yet to play in a losing Welsh side in six matches, but he fastened on to Phillips' shrewd pass only to shoot wide.

By the break there was little to choose between the teams. Nor was there afterwards. Scotland could perhaps claim a slight advantage in goal attempts, but the Welsh midfield of Mahoney, Flynn and Yorath were giving the 'home' team the edge in stability. Both sides brought on substitutes (Buchan for Jardine; Deacy for Sayer): both had players booked as the tension mounted (Donachie and Yorath). In the midst of this name-taking John Toshack was involved in one of the second half's two turning points. He was still on the comeback trail after sustaining a serious injury seven months earlier, and had not yet forced his way back into Liverpool's first team. On the hour he was presented with a clear opportunity to score at his beloved 'Kop' end – even though the 'Kop' happened to be wearing tammies. At an angle to the left, Toshack beat the offside trap and found himself with only Rough to beat. His lofted shot was dipping under the bar, onto which the Scottish keeper acrobatically turned it. Wales were as close as that.

Scotland struck back with verve. Davies did well to parry Dalglish's point-blank header, and Jordan drove frivolously too high. But eleven minutes from time came the second decisive incident, which heralded one of the most outrageous goals ever to disfigure a football match. A high ball hurled into the Welsh penalty area was pushed away by a raised hand. French referee Wurtz had had a splendid match up to that point, only to make one of the most critical errors of his life. He (along with many others at the time) adjudged the guilty hand to belong to David Jones. In fact it belonged to Joe Jordan. Masson scored from the penalty to give his side one of the most fortuitous goals imaginable. Monsieur Wurtz's magic wand had conjured a goal for Scotland from mid-air, and waved Wales out of the World Cup.

Dalglish's fine scoring header three minutes from the end, when almost the entire Welsh side were camped in the Scottish half, served no greater purpose than to relieve Scottish embarrassment. In reality it was the penalty which had taken Scotland to Argentina, not Dalglish. In reality the result was a travesty.

'Que Sera Sera, we're going to Argentina', chorused the Scottish throngs. If they had appreciated their debt to Monsieur Wurtz, they would have sung the Marseillaise. Yet in football, as in life, the celestial tribunal would ensure that the debt was rendered. Scotland would pay for their good fortune heavily, and with interest, the following summer.

WALES (0)0   SCOTLAND (0)2
Masson (pen), Dalglish

WALES: D Davies, R Thomas, J Jones, Mahoney, D Jones, Phillips, Flynn, Sayer (Deacy), Yorath, Toshack, M Thomas.

SCOTLAND: A Rough (Partick), S Jardine (Rangers) (*sub* M Buchan, Man U), W Donachie (Man C), D Masson (QPR), G McQueen (Leeds), T Forsyth (Rangers), K Dalglish (Liverpool), A Hartford (Man C), J Jordan (Leeds), L Macari (Man U), W Johnston (WBA).

World Cup Qualifying Group 6:

	P	W	D	L	F	A	PTS
SCOTLAND	4	3	0	1	6	3	6
Czechoslovakia	4	2	0	2	4	6	4
Wales	4	1	0	3	3	4	2

Other group results

Wales v Czechoslovakia   3-0

Czechoslovakia v Wales   1-0

World Cup Finals – ARGENTINA – June 1978

Scotland's qualification led to a prolonged ballyhoo quite unlike anything experienced in 1974 or, for that matter, at any other time. Taking their cue from the manager, large sections of the Scottish nation seemed swallowed up by a kind of xenophobic optimism which caused considerable disquiet among more discerning Scots and, frankly, derision from outside. Referee Wurtz's gift goal had turned Ally MacLeod into a much-needed Scottish national messiah.

MacLeod's apparently anti-English, anti-world, crusade was given impetus by England's later failure to qualify, which enabled Scotland for the second World Cup in succession to hog the British limelight. MacLeod's face beamed out from billboards and TV screens.

His managerial record was not exactly electrifying, consisting of ten years in the twilight world of part-timers Ayr United, followed by a mere eighteen months in the top flight at Pittodrie. But for Aberdeen lifting the League Cup prior to Willie Ormond's resignation, MacLeod probably would have remained the anonymous figure he had been until then. His early successes produced a widespread sentiment shared by many that 'cometh the hour, cometh the man'.

To be fair, the manager's excessive exuberance was not universally appreciated in Scotland. The fear that he was producing more hot air (coming close to predicting a Scottish victory in the World Cup) than sense gained credence during his final preparations for Argentina. Aside from a home fixture with Bulgaria, MacLeod did not seek to arrange warm-up matches against Continental or South American opponents, so depriving his players of any meaningful insight into alien styles of play. Instead, Scotland departed just a few days after a strenuous three-match schedule in the Home Internationals, all played at Hampden in the space of a week.

There were shrugs when Northern Ireland departed with a draw, sighs when the Welsh did likewise. But when England achieved a 1-0 victory you would have thought, listening to the manager's explanation, that Scotland had won. It was, apparently, only bad luck which had been responsible for Scotland's defeat. To compound matters, the Scottish players embarked on a lap of honour to celebrate their achievement in qualifying for Argentina. Laps of honour after a defeat – especially by England – were surely stretching credibility. One could sense many Scots wincing at the banality of it all – embarrassed players trying to smile as they trotted around Hampden's vastness. Several would later admit their misgivings: laps of honour were for victors, and Scotland had won nothing – yet.

Just before the Scottish squad departed for Argentina a send-off party was staged at Hampden. The supporters could come to show their appreciation, for the privilege of which they had to pay! How could it be that a nation so proud of itself and its football could stoop to so many indiscretions? One could almost anticipate the coming disaster.

MacLeod had named his World Cup squad of twenty-two before the Home Internationals. Brought up to date to include those three fixtures, the list read:

Gordon McQueen attended by Kenny Burns at Hampden Park in an international match against Wales. McQueen and Burns both took part in the 1978 World Cup campaign.

Name	Position	Club	Age	Caps	Goals
Alan Rough	goalkeeper	Partick	26	18	–
Jim Blyth†	goalkeeper	Coventry	23	2	–
Bobby Clark†	goalkeeper	Aberdeen	32	17	–
Sandy Jardine	full-back	Rangers	29	34	1
Stuart Kennedy	full-back	Aberdeen	24	3	–
Willie Donachie	full-back	Manchester C	26	30	–
Martin Buchan	central defence	Manchester U	29	28	–
Tom Forsyth	central defence	Rangers	29	19	–
Gordon McQueen*	central defence	Manchester U	25	20	3
Kenny Burns	central defence	Nottingham F	24	11	1
Bruce Rioch	midfield	Derby County	30	22	6
Don Masson	midfield	Derby County	31	16	5
Archie Gemmill	midfield	Nottingham F	31	26	2
Graeme Souness	midfield	Liverpool	24	6	–
Asa Hartford	midfield	Manchester C	27	24	3
Lou Macari	midfield/forward	Manchester U	28	22	5
Willie Johnston	winger	WBA	31	21	–
John Robertson	winger	Nottingham F	25	2	–
Joe Jordan	forward	Manchester U	26	30	7
Kenny Dalglish	forward	Liverpool	27	54	18
Joe Harper	forward	Aberdeen	30	3	2
Derek Johnstone*	forward	Rangers	24	13	3
		Averages	27.8	19.2	

*Players would not appear in the 1978 World Cup finals.
†Players who would not appear in the 1978 World Cup finals, nor play for Scotland again.

(Reserves: (uncalled upon) Jim Stewart, Willie Miller, John Blackley, Andy Gray, Arthur Graham, Ian Wallace).

For all his prickliness on the subject of England, MacLeod still named fifteen Anglos in his squad. Perhaps the only two surprise inclusions in the list were, firstly, Joe Harper from MacLeod's old stomping ground, Aberdeen, to the exclusion of the free-scoring Andy Gray; and secondly, the inexperienced John Robertson on the wing in place of former Don Arthur Graham. Gordon McQueen (having joined Joe Jordan at Old Trafford) had severely damaged knee ligaments against Wales. Although it was evidently doubtful that he could regain fitness, McQueen was not withdrawn from the travelling party, and there was no other orthodox centre-half included. With incomparable full-back Danny McGrain still incapacitated by his long-standing foot injury, and another regular full-

Graeme Souness lets fly for goal. Brazil defenders look on anxiously. A tense moment in the 1982 World Cup finals. Graeme played against Holland in the 1978 finals which Scotland won 3-2.

back, Willie Donachie, suspended from the first match owing to his booking at Anfield, MacLeod would have to field a totally improvised defence.

Group 4, in which Scotland found themselves, seemed a trifle kinder than that in West Germany. Certainly, MacLeod was happy with it. In 1974 Scotland had been pooled with the world champions, Brazil; now they had the World Cup runners-up, Holland. Instead of playing Zaire, Scotland would face Iran. What made 1978, on paper, more agreeable than 1974 was the identity of the supposed 'middle team' – that which, in theory, would be vying with Scotland for the second qualifying place, behind the Dutch. Four years earlier, the supposed 'middle team', Yugoslavia, had proved unexpectedly formidable. Peru, so the general opinion went, could not pose anything like the same threat to Scotland.

In 1974, shrewd judges had been found among the assembled footballing throngs who advised keeping an eye out for Scotland as possible dark horses. The same stories circulated in 1978, but with rather shakier foundations. MacLeod's boast about Scottish intentions to win medals evidently made an impression on his fellow managers and coaches, many of whom were happy to ignore Scotland's inability to win a game in the British Championships and the critical unavailability of key defenders. 'Scotland are a team to watch', spoke many wise football heads in Argentina.

Had those admirers peeped inside the Scottish camp at Alta Gracia, in the foothills of the High Sierras, their enthusiasm might have cooled. For all was not well with Scottish morale. From the first night it was clear that the gutter press was determined to find smoke and turn it into fire. It located a whiff and transformed it into an inferno. Stories of Scottish brushes with armed guards, boozing, gambling and womanising were transmitted around the globe, creating a lurid picture of rampant indiscipline and wantonness.

The Scottish players were already demoralised by failure, as in 1974, to exploit lucrative commercial bonus arrangements. Their tarnished public image, which bore little resemblance to the facts, upset them further – as did their hotel and the inadequacy of their training facilities, which threatened to exacerbate MacLeod's injury list. All boded ill – a state of affairs as yet unknown to the 500 or so Scottish supporters, tagging themselves 'Ally's Army', who had saved their pennies for the experience of a lifetime.

Ally's Army would not find themselves with the best of views. The pitch at Cordoba, the venue for Scotland's opening two matches, was remote from the spectators. First opponents were Peru. MacLeod had seen no reason to observe them beforehand – preferring a blinkered 'let them worry about us' philosophy.

Saturday, 3 June 1978
PERU v SCOTLAND   Cordoba 45,000

MacLeod's team selection for what appeared likely to be Scotland's decisive group match produced a hail of reproach. With the exception of Buchan as stand-in full-back for Donachie, MacLeod nominated the same team which had just lost to England. Despite Derek Johnstone's prodigious goal-scoring exploits for Rangers – he had bagged forty-one the previous season, not to mention both Scotland's goals in the British Championships – he was listed only among the substitutes. The centre-forward position went to the bustling Joe Jordan, who had managed just two goals for his country over the past four years. MacLeod was nothing if not loyal, but that commendable quality can be taken to extremes. His selection in midfield ignored the inescapable reality that his captain and vice-captain, Rioch and Masson, were both wretchedly out of form. Both had recently come together at Derby County, only for the Rams' ex-Scotland manager Tommy Docherty to deflate their confidence still further by publicly declaring them to have been 'bad buys', and slapping them both on the transfer list.

Competing against the 'bad buys' were the 'old men' of Peru. Hector Chumpitaz, Hugo Sotil and Teofilo Cubillas had all played in the exciting Peru team of 1970 which had reached the quarter-finals. They were now part of an ageing side which almost nobody seemed to take seriously. Scotland, or so it appeared, had only to run on to the pitch to be assured of victory – though it might have been pointed out that Rioch and Masson (and Gemmill on the bench) hardly constituted a youthful midfield. All three were in their thirties.

For fifteen minutes on a balmy evening everything seemed to be proceeding to plan. Scotland, playing in navy shirts and shorts, had taken control of the match and were a goal to the good. Quiroga – an eccentric goalkeeper who liked to spend as much time outside his penalty area as within it – couldn't hold Rioch's powerful shot, and Jordan pounced on the rebound. The scorer of Scotland's last goal in 1974 had opened his team's account in 1978.

From the restart you would have thought it was Peru who had scored. They immediately served notice that they were not the decrepit mugs they were taken to be. Cubillas might have played World Cup football all of eight years previously, but he had lost none of his pace and power, and quickly stamped himself as the game's most imposing presence. And as for the wingers, Munante and Oblitas, nobody had warned Scotland's inexperienced – and in the case of stopgap Buchan, painfully slow – full-backs of their electrifying speed. The lesson, it seemed, would never be learnt: in Switzerland in 1954 the Uruguayans' pace had ripped Scotland apart; four years later in Sweden the Paraguayans showed that they too could capitalise on their greater pace. In 1972 Peru had turned out at Hampden. Although the South Americans lost 2-0 on that occasion, Gemmill, Hartford and Donachie, survivors from that day, could vouch for their speed and control. Now, a goal behind, Peru, with their bright red diagonal sashes, proceeded to dissect the Scottish midfield and defence. Rough's goal led a charmed life. Cubillas ran free, with Rioch and Masson left in pursuit of shadows, unable to mark or contain him. Only Dalglish's dangerous lob threatened to break Peru's iron grip.

The only surprise was the length of time it took Peru to equalise. There were less than two minutes till the interval when another exhilarating move involving Cubillas and Valasquez created an opportunity for Cueto to blast past Rough. The red sashes danced with glee.

Peru's Inca magic continued to mesmerise the Scots in the second half. Just before the hour the game threw up its decisive moment. Cubillas challenged Rioch, the whistle blew, and Scotland had been awarded a penalty. The decision was not so scandalous as that against Wales, but was still debatable.

In view of Masson's previous lack of accomplishment, he could consider himself fortunate not to have been substituted. He was, however, Scotland's regular penalty taker, yet his lack of self-belief was fully demonstrated with his spot-kick, which sailed at catching height to Quiroga's right and was saved with contemptuous ease. Back in Scotland the armchair millions knew almost instinctively what lay in store. After seventy-one minutes Munante and Cueto scythed open the Scottish defence and Cubillas' blistering shot from twenty yards exonerated Rough from any blame. 2-1.

At long last Rioch and Masson were pulled off, and one wondered when was the last occasion a team had substituted its captain and vice-captain together under the eyes of the world. The thankless task of plugging the gaps fell to Archie Gemmill and Lou Macari, who, with Peru in full flow, might have preferred the comforting anonymity of the bench. No sooner were they on than Stuart Kennedy – rated a fast full-back in a Scottish context – was overwhelmed by Oblitas, whom he was compelled to bring down just outside the box. Cubillas' free kick was full of insult, curling round wall and goalkeeper to put Scotland out of their misery – for the time being. At the end both managers made revealing comments: 'The end of the world', sighed Ally MacLeod; 'I would like to congratulate Scotland and Mr MacLeod for the team they presented to us,' smiled Marcos Calderon. His words bit deep.

PERU (1)3   SCOTLAND (1)1
   Cueto, Cubillas 2   Jordan

PERU: Quiroga, Diaz, Chumpitaz, Manzo, Duarte, Velasquez, Cueto (Rojas), Cubillas, Munante, La Rosa (Sotil), Oblitas.

SCOTLAND: A Rough (Partick), S Kennedy (Aberdeen), K Burns (Nott'm F), T Forsyth (Rangers), M Buchan (Man U), B Rioch (Derby, capt.) (*sub* L Macari, Man U), D Masson (Derby) (*sub* A Gemmill, Nott'm F), A Hartford (Man C), K Dalglish (Liverpool), J Jordan (Man U), W Johnston (WBA).

Wednesday, 7 June 1978
IRAN v SCOTLAND   Cordoba 8,000

The aftermath of the Peru defeat was more traumatic than the game itself. At a press conference MacLeod appeared to disown his own players. Then it became known that Willie Johnston, one of two players chosen for mandatory dope tests, had given a positive result. He had – he insists unknowingly – taken 'stimulants', a cause for surprise only in view of the listlessness of his performance. Never mind the player, the whole team were now in grave danger of expulsion. Before the FIFA judiciary could convene, the SFA took swift steps to defuse the situation. 'Bud' was whisked out of Argentina, flown home, and had a life-ban slapped on him. He would never play for Scotland again. The severity of his punishment helped ensure that the team as a whole was not victimised – save for the jibes and taunts that now accompanied the mere mention of the word 'Scotland'.

There was only one redeeming aspect of the tragedy for Willie Johnston. Had Scotland won, his offence would automatically have resulted in the game being awarded to Peru. As it was, he was allowed to slip back into Britain largely unnoticed: but had his actions caused Scotland to forfeit a match they had actually won, the reception he would have received does not bear thinking about.

MacLeod knew as little about Iran as he did Peru. For Scotland, victory was imperative: defeat unthinkable. Iran had lost their first match 0-3 to the Dutch. Ideally, Scotland needed to surpass that score, otherwise – at best – be faced with elimination on goal difference as in 1974. Yet Iran were likely to be anything but pushovers. In their warm-up matches they had drawn with Yugoslavia and Bulgaria, and lost only 0-1 to Wales. Holland had themselves needed two penalties to push up their own winning margin. Iran were, furthermore, well versed in British soccer thinking: between 1974-76 they had been coached by the former Manchester United boss, Frank O'Farrell.

Scottish morale was pitifully low. Representatives of the SFA had to intervene to calm ill-feeling about financial incentives; then it was learned that the team line-up had been revealed to the press, not to the players. MacLeod, in fact, made several team changes, not all of them understandable. Graeme Souness, irrespective of his splendid form in helping Liverpool retain the European Cup, was listed only among the substitutes. So was Derek Johnstone, with his potential goal supply. Rioch and Masson were both missing – the former through injury to body; the latter to soul. Their replacements against Peru, Gemmill and Macari, lined up from the start. Gemmill was captain.

In defence, Tom Forsyth stood down to accommodate the return of Willie Donachie, while the shell-shocked Stuart Kennedy gave way to Sandy Jardine. Filling the two central defensive positions was the completely untried partnership of Kenny Burns and Martin Buchan. Up front, John Robertson filled the vacancy left by Willie Johnston's ignominious departure.

The match itself ranks as one of the worst ever to abuse the standards of play appropriate to the World Cup finals. Iran kept Scotland at bay more easily than they could have dreamt. If there was any constructive strategy to Scotland's play, none was detectable. MacLeod retained four permanent defenders to police Iran's two forwards. In fact, Iran could have stolen the lead after thirteen minutes. Rough had to move smartly to challenge Faraki, only for the ball to break into the goalmouth, where it was hoisted clear by Buchan without ceremony.

The interval was only two minutes away when Scotland were credited with a goal – no less valuable for its absurdity. Keeper Hedjazi emerged to gather Hartford's through ball. Under pressure from Joe Jordan and his own centre-half, Eskandarian, the goalkeeper could not prevent the ball breaking loose. Eskandarian panicked, turned, and rolled it back fifteen yards into his own net. One or two Scottish players registered delight: the rest did not know how to contain their blushes. Somebody up there liked Scotland – own-goals and silly penalties had paved their route to Argentina. If only the players could take advantage of His assistance instead of squandering it.

In the second half the aggrieved Eskandarian was cautioned for taking his revenge on Jordan. Buchan's active interest in the game ceased when he collided with Donachie and received a nasty head gash. MacLeod might have sent on a forward, but it was Tom Forsyth who pulled off his track-suit.

On the hour Iran sensationally – and deservedly – equalised. Danaiefard won the ball off Gemmill, skipped past Jardine, and shot past Rough from a tight angle. Within seconds, a lightning Iranian raid ended with Ghasempour foiled only by Rough's last-ditch intervention. The beating of Scottish hearts was audible.

For the last fifteen minutes Dalglish was substituted – not by Derek Johnstone, but by wee Joey Harper, who had not played international football for three years and would not do so again. Robertson's header, cleanly saved, was Scotland's last aggressive gesture. At the end, furious Scottish supporters screamed 'You only want the money' at manager and players.

The performance lost none of its awfulness in retrospect. At one poignant moment MacLeod had been pictured on the bench, abjectly holding his head in his hands. *The Times* summed up the whole shambles with brutal accuracy: 'Scotland came here to compare themselves with the best, and could not even run with the weakest'.

IRAN (0)1 SCOTLAND (1)1
  Danaiefard   Eskandarian (O.G.)

IRAN: Hedjazi, Nazari, Kazerani, Abdollahi, Eskandarian, Parvin, Danaiefard (Nhyebagha), Sadeghi, Ghasempour, Faraki (Rowshan), Jahani.

SCOTLAND: A Rough (Partick), S Jardine (Rangers), M Buchan (Man U) (*sub* T Forsyth, Rangers), K Burns (Nott'm F), W Donachie (Man C), L Macari (Man U), A Gemmill (Nott'm F, capt.), A Hartford (Man C), J Jordan (Man U), K Dalglish (Liverpool) (*sub* J Harper, Aberdeen), J Robertson (Nott'm F).

Sunday, 11 June 1978
HOLLAND v SCOTLAND   Mendoza 40,000

All pretence to Scottish self-respect had vanished. Never in their proud sporting history had Scotland presented such an abject performance before the world. Back home, windows were smashed in the offices of the Scottish Football Association. Billboards equating Scottish footballers with a certain make of motor car as 'running rings round the opposition' suddenly looked like a sick joke. To be tainted with Scottish football was now a leaden commercial liability. The day following the Iran humiliation was, for the manager and players, akin to a wake.

While Scotland were suffering their latest agonies, the Dutch were going through the motions with a goalless draw against Peru. Scotland, to all intents, were already out: Holland's draw meant that Scotland would be packing their bags unless they could win by three clear goals. Such a result against the World Cup runners-up overstepped the bounds of probability, and, in any case, did the Scottish players have the stomach for the fight? Did they want to live through their Argentine nightmare one second longer than was necessary? Many must have wanted to fly home as soon as possible.

If, however, Scotland were to obtain a favourable result from the Dutch, now was probably the most auspicious time to achieve it. Barring an unconscionably heavy defeat, Holland were already through to the second round. They had injuries to worry about, not least to their principal midfield architect Johan Neeskens. Evidently, the Dutch would not wish to exert themselves – unless they had to.

Moreover, the Dutch camp appeared even more unsettled than the Scots'. There were persistent rumours of disaffection over money. The squad was also shorn of the services of Cruyff, Van Hanegem, Peters, Kist and Geels, all of whom chose for personal reasons not to travel. There were, however, nine players from the 1974 finals still included. For the present tournament Holland hired the services of Austrian manager Ernst Happel, who had played against Scotland in Switzerland in 1954, and who was now seconded from his post at Bruges.

It appears that MacLeod's senior players now forced their own views on team selection upon him. Souness was at last given an outing, and Rioch also returned. In defence Kennedy and Forsyth resumed their places. The players to stand down were Jardine, Burns, Macari and – Robertson, which meant Scotland took the field without a recognised winger in an attempt to counter Dutch strengths in midfield.

In the small, cramped Mendoza stadium with its lush pitch, Scotland gave the powerful Dutch the fright of their lives. After just five minutes Rioch – given a free role further forward – headed Souness's cross against the angle of post and bar. Neeskens shortly lunged at Rioch, inflicted further damage to his own ribs, and took no further part – Boskamp deputising. Then Dalglish 'scored' only to have the goal chalked off through Jordan's earlier foul.

Rough had seen little action. But in the 34th minute Scotland's enterprise rebounded in their faces. Kennedy lost possession to Rep. The full-back chased back, the goalkeeper rushed out, and Rep was brought

John Robertson in full flight during the match against Brazil in the 1982 finals. He made one appearance in the 1978 finals against Iran.

down within a tartan sandwich. The referee gave a penalty, Gemmill was booked for protesting, and Rensenbrink notched the 1,000th goal in the history of the World Cup finals.

Rensenbrink's penalty effectively ended lingering Scottish dreams. They now needed four to qualify. But in the 44th minute they pulled back to all-square. The Dutch goal had been living under siege when Souness's probing centre was headed firmly down by Jordan for Dalglish to hook past Jongbloed.

The equaliser did wonders for Scottish confidence. They came out for the second half to find Holland had brought on Wildschut in place of Rijsbergen, injured through an earlier Jordan challenge. Within two minutes Scotland were in front. Souness, the inspiration behind his team's resurgence, chested down Dalglish's centre and was crudely bundled off the ball by Willy van der Kerkhof. Gemmill wasted no time in converting the penalty, and now Scotland had the whiff of a possible sensation.

The Dutch retaliated: Rough saved from Rep. But soon the traffic was again bearing down on Jongbloed. Dalglish headed over, Jordan headed wide, before the stadium and the watching·millions rose to their feet to acclaim a goal of pure genius. Out on the right Archie Gemmill embarked on a slalom run worthy of any skier. He wriggled past man after man, changing direction this way and that. The ball was poked through Krol's legs and now Gemmill had only Jongbloed to beat. The goalkeeper sprawled, the ball was flicked round him, and Scotland led 3-1. It was a moment to savour.

Scotland now had twenty-two minutes to find the fourth and – could it happen? – stay in the competition. But the ecstasy was abruptly stifled by Rep. Steaming through the middle he unleashed another example of Dutch power shooting. Rough was beaten high to his right from twenty-five yards to finally put paid to Scottish dreams. The Dutch had been stung into action: as soon as they needed to score they did so. They might well have equalised, too, as Scotland tailed away. At the death, Rene van der Kerkhof streaked away down the left. His shot beat Rough but flashed narrowly past the far post. For Scotland it was goodbye as expected, but the players' heads were held high as they left the pitch.

HOLLAND (1)2   SCOTLAND (1)3
   Rensenbrink (pen), Rep   Dalglish, Gemmill 2 (1pen)

HOLLAND: Jongbloed, Suurbier Krol, Poortvliet, Rijsbergen (Wildschut), Neeskens (Boskamp), Jansen, W van der Kerkhof, R van der Kerkhof, Rep, Rensenbrink.

SCOTLAND: A Rough (Partick), S Kennedy (Aberdeen), M Buchan (Man U), T Forsyth (Rangers), W Donachie (Man C), B Rioch (Derby, capt.), A Hartford (Man C), A Gemmill (Nott'm F), G Souness (Liverpool), K Dalglish (Liverpool), J Jordan (Man U).

Holland showed their mettle as the competition progressed, winning the second phase group completed by Italy, West Germany and Austria, before being beaten by Argentina in the Final. The host nation's ultimate triumph was perhaps the most farcical in the whole history of the World Cup. Outrageous refereeing decisions favoured them from start to finish. Every single match in which they won swung on an incident which went in their favour. Required to beat Peru by four goals to reach the Final, they managed six – but only after Peru had hit the post when 0-0. In the Final, Holland, handicapped by yet more refereeing connivance, still managed to strike wood in the final minute of normal time. They were three inches from the World Cup, which eventually went to Argentina, arguably the worst team ever to lift the trophy.

The fact that Scotland beat the eventual World Cup runners-up gave rise to endless misguided 'if onlys'. In reality, any win over a team which could have regarded a two-goal defeat as a triumph is a futile arguing point. Holland's ability to strike back at the Scots as soon as danger threatened emphasised the feebleness of Scotland's victory as a propaganda coup.

This is not to say that Scotland in their final match did not play the best football seen under Ally MacLeod. If anything, such a belated showing only angered the Scottish public further, highlighting the earlier failings. But such is the self-destruct quality so often apparent in Scottish football: the team they had to beat most of all was the one in the mirror.

Poor Ally MacLeod's short reign would inevitably soon be terminated. He was not so much a team manager as a cheerleader. His manifest failings in Argentina were not, of course, his fault, but that of the Scottish FA which appointed him. At a stroke all the good work of Tommy Docherty and Willie Ormond over the previous five years which had made Scottish international football something to be reckoned with had been undone. Everything would have to be built up again.

Group 4 – final positions

	P	W	D	L	F	A	PTS
PERU	3	2	1	0	7	2	5
HOLLAND	3	1	1	1	5	3	3
Scotland	3	1	1	1	5	6	3
Iran	3	0	1	2	2	8	1

Scotland appearances and goal-scorers:
World Cup qualifying rounds and final competition 1978

	A	G		A	G	
Dalglish K*	7	3	Jardine S*	3	–	
Jordan J*	7	2	Johnston W	3	–	
Rough A	7	–	McGrain D*	3	–	
Hartford A	7(2)	1	Macari L*	3(1)	–	
Donachie W*	5	–	Kennedy S	2	–	
Rioch B	5	–	Blackley J*	1	–	
Buchan M*	5(1)	–	Gray A	1	–	
Forsyth T*	5(1)	–	Gray E†	1	–	
Gemmill A	5(1)	2	Robertson J	1	–	
Masson D	4	1	Souness G	1	–	
McQueen G	4	–	Harper J*	1(1)	–	
Burns K	4(1)	–	Pettigrew W	1(1)	–	
			own goals		2	
24 players			caps	86	11	goals

Scottish League	25
English League	61
	86

Bracket signifies appearance was as a substitute
*Appeared in 1974 World Cup
†Appeared in 1970 World Cup

Scotland players celebrate David Narey's goal against Brazil in the
1982 World Cup finals.

CHAPTER 9

The 1982 World Cup

The task of restoring Scottish self-respect in the wake of the Argentine fiasco fell to Jock Stein. Irony of ironies, the job would have fallen to him a year earlier had he wanted it. But he was then still convalescing after a horrendous car accident, and was understandably averse to leaving Celtic when a lucrative testimonial was in the offing if he stayed.

In the days leading up to the 1978 finals the merry-go-round of Scottish club managers threatened to spin out of control, affecting nearly all the top clubs. Jock Wallace quit champions Rangers, who elevated John Greig from the playing staff to the hot seat. Celtic had had (for them) a wretched season. The time was considered appropriate for bringing in a younger face to keep in tune with developments at Ibrox. That face belonged to Billy McNeill, hero of Celtic's halcyon days, who vacated his job at Aberdeen only one year after succeeding Ally MacLeod. The Pittodrie club duly recruited Alex Ferguson, freed by St Mirren.

Stein, the most esteemed and successful manager in Scotland, thereby left his new appointment with Leeds United to take charge of the national team for the second time – he had, of course, guided Scotland's fortunes on a caretaker basis back in 1965. Now his job was to uplift Scottish football from the deepest depression in memory.

He did not have long to wait for competitive experience for his players. The preliminary rounds of the 1980 European Championships were already upon them, and a defeat had been recorded in Vienna. The end of the MacLeod interlude spelled the end for those two players inextricably associated with him – Rioch and Masson. Others – Lou Macari, Tom Forsyth and Joe Harper, not to mention Willie Johnston – also had no international future. (Masson and Macari were banned for airing their views to the press.)

Success for Jock Stein was not swift in coming. His team finished fourth out of five in the European Championships, behind Belgium, Austria and Portugal. In the summer of 1979 Scotland were beaten by Wales and England in the Home Internationals, and by world champions Argentina at Hampden. Peru were also invited to the national stadium, hopefully to provide sweet revenge. Even with home advantage Scotland could not turn the tables, requiring an own-goal to draw.

1980 was no better. In the British Championships Scotland again lost two out of three, including a Hampden defeat by England, followed by defeats in Poland and Hungary. By the time the 1982 World Cup qualifiers came round Stein had supervised his team on eighteen occasions and seen them lose on eleven, win on only five. There were rumblings of discontent in the Scottish press.

As part of the revolution within FIFA, which could be traced back to the ousting of Sir Stanley Rous from the Presidency in 1974 and his replacement by the Brazilian Joao Havelange, the number of finalists in 1982 would be increased from sixteen to twenty-four. In essence, this was to accommodate more teams from the third world, but it also meant more places available to European teams. In Scotland's group, *two* countries would qualify from Portugal, Sweden, Israel, Northern Ireland and Scotland themselves. Even allowing for Scotland's lack of success over the past three years, the nature of the opposition provided no cause for despondency.

The Qualifying Rounds

Wednesday, 10 September 1980
SWEDEN v SCOTLAND   Stockholm 40,000

Scotland opened their eight-match qualifying programme in front of a 40,000 crowd in Stockholm's Solna Stadium. For a country comprising, in the main, part-time players, Sweden had a most creditable record in the World Cup. They had appeared in the final stages of seven of the eleven previous competitions, reaching the semi-finals back in 1938, finishing third in 1950, and ending up losing finalists in 1958. They had not been defeated at home in a World Cup eliminator for fifteen years.

This record of accomplishment in the cup of cups was something of a mystery. Sweden had no pedigree in the European Championships and their recent form was wretched. They had been held to a draw by tiny Luxembourg, and so far in 1980 had mustered just one win from six outings. This was their second home match in the current round of qualifiers, having already been held to a 1-1 draw by the unfancied Israel. Scotland's own past file on matches with Sweden made for poor inspection: in 1977 at Hampden Scotland had registered their first win in four attempts. Clearly it was to be a match between two teams more accustomed to defeat than victory. Whichever of them won would have little to brag about.

Swedish coach Lars Arnesson had one vastly experienced player in his ranks. Goalkeeper Ronnie Hellstroem was lining up for the 76th time in a Swedish jersey, having represented his country in the World Cup finals of 1970, 1974, and 1978. Hellstroem earned his wages in West Germany with Kaiserslauten, yet with just one further exception – Hasse Borg of Eintracht Brunswick – the present Swedish team was composed entirely of home-based part-timers.

Sweden's only recent footballing landmark had been created the previous year when Malmö reached the final of the European Cup – losing to Nottingham Forest. This enabled Malmö's Erlandsson and Forest's John Robertson to renew their acquaintance. Kenny Burns had also been in that triumphant Forest side, though he was for the moment out of international favour. Stein had now experimented with six pairings in central defence in recent games. In Stockholm it would be the turn of Liverpool's elegant Alan Hansen and Aberdeen's Alex McLeish. McLeish's Pittodrie captain, Willie Miller, was pushed forward into a defensive midfield role, and a third member of Aberdeen's championship-winning side, the flame-haired Gordon Strachan, won his own sixth cap.

The team had a welcome streak of experience running through it. Six players had taken part in the 1978 campaign – Rough, McGrain, Dalglish, Andy Gray, Robertson and ... Archie Gemmill, now with Birmingham and once again Scottish captain. Frank Gray – brother of Eddie not Andy – had already won eight caps at left-back.

Since taking charge, Stein had watched his players perform in Austria, Portugal, Norway, Belgium, Poland and Hungary. He had seen them lose to them all – bar Norway – so would obviously be well satisfied with a draw in Stockholm. To this end he attempted to instil the virtues of workmanship rather than flair into his players. Robertson dropped deep, leaving Andy Gray (a £1½ million buy for Wolves) and Kenny Dalglish as lone front runners.

Dalglish soon found room for an early shot at goal, but most of the first-half excitement was generated by the Swedes. One flowing intricate move after twenty minutes climaxed with a Sjoberg glancing header which brushed an upright. Eight minutes before the break Miller's clearance was picked up by Nilsson and struck back viciously on to Rough's post. The ball rebounded off the goalkeeper and was belted away by McLeish. Miller's twenty-yard drive over the top brought the first half – in which chances at both ends had been scarce – to a close.

It was evident as the second half unfolded that one goal was likely to settle the match. The Swedes had thus far come closest, and Andy Gray now popped up to clear Gustavsson's dangerous free kick. Both sides looked to manufacture a penalty, each having their moments of hope. But

A determined Gordon Strachan in action against Brazil in the 1982
World Cup finals. Looking on is Graeme Souness.

the goal which did break the deadlock was far more worthy. It fell to Scotland, was unexpected inasmuch as it was more or less their first clear-cut chance, but was sufficiently noble as to raise many a Scottish roof. In the 72nd minute the diminutive Strachan dispossessed Erlandsson, exchanged passes with the tinier Gemmill, advanced at an angle on the left and fired along the ground inside the far post. Scottish patience had been worthwhile, for it was a textbook goal.

With Tottenham's Steve Archibald on for Dalglish, Scotland held out till the end to record a rare away victory. 'Professional' and 'disciplined' were the adjectives used to describe the performance, with a moment of Strachan magic worthy of the winning side. An away win to open the account was just what the doctor ordered. It turned out to be a bleak evening altogether for Scandinavia, Norway going down 0-4 at Wembley.

SWEDEN (0)0   SCOTLAND (0)1
                                    Strachan

SWEDEN: Hellstroem, Gustavsson, Borg, Bild, Arvidsson, Erlandsson (P Nilsson), Ramberg, Nordgren, T Nilsson, Sjoberg, Ohlsson.

SCOTLAND: A Rough (Partick), D McGrain (Celtic), F Gray (Nott'm F), W Miller (Aberdeen), A McLeish (Aberdeen), A Hansen (Liverpool), K Dalglish (Liverpool) (*sub* S Archibald, Spurs), G Strachan (Aberdeen), A Gray (Wolves), A Gemmill (Birmingham, capt.), J Robertson (Nott'm F).

Wednesday, 15 October 1980
SCOTLAND v PORTUGAL   Hampden 61,000

Sweden had now let slip three points from two home games. They would evidently be struggling to qualify. If Scotland could now overcome Portugal at Hampden, a psychologically imposing gap would be opened up over two of their principal rivals. Portugal, unlike Sweden, had no tradition at all in the World Cup. They had reached the finals only once, in 1966, when they had finished a splendid third. Nor had they ever appeared in the later stages of the European Championships. Portugal's footballing fortunes were largely invested in their leading club, Benfica, five times European Cup finalists in the 1960s. With the 1982 World Cup finals to be held in neighbouring Spain, and huge travelling support guaranteed, Portugal were desperate to qualify.

Portugal were no strangers to Scotland. This would be the ninth meeting since the War. Scotland had won three and lost one at Hampden; and had achieved only a solitary draw in Lisbon. Portugal had played in Glasgow as recently as March 1980 in the European Championships. Scotland had won that match comfortably, 4-1, though with both teams already eliminated it had been contested in an air of bonhomie and anti-climax, not blood and thunder.

Not surprisingly, the Portuguese, for whom this was their inaugural fixture in the current series, prepared with determination and diligence. Their new coach, Julio Cernadas Pereira, cancelled the domestic league programme so as to concentrate minds and resources on the international. In contrast, there were no postponements to the Scottish or English Leagues – despite England's own World Cup fixture in Romania.

Portugal's captain was a thirty-two year old goalkeeper from Benfica, Manuel Bento, who was reputedly given to flights of eccentricity. He had not performed with distinction on his recent visit to Hampden, nor against Liverpool in the European Cup quarter-finals back in 1978. With key players missing – including sweeper Humberto, Alves in midfield, and Alberto, who had scored Portugal's winner against Scotland in Lisbon in 1978 – it was expected that Portugal would come in search of a goalless draw.

In the attempt to frustrate that objective Stein retained virtually the same team which had been victorious in Stockholm. The solitary change was caused by the absence of Alex McLeish with knee ligament trouble. Miller fell back to partner Hansen, and Graeme Souness returned to midfield.

Scotland enjoyed so much possession as to invite accusations of gluttony. Alan Rough might easily have brought his sandwiches with him, so idle was he. But Bento and his countrymen were resolute that thou shalt not pass. In the first half Scotland found no chink in the Portuguese armour. A Dalglish swivel and shot, ably smothered by Bento, and a Souness long-range effort which flashed over the bar were as near to a goal as Scotland could come. Their opponents contrived just one scoring opportunity, but it turned out to be the most inviting of the match. Costa worked the ball down the left, and when it was cut back Fernandes, with the goal yawning, brushed the cobwebs from Rough's left-hand post. Small wonder Fernandes gave a look of concentrated anguish: his team would not come so close again.

For the second period Portugal abandoned any pretence at searching for a goal, and were quite content to permit Bento to make a hero of himself. This he was perfectly willing to do, brushing himself down from an earlier collision with Miller to become the most unpopular man on Hampden's terraces. Straight from the restart he plunged to his right to divert

Dalglish's fierce shot-on-the-turn. The same Liverpool player then tumbled twice without gaining the desired penalty.

The Portuguese hauled off their two notional strikers, Chalana and Jordao, but Stein kept his own substitutes on the bench. Souness thundered a mighty shot through a ruck of players but Bento clutched the ball and stubbornly declined to drop it. Scotland's build-ups through the middle were becoming all too predictable. Robertson, playing deep, could rarely escape the attentions of Gabriel, and only McGrain's thrilling sorties up the right touchline offered a hint of the unexpected. Four minutes from time a Strachan drive was deflected straight into the grateful Bento's waiting arms and that was that. Portugal had got what they had come for – but Scotland still had three points to show from their first two matches. Jock Stein would happily have settled for that beforehand, and besides, he had more cause to smile than Ron Greenwood. England lost in Bucharest.

SCOTLAND (0)0   PORTUGAL (0)0

SCOTLAND: A Rough (Partick), D McGrain (Celtic), F Gray (Nott'm F), G Souness (Liverpool), A Hansen (Liverpool), W Miller (Aberdeen), G Strachan (Aberdeen), K Dalglish (Liverpool), A Gray (Wolves), A Gemmill (Birmingham, capt.), J Robertson (Nott'm F).

PORTUGAL: Bento, Gabriel, Pietra, Simoes, Larangeira, Fernandes, Eurico, Costa, Chalana (Sheu), Dos Santos, Jordao (Nene).

Wednesday, 25 February 1981
ISRAEL v SCOTLAND   Tel Aviv 35,000

Scotland were not in the habit of playing football matches in the freezing month of February. That they did so now was due entirely to the fact that their hosts were Israel, basking in the comparative warmth of the eastern Mediterranean. The inclusion of Israel in a European World Cup section owed its illogicality to politics. Geographically, Israel belonged to Asia but was not welcome among the Asian confederation of FIFA and had been expelled in 1976. Israel had then been refused entry to the Central and South American confederation, and eventually had to seek soccer refuge as an honorary constituent of Europe.

Group 6 was now beginning to take shape. Portugal were out in front with five points from three matches. Israel had so far proved unexpectedly resilient, losing just one of their opening four games and forcing goalless draws at home to Northern Ireland and Sweden. They had recently beaten

Austria in a friendly, and had been preparing for the visit of Scotland for several weeks in almost monastic seclusion. Clearly there were going to be no presents for Scotland in the Ramat Gan Stadium in Tel Aviv.

Israeli football was heavily influenced by the English game: English League matches were televised every week; the Israel team manager was an Englishman, Jack Mansell; and the country's most capable player, Avi Cohen, was in and out of Liverpool's first team. His Anfield colleagues, Souness and Dalglish – familiar with Cohen's ability – would ensure that no complacency undermined Scottish preparations.

Other Israelis to guard against included their veteran central defender from the 1970 World Cup finals, Ytszak Shum, and a pair of speedy front runners, Damti and Sinai. The former had sixty-two internationals behind him, the latter none. Levi was also making his debut. If he and the rest could play like Avi Cohen, Scotland were likely to be stretched.

Stein made a few changes. Willie Miller had recently served a suspension and was lacking match fitness. McLeish and the reinstated Kenny Burns teamed up for the first time in front of Rough. With Strachan out through a serious stomach injury, Ipswich's goal-getting midfielder John Wark made a comeback. Andy Gray dropped down among the substitutes, allowing Steve Archibald to play at centre-forward. Archibald and Wark were the English First Division's leading scorers.

Sporting red shirts and navy shorts, Scotland tried to seduce the rain-soaked crowd by distributing flowers before the kick-off. But lest anyone interpret this as a Scottish peace-offering, Burns promptly clattered Damti once play commenced.

The more discerning Scottish players appreciated that this could be one of their trickiest fixtures, and they were proved correct. When the teams tramped off at the conclusion of the first forty-five minutes Israel had everything but a goal to show for their all-round superiority. Playing to a methodical 4-4-2, in white shirts with blue sleeves, the home side were much the more organised. With Avi Cohen orchestrating his team from the sweeper position, several excellent chances were fashioned, most of them foiled by the admirable Rough. After just twelve minutes Tabak raced into the box to be frustrated by a courageous plunge on the part of the Scotland goalkeeper. In midfield, Wark and Gemmill were in danger of being swept into the West Bank.

Midway through the half a silky-smooth Israeli move culminated in Tabak pushing the ball through to Damti, clear on the right, who carelessly shot into the sky. Tabak then tried himself, Rough blocking the ball with his legs. Souness's 37th minute attempt which sailed wide was Scotland's only serious reply. Shortly before the half-time whistle McLeish lost sight of the ball, Damti didn't, but Rough again came to the rescue. 'A shambles' was how Jock Stein described his side during that worrisome three-quarters of an hour.

The Scottish manager must have delivered inflammatory words in the dressing room, for there was a perceptible uplift in the Scottish performance thereafter. John Wark, looking uncomfortable without the Ipswich support provided by Franz Thiyssen and Arnold Muhren, did not reappear. Burns pushed forward into midfield and Miller lined up to partner McLeish in defence. Robertson switched to the right to noticeably good effect. Within nine minutes Scotland were ahead. Robertson swung over a corner, McLeish nodded it back, and the ball fell at hip height to Dalglish loitering with intent on the six-yard line. Dalglish had suffered a mild concussion earlier in the match and had contemplated coming off at half-time. He would be glad he didn't, for he was now the toast of Scotland, winding into a ferocious volley which, fortunately for a hapless defender on the goal-line, missed decapitating him by inches. It was Dalglish's 24th goal in his 78th international.

The goal worked wonders for Scottish confidence, but did not prevent the Israelis looking perfectly capable of equalising. Rough was busy till the end, and Frank Gray once belted clear with the Scottish goal under siege. Andy Gray replaced Dalglish and might have scored with an instant volley, yet the final whistle could not come quickly enough for Scotland. Dalglish had scored from one of only two real chances which had come their way. Stein was not lulled into complacency. Scotland's play had not been pretty to watch, but they had managed another welcome away win.

ISRAEL (0)0   SCOTLAND (0)1
                                          Dalglish

ISRAEL: Mizrahi, Mahness, J Cohen, Ekhois, A Cohen, Barr, Shum, N Cohen, Sinai, Damti, Tabak.

SCOTLAND: A Rough (Partick), D McGrain (Celtic), F Gray (Nott'm F), G Souness (Liverpool), A McLeish (Aberdeen), K Burns (Nott'm F), J Wark (Ipswich) (*sub* W Miller, Aberdeen), K Dalglish (Liverpool) (*sub* A Gray, Wolves), S Archibald (Spurs), A Gemmill (Birmingham, capt.), J Robertson (Nott'm F).

Wednesday, 25 March 1981
SCOTLAND v NORTHERN IRELAND   Hampden 78,000

Scotland's record to date of two away wins and no goals conceded in three games was most un-Scottish, an indication of Stein's determination to instil functionalism and consistency into his squad – dispensing with the fancy stuff. Alan Rough's 270-minute shut-out equalled the record established by Jim Cruickshank back in 1970.

Whether Northern Ireland were likely to end that sequence depended on whether they offered themselves like lambs to the slaughter as so often in the past, or played to their new-found potential as cultivated by manager Billy Bingham. Northern Ireland were defending British champions, the first time they had ever won the championship outright. They had also beaten Scotland in Belfast in 1980. Prior to that, the 'troubles' had necessitated that all Scotland-Ireland matches since 1970 be played at Hampden – Scotland winning five, Ireland three.

In Group 6 to date, Northern Ireland had three points to show from three matches, having lost a mite unfortunately by the only goal in Portugal. The Irish team welcomed back Pat Jennings in goal after an eight-match absence (he had first played for his country in 1964: this was his 84th cap), but were handicapped by the omission through injury of Martin O'Neill. Sammy McIlroy needed a late test on his knee before being passed fit.

The balance of the Scotland team was not to Jock Stein's satisfaction. He found himself with an abundance of quality central defenders and strikers, but a dearth of talent in midfield – the department where Scotland had been strongest in 1974 and 1978. This weakness was illustrated by Stein's having to play surplus defenders like Burns and Miller as make-do midfield operators.

Jock Stein, too, had injuries depleting his squad, notably those to Graeme Souness and Kenny Dalglish. It was the first match Dalglish had missed after a run of forty-three consecutive caps. John Wark, who deputised for Souness, had recently been voted the English 'Player of the Year'. In attack, Stein overlooked the claims of all the leading goalscorers in the Scottish Premier Division: McGarvey and Nicholas (Celtic); Sturrock and Dodds (Dundee Utd); McGhee and McCall (Aberdeen); McAdam and McDonald (Rangers).

The early play was scrappy and tense, and McLeish's nudge on McIlroy provoked Irish howls for a penalty. Archibald's answer was to spin on McGrain's pass to crash the ball against the base of Jennings' post. Then it was Ireland's turn, McIlroy racing clear, only to be victim to Miller's professional foul for which the Aberdeen captain was cautioned. Scotland saw more of the ball in the wet conditions but their use of it relied more on muscle than finesse. Glimpses of goal still came their way. Burns and Wark produced a double-act to carve into the Irish defence, but Archibald's final shot was repulsed by Chris Nicholl's spectacular diving clearance. Miller also struck the ball sweetly, but it was deflected into the heavens. All Ireland had to offer for their first-half puff was a McCreery run and shot which he couldn't keep low enough to trouble Rough.

If Scotland shaded the first half they were decidedly inferior for much of the second. Within three minutes McIlroy's centre was nodded goalwards by Billy Hamilton – playing in the English Third Division with Burnley. Alan Rough flung himself sideways to turn the header against a post. McLeish cleared up the rebound. Rough then brought injury upon himself when disputing possession with Hamilton.

Scotland's difficulties were directly attributable to their midfield, where Gemmill, Wark, Burns and Robertson were unable to prize open their opponents' grip – with McIlroy looking the best player afield. In desperation, Miller and Burns switched positions, and Scotland relied ever more heavily on the forward surges of McGrain. Sammy Nelson's name entered the referee's notebook for a crude challenge on Wark, but with twenty minutes left to play Ireland opened the scoring. McClelland was fouled by Burns out on the touchline. McIlroy flighted over the free kick and Hamilton stole in to plant an emphatic header just inside Rough's left-hand post. It was Scotland's first lost goal of the 1982 World Cup.

Ireland's goal stung Scotland into action, and within five minutes they had erased the deficit with the most incisive move of the match. Miller and Wark both had shots charged down before combining to put Scotland level. Willie Miller's inch-perfect pass bisecting the Irish defence was synchronised with Wark's forward burst. The Ipswich player composed himself to slot the ball wide of the advancing Jennings. The Hampden jeers of 'What a load of rubbish' were substituted in mid-refrain by 'We'll support you evermore'.

Scotland now seized the initiative. Asa Hartford came on for Kenny Burns; Derek Spence for Billy Hamilton. Rough had been struggling ever since his earlier knock, and with the play now concentrated at the other end, St Mirren's Billy Thomson deputised for the final ten minutes. The roused Scots created just one more chance, Gray setting up the opportunity for Archibald to blaze over.

After having played all their opponents once, Scotland had harvested a crop of six points. A further six from the second half of the schedule would see them through with something to spare.

John Wark keeps his eye firmly on the ball to avoid a sliding tackle in the Seville match against Brazil during the 1982 finals.

SCOTLAND (0)1   NORTHERN IRELAND (0)1
   Wark   Hamilton

SCOTLAND: A Rough (Partick) (*sub* W Thomson), D McGrain (Celtic), F Gray (Nott'm F), K Burns (Nott'm F) (*sub* A Hartford, Everton), A McLeish (Aberdeen), W Miller (Aberdeen), J Wark (Ipswich), S Archibald (Spurs), A Gray (Wolves), A Gemmill (Birmingham, capt.), J Robertson (Nott'm F).

NORTHERN IRELAND: Jennings, J Nicholl, C Nicholl, J O'Neill, Nelson, McCreery, McIlroy, McClelland, Cochrane, Armstrong, Hamilton (Spence).

Tuesday, 28 April 1981
SCOTLAND v ISRAEL   Hampden 62,000

Six points from four matches was a healthy position to be in: a meagre three goals scored in those matches was less comforting. Stein felt changes were needed for the task of running up a big score against Israel. The manager nominated the most adventurous formation he had yet contemplated, with his midfield entirely reconstructed. Miller, Burns, Wark and Gemmill stood down – with Andy Gray unfit. Alex McLeish and Alan Hansen were partnered in defence for the first time since their encouraging display in Stockholm. Souness and Hartford were brought together in midfield, and Celtic's Davie Provan was brought in to give balance to John Robertson wide on the flank. It was Provan's fifth international appearance, but the previous four had all been as substitute. Taking over from Gray was the bustling figure of Joe Jordan, recalled to international duty for the first time in eleven months. In the absence of Gemmill, who had pulled on a Scottish shirt for the last time, Danny McGrain was granted the captaincy for only the second time in his career.

Israel, with just five goals conceded from five games, were proving to have a profound influence on the outcome of Group 6. They made one change from the side which deserved better than defeat against Scotland in Tel Aviv, and almost caused an early sensation at Hampden. Mahness's through ball on the left found Tabak with only Alan Rough between him and goal. Tabak squandered the chance, shooting hurriedly and wildly. But in the eleventh minute Israel manufactured a second golden opportunity. Tabak again caused the danger. Rough – the Scottish Football Writers 'Player of the Year' – plunged to parry, then blocked Damti's follow-up.

Thanks to Rough, Scotland had been reprieved and now they applied some pressure themselves. Keeper Mizrahi thwarted Andy Gray, but a goal was not long postponed. After twenty-one minutes Archibald and

Robertson exchanged passes, and the winger was hauled down by Mahness. Robertson took responsibility for the penalty, directing the ball into the net via a goalpost.

With the pressure lifted, Scotland piled men forward. On the half-hour Archibald raced on to Hartford's glided pass and was carelessly felled by Shum. Robertson lined up his second penalty and struck it to the same side of Mizrahi – this time not requiring the assistance of Scottish timber. There might even have been a third goal before half-time. McLeish's thumping header crashed on to the bar and bounced down in front of the goal-line. Archibald tried to force the ball in, but Mizrahi saved.

There was no satisfying Scotland. Israel were made to look like the pretenders they were. Eight minutes into the second half Jordan engineered goal number three. He was enjoying a distinguished return, winning the ball regularly and distributing it with accuracy. Now he touched the ball on to Souness who spread it wide to Provan. The Celtic winger was presented with a clear sight of goal, cracking his shot wide of Mizrahi.

Israel were now in danger of leaving battered and bruised, but redeemed themselves by pulling a goal back after fifty-eight minutes. Rough again got behind Tabak's drive, but Sinai was free to sweep home the rebound. It was only Israel's second goal from six matches, but it had no effect on dampening the Scottish ardour. Frank Gray's centre was headed out to Robertson, who hammered it back hard against a post. Jordan's header was cleared off the line, while Archibald's was flicked over the bar by Mizrahi.

Chances were now falling to Scotland with gay abandon. Souness had a shot saved; Archibald a goal disallowed. In the midst of Scotland's pressure Israel broke away to bring another fine save from Rough. The goalkeeper thereafter resumed his meditation as first Provan, then Archibald, came close to scoring their team's fourth. Mizrahi performed with valour till the end.

Scotland's win put them well clear of the pack in Group 6. The following day Northern Ireland achieved perhaps the most significant result in the group so far, defeating Portugal 1-0, controversially, at Windsor Park. The Irish were now second to the Scots, and Portugal's threat began to recede.

SCOTLAND (2)3   ISRAEL (0)1
   Robertson (2 pens), Provan   Sinai

SCOTLAND: A Rough (Partick), D McGrain (Celtic, capt.), F Gray (Nott'm F), G Souness (Liverpool), A McLeish (Aberdeen), A Hansen (Liverpool), D Provan (Celtic), S Archibald (Spurs), J Jordan (Man U), A Hartford (Everton), J Robertson (Nott'm F).

ISRAEL: Mizrahi, Mahness, J Cohen, Ekhois, A Cohen, Barr, Shum, Zeituni, Sinai, Damti, Tabak.

Wednesday, 9 September 1981
SCOTLAND v SWEDEN   Hampden 82,000

Scotland hung up their boots for the summer months with the hardest part of their quest already accomplished. Five matches had been played: eight points garnered. The visit of Sweden was Scotland's final home tie. Two points from it might well secure qualification. There remained uninviting trips to Belfast and Lisbon to follow, where points might not be so easy to come by.

In June Sweden had done themselves a power of good with home wins over Northern Ireland and Portugal. From being potential wooden spoonists, they had now given themselves a strong chance of qualifying if they could gather wins in Glasgow and Lisbon. Only two of the Scottish team beaten 1-0 in the first match were retained for the second, Lars Arnesson axing his ageing 'stars' and packing his side with younger, hungrier players.

The wisecracks on the Hampden terraces and in the Scottish changing room prior to the match were centred on England, who earlier in the day had unaccountably been beaten in Norway, seemingly to ensure their own demise. Wales also lost in Czechoslovakia, and as things stood Scotland seemed poised to qualify, unburdened by British rivals, for the third time in succession.

Of the team which sank Israel, only Souness and Archibald were missing – both through injury. Wark and Dalglish were the obvious replacements. John Wark had yet to settle in a Scotland shirt, but by the close of the previous season he had bagged fifty-six goals in all competitions – an extraordinary number for a forward, never mind a midfield player. A month into the new season he had already mustered eight. Strachan was not yet back into international reckoning, which did not displease the Swedes.

There was, as ever, much debate about the inclusion of Joe Jordan. His robust approach was something which inflamed passions but irritated the purists. He was now playing in the Italian League, where he had netted seven goals from his first nine matches with Milan. This achievement was worthy of comment, for whatever Jordan's strengths, being a proven goalscorer was not one of them. It says much for his timing, because although it had been Jordan's headed goals against the Czechs which had taken Scotland to the 1974 and 1978 finals, overall he had scored just eight times in forty-seven internationals – a paltry return. Hence the value of Wark.

Against Sweden, Scotland began with panache. Both Provan and Robertson were prominent in early flourishes. Wark, surrounded by defenders, reached Robertson's free kick and watched his header roll infuriatingly along the goal-line. Dalglish found space for a clean header from Provan's cross, but his aim was wanting. In the twentieth minute the Swiss referee blew for a questionable foul on Jordan. Robertson flipped the ball to the near post, where Jordan projected a searing diving header high and wide to Ravelli's left. It was the kind of goal which only Jordan could score, and the arguments over his inclusion in the team were temporarily adjourned.

For the remainder of the half, Scottish skill and power – with Hartford always in the action – was as impressive as anything yet witnessed under Stein. Passion and patience were mixed into an irresistible force. Jordan outjumped Borgesson at will, and the Swedes could offer only the offside trap to frustrate their opponents. A Hartford 'goal' came to nothing through offside, before Wark and Dalglish combined exquisitely to create a chance blocked by the keeper. The Swedes could do nothing to impede McGrain's threatening surges down the right.

The interval must have provided more potent refreshment to the Swedes than the Scots. With nothing to lose, the visitors looked more constructive and positive. Within two minutes Rough was asked to make his first serious intervention of the evening. Worse was to follow. The Scottish keeper misjudged a swirling centre, Bjornlund fired towards goal, and McGrain earned the gratitude of his countrymen when intercepting the shot.

Scottish cohesion was now consigned to the memory, passes went where they oughtn't, and the game was much more open. Swedish substitute Hallen brought down Dalglish in full flight and was booked. Soon, Dalglish was withdrawn in favour of Andy Gray, while the Swedes brought on a fresh winger – Nilsson for Svensson. Jordan was cautioned for timewasting, before the game was finally settled seven minutes from time. With the Swedes enjoying their busiest spell of the match, Borgesson tackled Gray. The forward went down, the referee pointed to a small, white circle, and Robertson despatched the penalty. Gray's later televised confession that he had conned the ref by taking a dive did not amuse the Swedes – nor Jock Stein, who would rather he had kept his mouth shut. Over the ninety minutes there was no doubting Scottish supremacy, except for the referee's complicity in both goals. It would now take a freakish series of results to stop Scotland reaching the World Cup finals in Spain.

SCOTLAND (1)2   SWEDEN (0)0
   Jordan, Robertson (pen)

SCOTLAND: A Rough (Partick), D McGrain (Celtic, capt.), F Gray (Leeds), J Wark (Ipswich), A McLeish (Aberdeen), A Hansen (Liverpool), D Provan (Celtic), K Dalglish (Liverpool) (*sub* A Gray, Wolves), J Jordan (AC Milan), A Hartford (Everton), J Robertson (Nott'm F).

SWEDEN: T Ravelli, Erlandsson, Hysen, Borgesson, Fredricksson (Hallen), Borg, A Ravelli, Bjornlund, Larsson, Sjoberg, Svensson (Nilsson).

Wednesday, 14 October 1981
NORTHERN IRELAND v SCOTLAND   Belfast 35,000

Scotland had to wait five weeks for the opportunity to clinch a place in Spain. One point from the trip to Windsor Park would put the issue beyond doubt. As for the Irish, victory alone, it seemed, would suffice to keep their own odds favourable. Portugal were entertaining Sweden the same evening.

The Scots had vivid memories of their 1980 defeat in Belfast. The present match would evidently be a cliff-hanger, with no British love wasted on the opponents. Stein may not have instructed his players to adopt safety-first, negative tactics, but it did not take a shrewd man to realise that Scotland might need to do much defending, and that the team would be picked accordingly. Unfortunately, those redoubtable defenders Danny McGrain and Alex McLeish were unfit, as was Joe Jordan. West Ham's Ray Stewart took over at right-back for his fourth cap, while Willie Miller performed a straight Aberdeen swop for McLeish. Archibald resumed the central striker's duties from Jordan.

In the 1-1 Hampden draw the Scottish midfield had comprised Wark, Burns and Gemmill. Two of these, Burns and Gemmill, had reached the end of their international careers, with Wark rested. The three replacements in Belfast were Souness, Strachan (playing his first

Steve Archibald strikes at goal in the match against the Soviet Union played at Malaga in the 1982 finals. In all, Steve made 9 appearances for Scotland, including qualifying rounds, during that campaign.

international for a year) and Hartford – who had just returned to Manchester City from Everton, and who was handed the captaincy of his country for only the second time. With their Irish counterparts – McIlroy, O'Neill and McCreery – equally formidable, the game was likely to be fiercely contested in midfield. The Irish, in fact, had the makings of one of their finest teams. Of their last thirteen fixtures they had lost only three, and in fifteen matches in Belfast dating back to 1975 only Holland and England (three times) had emerged triumphant.

The game spelled action and high excitement from start to finish. The early play saw Scotland enjoying more than their share of fiery possession. Souness's shot was too high, and one marauding solo burst by Strachan brought a sharp save from Pat Jennings. For Ireland, the balding Noel Brotherston was involved in all their constructive moments, on one occasion cutting inside to hook O'Neill's centre over the top. Shortly before the interval Dalglish accelerated past Chris Nicholl, but his cut-back across the face of the goal narrowly eluded the straining leg of Archibald. McIlroy retaliated with a drive which passed uncomfortably close to Rough's goalpost.

The half-time breather provided pause for reflection. Scotland had searched in vain for a goal. Now the priority was to avoid losing one. Not that they had much choice about second-half tactics. Ireland resumed as if demented, grabbing the game by the scruff of the neck and twisting it until Scottish vertebrae threatened to snap. Hartford and Co were swept contemptuously aside as Ireland surged forward in search of the all-important victory.

Ireland's forward momentum left inevitable gaps in the rear. Chris Nicholl's misplaced back-pass rolled wide of his own post when it could easily have gone in. The omnipresent Strachan set up a chance for Archibald which curled tantalisingly over the bar. But these fleeting Scottish opportunities were eclipsed by the activity at the other end. Chris Nicholl's attempt at the correct goal passed even closer than the unintentional one at his own. A corner carelessly conceded by Strachan produced further Scottish palpitations. A goalmouth melée ensued before a hidden green shirt belted in a shot. Rough parried, only for Gerry Armstrong to power back the rebound, which was hacked off the line by Hartford.

As the game entered its final ten minutes, Scotland were simply hanging on any way they could. Andy Gray replaced the exhausted Strachan, Dalglish dropped back into midfield, and on the final whistle Hamilton's firm header was juggled on the goal-line by Alan Rough. Would he or wouldn't he drop it? He didn't, and Ireland had been denied.

Scotland were euphoric at qualifying, not inclined to dwell on probably their least impressive ninety minutes of the whole campaign. But Irish dejection turned to cheers a couple of hours later when news from Lisbon told of a Swedish victory. As it turned out, Scotland could have lost but still qualified, and all Ireland had to do now was beat Israel to join them in sunny Spain.

NORTHERN IRELAND (0)0   SCOTLAND (0)0

NORTHERN IRELAND: Jennings, J Nicholl, C Nicholl, J O'Neill, Donaghy, M O'Neill, McIlroy, McCreery, Brotherston, Armstrong, Hamilton.

SCOTLAND: A Rough (Partick), R Stewart (West Ham), A Hansen (Liverpool), W Miller (Aberdeen), F Gray (Nott'm F), G Strachan (Aberdeen) (*sub* A Gray, Wolves), G Souness (Liverpool), A Hartford (Man C, capt.), J Robertson (Nott'm F), K Dalglish (Liverpool), S Archibald (Spurs).

Wednesday, 18 November 1981
PORTUGAL v SCOTLAND   Lisbon 10,000

It was time to take stock. Scotland's achievement could be viewed from two contrasting perspectives. They had won their group with a match to spare. They were unbeaten after seven matches, and Alan Rough had conceded a miserly two goals. These statistics were not the kind which were commonly associated with Scotland. Jock Stein deserved every credit for the way he had instilled an unprecedented functionalism and professionalism into Scottish football. Few Scots would welcome the comparison, but their team's dour, unadventurous outlook was more in keeping with that expected of England over the years, at a cost of sacrificing much of the flair which was thought to be a Scottish prerogative. Qualifying for World Cup finals required work; damned hard work.

Realist that he was, Stein would also have appreciated that, looked at match-by-match, Scotland's performances were not as praiseworthy as the overall record would suggest. Three of their eight goals had been penalties – at least one awarded in error. As regards the away form, five points from the visits to Stockholm, Tel Aviv and Belfast was an achievement almost without compare, but again the ball had rolled kindly for Scotland on occasions. Had one, or even two, of those games been lost by the odd goal Scotland could have had no cause for complaint. In fact, in most of Scotland's matches the tide could have turned against them at a critical juncture. Jock Stein appeared to have two things going for him: the shrewdest of football brains, and that priceless knack of having his teams make their own luck.

Portugal's team were in crisis, having slumped from their opening burst to lose four matches in a row – the last being a 4-1 drubbing in Israel. The Portuguese nation were mourning their team's absence from the finals in Spain. It was as well that Scotland had matters sewn up, however, for Lisbon was not a happy hunting ground for Scottish footballers. They had drawn there, 2-2, in 1950, but on their three subsequent visits had lost – and failed to score.

Scotland's trip to the Stadium of Light could now be regarded as something of a luxury. Only Frank Gray of the starting line-up had played there in the European Championship defeat of 1978. Of Stein's regulars, McGrain and McLeish were still out through injury, and a late training knock to Alan Rough presented Billy Thomson with a rare appearance. The make-up of the side had a positive look about it, with Davie Provan reinstated and a fourth cap granted to Paul Sturrock, who had already found the net thirteen times for Dundee United in the new season. John Robertson (with a caution hanging over him) and Kenny Dalglish were the players who made way.

Playing with all the freedom to which their success entitled them, Scotland took the lead after only nine minutes. Ray Stewart tossed back Bento's misdirected clearance. The keeper was helplessly stranded as Sturrock coolly clipped the ball over his head. It was his first goal for his country, and the buoyant scorer raced into the net to cuddle the ball.

Souness and Strachan had been the instruments behind Scotland's resourceful opening, but Portugal hit back with verve. Hansen's last-ditch tackle thwarted the menacing Oliveira. The same forward's next effort was beaten out by Thomson, but after thirty-three minutes Portugal carved out the equaliser they had been threatening. Romeu unleashed a shot from way out which Thomson couldn't hold. Manuel Fernandes was handily placed to stroke home the loose ball.

For the second half Scotland switched their full-backs. Stewart moved over to the left to accommodate Stuart Kennedy, who had come on shortly before the interval to replace Frank Gray, the victim of shoulder injury. The readjustment did not inspire confidence, and it took only eleven minutes for Portugal to go in front. Miller's challenge on the edge of the box failed to dispossess Fernandes, who strode on to shoot past Thomson. Pleased as Fernandes was with his two goals, he would probably have been willing to swop both for the one he missed at Hampden.

Scotland continued to live dangerously. Up front, Sturrock was left to pose whatever threat Scotland presented. Archibald had now failed to score in any of his six World Cup outings, and he made way for Dalglish. Thereafter Scotland brightened considerably. Provan tried his luck and saw his shot parried by Bento; and Dalglish was only just wide.

The defeat spoiled Scotland's unbeaten record, but theirs was the proud distinction of heading Group 6. For good measure, the same evening, Northern Ireland beat Israel to qualify alongside Scotland, while down at Wembley England secured the necessary result against an apathetic Hungary to bring the British contingent up to three. Not since 1958, when all four home countries reached the finals, would the British nations be so generously represented in the world's premier football championship.

PORTUGAL (1)2	SCOTLAND (1)1
Fernandes 2	Sturrock

PORTUGAL: Bento, Frixo, Simoes, Teixeira, Eurico, Dito, Jaime, Romeu, Fernandes, Oliveira, Costa.

SCOTLAND: W Thomson (St Mirren), R Stewart (West Ham), F Gray (Leeds) (*sub* S Kennedy, Aberdeen), G Souness (Liverpool), A Hansen (Liverpool), W Miller (Aberdeen), D Provan (Celtic), G Strachan (Aberdeen), S Archibald (Spurs) (*sub* K Dalglish, Liverpool), A Hartford (Man C, capt.), P Sturrock (Dundee U).

World Cup Qualifying Group 6:

	P	W	D	L	F	A	W	D	L	F	A	PTS
			HOME						AWAY			
SCOTLAND	8	2	2	0	6	2	2	1	1	3	2	11
N. IRELAND	8	3	1	0	5	0	0	2	2	1	3	9
Sweden	8	2	1	1	5	2	1	1	2	2	6	8
Portugal	8	3	0	1	7	3	0	1	3	1	8	7
Israel	8	1	2	1	4	2	0	1	3	2	8	5

Other group results

Israel v N. Ireland	0-0
Sweden v Israel	1-1
N. Ireland v Sweden	3-0
Israel v Sweden	0-0
Portugal v N. Ireland	1-0
Portugal v Israel	3-0
N. Ireland v Portugal	1-0
Sweden v N. Ireland	1-0
Sweden v Portugal	3-0
Portugal v Sweden	1-2
Israel v Portugal	4-1
N. Ireland v Israel	1-0

World Cup Finals – SPAIN – *June/July 1982*

Jock Stein had two friendlies, plus the Home Internationals, to act as target practice before the Big Event. The first of these was in Valencia against the World Cup hosts Spain, Scotland trailing away to a disappointing 3-0 defeat. Holland, World Cup runners-up in 1974 and 1978, but failing to qualify for 1982, were beaten 2-1 at Hampden.

Before the British Championships got underway, however, events elsewhere threatened dire repercussions for the World Cup. The Argentine invasion of the Falkland Islands and the build-up of hostilities which followed led to intense speculation that the three British teams would pull out. The British public, or so it was thought, would not stomach the prospect of their footballers participating in the glamour of a soccer tournament while Britain's armed forces were fighting for their lives in the South Atlantic. Certain prominent Scottish players were forthright in their belief that Scotland should not compete.

Should Argentina at any stage have to play a British country there seemed little hope of the fixture going ahead. But such a situation was highly

Alan Hansen resists a challenge in the 1982 World Cup match against Brazil.

unlikely to arise. The draw dictated that Argentina could not meet England or Northern Ireland except in the World Cup Final itself. Even for Argentina to face Scotland required some conspiracy on the part of the gods. Only if one of them finished first, the other second, in their respective opening groups would they meet up in the second round.

As the weeks passed the near-certainty that Britain would withdraw passed into probability, then a possibility, before the whole question simply died in its own silence – despite the mounting casualty rate in the war. The Scottish popular press changed its tune: one day clamouring for Britain's teams to pull out, the next conveniently hoping nobody had taken their strictures seriously.

The draw itself had been made back in January, and was the stuff of farce. Miniature footballs containing miniature national flags held the key to each country's fortunes. The balls were juggled in whirling lobster pots. To begin with, some balls – including Scotland's – were allocated to the wrong groups, so the whole procedure had to restart from scratch. Then one of the balls broke and choked its lobster pot.

When all was settled, six groups of four teams were neatly arranged. There had been nothing to prevent Scotland, England and Northern Ireland all landing up in the same section, but thankfully that dreary prospect did not materialise. England, ludicrously, had even been seeded in their group, despite their appalling record in the World Cups of 1974 onwards.

The Scotland manager and players did not conceal their disappointment at the composition of their own section, which threw up a near replica of the situation in 1974. The lesson was now truly learnt: it was bad news to have to face the expected weaklings in the first match, in this instance New Zealand. The second game, as in 1974, was against Brazil. The concluding fixture – again a repeat of 1974 – was likely to prove the decisive match. Eastern Europe provided the opponents: Yugoslavia then, the Soviet Union now.

Even at the blueprint stage, Scotland once again looked like having their fate settled by goal difference – at best. Ill-conceived and premature mutterings were heard to the effect that Scotland had drawn the toughest group of all. As it turned out, this was not the case, but Scotland's insistence on believing they'd drawn a bad hand continually seemed to prey on their minds. Their confidence was not boosted by losing at Hampden for the third successive time to England, with the match against New Zealand less than three weeks away. Stein announced his pool of players following the England defeat:

Name	Position	Club	Age	Caps	Goals
Alan Rough	goalkeeper	Partick	30	48	–
George Wood†	goalkeeper	Arsenal	29	4	–
Jim Leighton *	goalkeeper	Aberdeen	23	–	–
Danny McGrain	full-back	Celtic	32	60	–
Frank Gray	full-back	Leeds United	27	22	1
George Burley *	full-back	Ipswich	25	11	–
Alex McLeish	central defence	Aberdeen	23	15	–
Willie Miller	central defence	Aberdeen	27	17	1
Alan Hansen	central defence	Liverpool	26	14	–
Allan Evans	central defence	Aston Villa	25	3	–
David Narey	central defence/ midfield	Dundee United	25	13	–
Gordon Strachan	midfield	Aberdeen	25	11	1
Graeme Souness	midfield	Liverpool	29	24	–
Asa Hartford	midfield	Manchester C	31	49	4
John Wark	midfield	Ipswich	24	15	3
Davie Provan *	winger	Celtic	26	9	1
John Robertson	winger	Nottingham F	29	21	6
Kenny Dalglish	forward	Liverpool	31	86	25
Ally Brazil	forward	Ipswich	23	7	–
Steve Archibald	forward	Tottenham	25	14	3
Paul Sturrock *	forward	Dundee United	25	17	1
Joe Jordan	forward	A C Milan	30	51	10
		Averages	26.8	23.1	

*Players who would not appear in the 1982 World Cup finals.
†Players who would not appear in the 1982 World Cup finals, nor play for Scotland again.

Jock Stein had continued to instil that most invaluable commodity – experience – into his squad. Long gone were those foolish days when players could be asked to make their debuts by being pitched into the World Cup finals. With each tournament in which Scotland had participated the average number of caps awarded per man had steadily increased:

World Cup	Ave. No. of caps
1954	4.8
1958	9.9
1974	13.9
1978	19.2
1982	23.1

West Ham's Ray Stewart and Celtic's Tommy Burns were left out of the manager's plans at the last moment. There was one completely unexpected inclusion in the squad. Over the previous couple of years Jock Stein had made frequent changes to his central defensive partnership. In his final warm-up matches he suddenly introduced Allan Evans – a big, bustling, conventional stopper from Aston Villa – into his side, and began a belated experiment with a sweeper system that came a mighty cropper against England. Otherwise, the squad was packed with those players who had secured Scotland's fine record in the qualifying stages. For Kenny Dalglish and Joe Jordan it would be their third experience of the World Cup finals.

Stein arrived with his players at their Sotogrande headquarters on the Costa del Sol, within sight of Gibraltar, after a relaxing interlude in adjoining Portugal on the Algarve. His was a diplomatic, cautious attitude when questioned about his team's chances – which carried far more conviction, and threat, than the rhetoric of Ally MacLeod four years earlier. Nevertheless, Scotland were once again the team being tipped as possible dark horses. All they needed, it seemed, was to suffer defeat by England at Hampden to have everyone raving about them.

Group 6 opened with the much-heralded meeting of Brazil and the Soviet Union. Bearing in mind the experience of 1974, Scotland did not want that opening fixture to end in a draw. The entire Scottish camp was heartened when Brazil came from behind to win 2-1. Now the pressure was truly on the Russians if they wanted to qualify.

Tuesday, 15 June 1982
NEW ZEALAND v SCOTLAND   Malaga 28,000

Having New Zealand appear in a world soccer, as opposed to rugby, championship was an oddity to ponder. They had qualified by the longest route of any, claiming the second Asia/Oceania place on offer, behind Kuwait, only after a play-off with China in Singapore. En route they had established a new record score in a World Cup qualifier when overwhelming Fiji 13-0. After fifteen matches, and travelling distances commensurate with a voyage to the moon, New Zealand finally earned their passport to Spain.

Facing New Zealand was, for Scotland, being asked to play a good old-fashioned British cup-tie. Manager John Adshead had naturally weaned his players on British methods. Indeed, three of them had been born in Scotland, and several others had experience of playing in the English League.

Jock Stein's team selection kept faith with those players brought in for Scotland's warm-up fixtures. Allan Evans – now the proud possessor of a European Cup medal with Villa – lined up for his fourth cap alongside Alan Hansen, to the exclusion of the tried and tested pairing of Miller and McLeish. In attack Stein continued to make use of Alan Brazil, unused in the eliminators, but looking deadly sharp for Ipswich. Brazil was included in preference to the more conventional front runners, Jordan and Archibald. Brazil had not yet scored in any of his seven internationals, but it was his 23rd birthday and he would be looking for a double celebration.

The British nation was in festive spirits: the Argentine garrison at Port Stanley had just surrendered. Now Scotland must learn from the mistakes against Zaire and Iran and hand New Zealand the hiding of their lives.

The pitch at Malaga's La Rosaleda Stadium was to the delight of all footballers; the heat and the humidity to none. New Zealand wore all-white, perhaps trying to invite associations with Real Madrid or Leeds United. Scotland felt quite at home. Their supporters were everywhere to be seen and heard, and one banner proclaimed 'Don't worry lads, Ally MacLeod is in Blackpool'. The tanoy gave a tinny rendition of 'Scotland the Brave', and battle began.

New Zealand must have been encouraged by the amount of early possession won, though Rough was untroubled and John Robertson looked decidedly in the mood. So did Strachan, and it was his exhilarating run after eighteen minutes which loaded the gun for Scotland's first goal. He jinked his way from inside his own half into the Kiwi penalty area and threaded the ball ahead to Dalglish. The finish was clinical, Dalglish wheeling to clip the ball across Van Hattum and into goal. The tension lifted visibly, but returned for an instant when Hansen passed back to a goal-keeper a.w.o.l. Rough had to scamper back to claim the ball under his crossbar.

On the half-hour Scotland increased their lead. McGrain fed Strachan, who tee'd up a chance for Ally Brazil, which Van Hattum couldn't hold. There, vulturing on the remains, was John Wark, poking the ball back underneath the keeper's body. Two minutes later it was Strachan again, projecting a slide-rule cross on to Wark's head. The ball glanced inside Van Hattum's right post and Scotland were three up. Not only that, they were performing handsomely. The watching Brazilians and Russians must have sat in dry-mouthed silence at the spectacle of a Scottish team for once doing everything right. Until the interval Scotland were queuing up to score, winning a rash of corners and bringing a lightning save from Van Hattum following a cruel deflection. The nearest New Zealand came was a Steve Wooddin drive which squirmed out of Rough's clutches and was saved only at the second attempt.

One can imagine Stein's interval comments: 'keep it steady, and more of the same'. The second part of his instructions seemed ripe for fulfilment as, upon the resumption, Evans nodded Robertson's cross close – but not close enough. Boath almost put through his own goal and Brazil blazed wastefully over from Dalglish's neat pull-back. The birthday boy ought to have made it 4-0 but, exhausted by the heat, he was substituted by Archibald and within seconds it was 3-1. Scotland captain McGrain was pressurised by Kiwi captain Steve Sumner – once of Preston North End. McGrain's pass back was suicidally short and Sumner nipped in to tuck the ball into goal off Rough's body.

Would this be an isolated, inconsequential setback, or a presage of disaster? It might have been the former had Archibald done better than hook the ball over the top: it emphatically became the latter when, twenty minutes into the half, Hill delivered a long speculative pass from deep in his own half. The ex-Tranmere Rovers player, Wooddin, found himself free in space as he advanced to power the ball past Alan Rough from eighteen yards. 3-2, and now all Scotland's habitual self-destruct buttons had been activated. Sensing a sensation, New Zealand whipped off their sweeper for a forward player and urged themselves to new heights.

It was now a case of whether Scotland could hold out, but in the 74th minute they made the game safe. At a Scottish free kick players feigned disagreement among themselves, leaving Robertson to flip the ball exquisitely into the top corner. The scorer stood there motionless, arms above his head, as if he'd just fathered quintuplets. Ten minutes from time Strachan's corner fell neatly on to Archibald's head for the fifth. The brilliant but drained Strachan – architect of four Scottish goals and indubitably Man of the Match – was given a breather, Narey taking his place. Frank Gray was denied a sixth by Van Hattum's sharp save, but afterwards attention did not focus on Scotland's five loaves, but on New Zealand's two fishes, which now threatened to lodge painfully in Scotland's gullet.

NEW ZEALAND (0)2	SCOTLAND (3)5
Sumner, Wooddin	Dalglish, Wark 2, Robertson, Archibald

NEW ZEALAND: Van Hattum, Hill, Elrick, Mackay, Malcolmson (Cole), Almond (Herbert), Rufer, Boath, Wooddin, Sumner, Cresswell.

SCOTLAND: A Rough (Partick), D McGrain (Celtic, capt.), F Gray (Leeds), G Souness (Liverpool), A Hansen (Liverpool), A Evans (A Villa), G Strachan (Aberdeen) (*sub* D Narey, Dundee U), K Dalglish (Liverpool), A Brazil (Ipswich) (*sub* S Archibald, Spurs), J Wark (Ipswich), J Robertson (Nott'm F).

Friday, 18 June 1982
BRAZIL v SCOTLAND   Seville 47,000

For a country which hadn't won the World Cup for twelve years, Brazilian mystique in 1982 was remarkably undimmed. They had galloped through a European tour inflicting defeats on England, France and West Germany in the process. In Spain, Brazil's very presence seemed to induce reverence in the press, public and opposition. In beating the Soviet Union 2-1, Brazil had looked magical at times – curiously mortal at others. In midfield, coach Tele Santana could boast a combination of frightening speed, grace and power. For any one team to have Socrates, Zico, Falcao and Cerezo (missing against Russia) in its ranks was simply unfair to its opponents.

Brazil's problems lay elsewhere. Their goalkeeper, Waldir Peres, like others before him, was – in a word – inept. The left-back, Junior, supreme venturing forward, was less assured when defending. The attack contained no Garrincha, no Pele, no Tostao, no Jairzinho. Instead it relied on an erratic winger, Eder, and a transparently sub-standard centre-forward, Serginho. Such was the all-pervading brilliance of the Brazilian midfield that deficiencies elsewhere were apt to be overlooked – by the public if not by the professionals. It was to be hoped that Stein would not overlook them. Scotland would be delighted with a repeat of the goalless draw achieved in West Germany eight years to the day previously. They had faced Brazil once since, going down 2-0 in Rio in 1977, so still had only one goal to show from five matches against the triple World Cup winners.

The Scottish manager now had to juggle with competing factors. Some of his players were still suffering the heat effects of Malaga. In Seville, 150 miles inland, it would be even hotter. Adding to Stein's calculations was the realisation that, much as a good result was now desirable, it was not imperative. The Russia match was still going to hold the key to Scotland's fortunes. Put simply, it was preferable that Scotland lose heavily, but remain fresh, rather than drain themselves in an attacking frenzy which left them exhausted without time to recover for their crunch game.

Weighing his options, Stein made four changes. In defence, the Tannadice utility player, David Narey, switched for McGrain (Souness assuming the captaincy). Willie Miller took over from Allan Evans, whose international star fell as swiftly as it had risen. In midfield, Stein opted to counter the Brazilian quartet with his own quintet. This required Dalglish and the still-dehydrated Alan Brazil to step aside for Asa Hartford and the lone Scottish striker – Steve Archibald. The game provided a personal landmark for Alan Rough. It was his fiftieth international, a figure reached by only six previous Scotsmen.

Among the 47,000 spectators in the Benito Villamarin Stadium a lone Scottish piper did his utmost to be heard above the drumming rhythm of the samba. On the pitch, Scotland were content to play patiently, and with Brazil operating at a virtual walking pace there were few early scares at either end. Rough was periodically employed gathering up back passes, but he was stranded as the loping Socrates headed carelessly into the side-netting.

Scotland's moment to treasure arrived after eighteen minutes, during which they had fully held their own. Souness, co-ordinating his team's every breath, swung the ball over from left to right, where Wark climbed to head back into the path of Narey. The Dundee United player had taken time off from policing Eder and Junior to stride into the enemy's nerve centre. Escaping Luizinho's challenge, Narey unleashed a sizzling drive with the outside of his right foot, which veritably screamed its way high to Waldir Peres' left. It was a peach of a goal, and now Scotland sensed a miracle.

With Miller winning all the tackles expected of him, and some that weren't, Scotland looked relaxed and comfortable – other than when Eder's angled chip landed on top of the net. Twelve minutes from the break it needed the scarlet-clad Costa Rican referee Luis Calderon to abet Brazil's endeavours to equalise. Hansen's challenge on Cerezo was scarcely illegal, but Brazil were awarded a free kick twenty paces in front of Rough. To Brazil such a prize was tantamount to a penalty, given the nominal inconvenience of the 'wall'. Zico aimed for a six-inch gap inside Rough's left-hand post. And found it.

Shortly afterwards Serginho, under pressure, headed Eder's swinging centre a shade too high, and Scotland were beginning to reel. When Robertson's clever dribble and Wark's flick-on ended with Waldir Peres saving at the feet of Archibald, Scotland's last effective chance of taking the game had passed.

Scotland's legs looked heavy in the second half. Within three minutes Socrates bewildered Narey, and Hansen conceded a corner. Junior swung it towards the near post, where centre-back Oscar, with not a ghost of interference, thumped a close-range header past Rough. It was, to coin a phrase, a 'British' type of goal – and a criminal one to give away. Scotland were now on the ropes: Zico went close, then closer still.

Nineteen minutes into the half Brazil contributed a dazzling goal. A silky move, during which Narey was 'nutmegged', saw the ball splayed wide to Eder. As Rough came out, Eder floated the ball over his head for a goal probably beyond Scottish compass.

Stein now sent on Dalglish and McLeish for the spent Strachan and

Hartford. They made little impact, though Robertson did cut in to shoot narrowly over. Brazil were now cruising, oozing contempt for their vanquished foes, and happy to turn on the exhibition stuff. Three minutes from time they worked an exhibition goal. An entrancing build-up climaxed with a square pass to Falcao, who crashed it through a shadow-chasing Scottish defence and in off the far post. Scotland had been taught an almighty lesson.

BRAZIL (1)4   SCOTLAND (1)1
   Zico, Oscar, Eder, Falcao   Narey

BRAZIL: Waldir Peres, Leandro, Oscar, Luizinho, Junior, Cerezo, Falcao, Socrates, Serginho (Paulo Isidoro), Zico, Eder.

SCOTLAND: A Rough (Partick), D Narey (Dundee U), F Gray (Leeds), G Souness (Liverpool, capt.), A Hansen (Liverpool), W Miller (Aberdeen), G Strachan (Aberdeen) (*sub* K Dalglish, Liverpool), A Hartford (Man C) (*sub* A McLeish, Aberdeen), S Archibald (Spurs), J Wark (Ipswich), J Robertson (Nott'm F).

Tuesday, 22 June 1982
SOVIET UNION v SCOTLAND   Malaga 38,000

It was with a sense of déja vu that Scotland prepared for their showdown with the Soviet Union. Eight years earlier Scotland had been in exactly the same position against Yugoslavia. Their opponents needed only to draw to survive. For both states of affairs the Scots had only themselves to blame. In 1974 they rued their failure to turn the screw against Zaire. Now, their inability to emulate the Russians in restricting Brazil to a one-goal victory put Scotland at a disadvantage. Had Scotland not tossed away a couple of goals in the direction of New Zealand, the Russians would have taken the field against the Kiwis wanting a minimum of four – a far from comfortable task. Needing only two, they ticked them off – plus a third – without ever playing well. Jock Stein tried to turn the situation to his players' advantage, suggesting they were better equipped to fight for a win than hang on for a draw. It was scatterbrained logic (for it hardly flattered his side) but a sensible morale-booster.

   Scotland had lost both their previous matches with the Soviet Union – 0-2 at Hampden in 1967, 0-1 in Moscow in 1971. Those judges most entitled to an opinion – the managers of Brazil and New Zealand – were united in their prediction of a Soviet victory in Malaga. Eder's late winner had brought about the Russians' first defeat in twenty-three games. Their

Scotland midfield player Paul McStay (Celtic) on the ball against
Iceland in 1984. Scotland won this qualifying match played at
Hampden Park 3-0. Paul McStay scored 2 goals.

powerful, sleek team contained some redoubtable players. Desaev, the goalkeeper, and Chivadze the sweeper (and captain) were widely canvassed as the best at their position in the World Cup. Up front, coach Constantin Beskov would rely on the Soviet Player of the Year, Ramaz Shengelia, and the fitfully brilliant left-winger, Oleg Blokhin – European Footballer of the Year back in 1975.

There was much speculation about the identity of the Scottish team. Alan Rough – not for the first time in his life – was receiving adverse comment. In the event, Stein made just one change, shedding one of his surfeit of midfield players brought in to face Brazil – Asa Hartford – in exchange for target man Joe Jordan. With Jordan and Archibald spearheading the attack, there was little doubt about the aerial tactics Scotland would want to employ.

It is not often that Scottish sides are described as predictable or consistent. But for the third match running they spent the first forty-five minutes playing in a manner to draw praise from all-comers. The Russians may have been happy to sacrifice the midfield, but they were anything but happy in the face of Scotland's virile opening. Souness looked even sharper than he had against the Brazilians. Scotland almost took an early lead when Jordan launched himself at Robertson's centre and was forced to watch Desaev make the save of the night, plunging to touch the header away.

At the other end Rough managed to parry a Blokhin effort, before Scotland sensationally took the lead on the quarter hour. In the middle of the pitch Chivadze was challenged by both Jordan and Archibald. Archibald won the ball and stroked it ahead into the path of Jordan. It was one against one: the scorer of World Cup goals in 1974 and 1978 versus one of the world's top goalkeepers. One wondered whether Jordan had the composure, never mind the skill, to score. The sceptics were shamed as he slotted the ball with ruthless precision between keeper and near post.

For the third successive match Scotland were in front – a luxury denied them in 1974 and 1978. Surely they could hang on this time. The Russians emerged from their shell but Scotland continued to look assured in everything they did. Miller looked unbeatable, Strachan inexhaustible, Robertson unstoppable. Souness was not too particular how the Russians were softened up, and some of his interventions – especially on Shengelia – were not for the squeamish.

Before half-time Jordan headed wide, and Strachan's impudent burst forced Desaev to turn his cross-shot away from the lurking Wark. The busy keeper then leapt to keep out Jordan's hook. For their part, the Russians were not without their moments. One Blokhin drive was on target, another not. On the stroke of half-time Chivadze's penetrating run and interchange with Shengelia was unceremoniously interrupted by Souness.

Scotland could have made the game safe in the first three minutes after the interval, Archibald, Wark and Robertson taking turns to pepper the Soviet goal. The Russians showed few signs of an equaliser when, after an hour, they found it. Gavrilov carried the ball into the Scottish area, whence it flew around as if on a pinball table. Chivadze's miscued shot would have carried no danger had Rough been where he ought – in his goal. But the keeper had needlessly strayed from his line and the ball bounced almost insultingly over his shoulder before trundling into the net.

If the score stayed at 1-1, Scotland were out. Demianenko lashed a shot wide of Rough's post and now Scotland were becoming desperate. Danny McGrain and Ally Brazil came on for the fatigued Strachan and Jordan, with Narey pushed forward into midfield.

Five minutes from the end Scotland committed their second act of kamikaze. Out on the touchline Miller and Hansen – an ill-fitting double act whenever they played – converged to clear the ball, which broke amid all the confusion for Shengelia to home in on the unprotected Rough. Shengelia scored as coolly as Jordan had earlier from a similar situation. Scotland were now well and truly out of the World Cup. Souness's cleverly worked goal at the death (shades of Jordan in 1974), which went in off the post, restored pride but not satisfaction.

USSR (0)2	SCOTLAND (1)2
Chivadze, Shengelia	Jordan, Souness

USSR: Desaev, Sulakvelidze, Chivadze, Baltacha, Demianenko, Borovsky, Shengelia, Bessonov, Gavrilov, Bal, Blokhin.

SCOTLAND: A Rough (Partick), D Narey (Dundee U), F Gray (Leeds), G Souness (Liverpool, capt.), A Hansen (Liverpool), W Miller (Aberdeen), G Strachan (Aberdeen) (*sub* D McGrain, Celtic), S Archibald (Spurs), J Jordan (AC Milan) (*sub* A Brazil, Ipswich), J Wark (Ipswich), J Robertson (Nott'm F).

The statistics tell the tale that for three World Cups in succession Scotland had been eliminated on goal difference. It is sequences like that which give statistics a bad name, for they conceal the reality that Scotland were always chasing the improbable in their final matches. On each occasion their opponents were in the driving seat. They – Yugoslavia, Holland, and now the Soviet Union – were unwilling to be budged and Scotland were ill-equipped to budge them. Scotland never did more than flirt with success, as if it was some beautiful woman tantalisingly out of reach. Last-minute equalisers might restore self-respect but they should not be permitted to distort the harsh truth that Scotland never quite deserved to progress further. Their elimination was always their own fault, nobody else's. In 1974 they were knocked out quite simply because they couldn't score goals; in 1982 because they couldn't prevent them.

In many ways Scotland emerged with considerable credit from the 1982 World Cup, measured by the dignified conduct of manager and players off the pitch, and the positive, adventurous, and – at times – effective football realised on it. It was Gordon Strachan, not one of the Brazilians, who was voted by the Spanish press the outstanding player of Group 6, and he was also voted into a world team. Set against these credits was the lengthy debit column – the team's tactical naïveté and technical limitations which were ruthlessly exposed. Scotland took a much-coveted early lead in each match they played, only to ship an alarming total of eight goals. Of those eight, seven were in the second half as Scotland's discipline and composure wilted. At least five of the eight (both New Zealand's, both the Soviet Union's, and Oscar's header for Brazil) owed nothing to attacking virtuosity and everything to fragile defending. An eight-goal debit column could hardly commend success.

In 1958, the last occasion when Britain had mustered a broad-fronted assault on the World Cup finals, it was Scotland who were the first to return home. Likewise in Spain, while the Scots pondered where it all went wrong, England and Northern Ireland remained to do battle in the second round – though they progressed no further.

It had been an oft-heard comment of Jock Stein's that his team had been included in the toughest of all groups, and that had they been allocated to any other section Scotland would doubtless have qualified. This unwarranted notion should have been exorcised by the demise of Brazil and the Soviet Union in the second phase. Poland comfortably disposed of the Russians. As for Brazil, this is what Jock Stein had to say following his team's heavy defeat: 'We lost to a rather special team in Brazil ... barring some catastrophe they will win the World Cup for sure'.

In fact, it did not take a catastrophe to beat Brazil, merely their own shortcomings. There came a time when the incomparable magic of the midfield could no longer paper up the cracks in front of, and behind, it. Italy – whose form in the first round had been thoroughly wretched – capitalised on appalling defensive lapses to show Scotland how to bring the over-confident Brazilians down to size. They were beatable after all. Verily, the most attractive side in the world was not necessarily the best.

So neither Brazil nor the Soviet Union reached even the semi-finals, never mind the Final. Their respective conquerors, Italy and Poland, had both emerged from Group 1, which on paper did not seem as star-studded as Group 6. But paper, as Jock Stein should have known, burns easily.

In one semi-final Italy met Poland a second time before winning through to the Final, there to meet the most unpopular team in Spain. West Germany's route was littered with good fortune and chicanery. They had lost to the no-hopers of Algeria, connived with the Austrians so that both might qualify, watched helpless in the stands as England failed to beat Spain, and then overcame the French in a penalty shoot-out after trailing by two goals and after their goalkeeper had all but killed Battiston with a forearm smash.

To the cheers of football lovers everywhere, the Germans met their come-uppance in the Final. Italy – not Brazil – were indubitably worthy winners of the 1982 World Cup.

Group 6 – final positions

	P	W	D	L	F	A	PTS
BRAZIL	3	3	0	0	10	2	6
SOVIET UNION	3	1	1	1	6	4	3
Scotland	3	1	1	1	8	8	3
New Zealand	3	0	0	3	2	12	0

Scotland appearances and goal-scorers:
World Cup qualifying rounds and final competition 1982

	A	G		A	G
Gray F	11	–	Gray A*	6(3)	–
Robertson J*	10	4	Gemmill A*	4	–
Rough A*	10	–	Jordan J†	3	2
Hansen A	9	–	Provan D	3	1
Archibald S	9(2)	1	Narey D	3(1)	1
Souness G*	8	1	Burns K*	2	–
McGrain D*†	8(1)	–	Stewart R	2	–
Miller W	8(1)	–	Brazil A	2(1)	–
Dalglish K*†	8(2)	2	Thomson W	2(1)	–
Strachan G	7	1	Evans A	1	–
Wark J	6	3	Sturrock P	1	1
Hartford A*	6(1)	–	Kennedy S*	1(1)	–
McLeish A	6(1)	–	caps	136	17	goals

25 players

Scottish League	49
English League	85
Italian League	2
	136

Bracket signifies appearance was as a substitute
*Appeared in 1978 World Cup
†Appeared in 1974 World Cup

Davie Cooper (Rangers) displays his skills in an international match against East Germany. He played in most of Scotland's qualifying games in the 1986 World Cup tournament. With his wing trickery and skill at free-kicks he should be an asset in the finals in Mexico.

CHAPTER 10

The 1986 World Cup

The modern international footballer faces an exhausting schedule. No sooner have the echoes of one competition faded away than the noises of the next begin. Straight after the Spain World Cup came the qualifying rounds for the 1984 European Championships. If Scotland could claim modest success from their most recent efforts in global tournaments, they were more embarrassed by the continental stage. Jock Stein led his Spanish veterans into Europe only to watch them sink to the bottom of a mediocre group completed by Belgium, East Germany and Switzerland. In view of Scotland's chronic travel sickness it was again a cause for disappointment that their three away fixtures yielded no points whatsoever. Once more the press knives were waving in the direction of Mr Stein.

On the domestic front, however, a Scottish club side was busy making headlines. Only twice had a European trophy adorned a Scottish boardroom – Celtic and Rangers taking the honours in 1967 and 1972 respectively. Such was the stranglehold that these two titans had on the Scottish scene that it was cause for raised eyebrows if another club lifted a Scottish trophy, never mind a European one. Yet this was Aberdeen's achievement in May 1983, returning from Gothenburg clutching the European Cup-Winners Cup. Dons' manager Alex Ferguson had shrewdly invited Jock Stein along to lend his massive experience to a Scottish cause. The switching regional fortunes of Scottish football at this period meant that Aberdeen players began to hog the international limelight to an extent only paralleled by the Old Firm in years gone by.

Until the commencement of the 1984-85 season there seemed little sign that the robust health of Scottish club football would spill over on to the national eleven. The annual Home International Championships were staged for the last time in 1983-84, Scotland propping up the group on goal difference. That meant a wooden spoon in Europe had been followed by another at home; and an emphatic defeat in France by the European champions clearly demonstrated the gulf which existed between Scotland and the cream of European soccer.

But fate was determined to have the last word on the demise of the British Championships. Wales and Northern Ireland were still smarting at the implied insult of Scotland and England not wishing to play them in future. So FIFA provided them with an opportunity for revenge, and to refurbish their empty coffers. The draw for the qualifying rounds of the 1986 World Cup, the finals of which would be staged in Mexico, pitched the Irish into the same section as England, and paired Wales with Scotland in the same group as Spain and Iceland.

It is a sign of these congested times that with each successive World Cup the qualifying arrangements become ever more tortuous and complex. With 121 countries entering FIFA's premier tournament there were bound to be administrative headaches. Half the European groups comprised five teams with the top two to qualify. The other three sections, including Group 7 which housed Scotland and Wales, consisted of only four teams. Just the winners would progress automatically to Mexico.

FIFA's original intention was that the runners-up in the European four-team groups would take part with countries from Asia or the Antipodes in a worldwide free-for-all for a second bite at the cherry. Swamped with protests against such a protracted ordeal, FIFA simplified its arrangements. In the case of Scotland, the revised plan was not at all to their displeasure. When the administrative dust had settled Scotland and Wales knew that to finish second in Group 7 would lead to a two-way play-off with the winners of the Oceania section.

By the time the World Cup eliminators were under way, Scotland's fortunes had taken a turn for the better. A touchline ban on assistant manager Jim McLean meant that a successor was necessary. The job went to Aberdeen's Alex Ferguson, who insisted on the title 'coach', not 'assistant manager'. Thereupon the Stein-Ferguson ticket inspired the Scots to wallop the powerful Yugoslavs 6-1 at Hampden, with the visit of Iceland just five weeks away.

The Qualifying Rounds

Wednesday, 17 October 1984
SCOTLAND v ICELAND   Hampden 53,000

An opening home fixture against the group whipping boys is designed to produce two points, head the table from the start, and put all the pressure on your strongest rivals. A setback here could wreck Scotland's entire programme. Already, Iceland's unexpected 1-0 home victory over Wales in September looked like casting a blight on Wales' qualifying aspirations.

Jock Stein's team was unrecognisable to that which partook of the 1982 World Cup campaign. Only four veterans of Spanish battles remained: central defenders Willie Miller and Alex McLeish; skipper Graeme

Three members of Scotland's World Cup squad. From left – Graeme
Souness, Jim Leighton, Kenny Dalglish.

Souness, now playing in Italy with Sampdoria; and the indestructible Kenny Dalglish. The Liverpool legend, though dropped from the Anfield first team for the first time in his illustrious career, stepped out for his fourth World Cup as a sprightly 33-year old.

Aberdeen's bandy-legged keeper, Jim Leighton, taken to Spain as a virginal second understudy to Alan Rough, was promoted to first-team guard duty thereafter. Protected by Miller and McLeish, Leighton completed the Pittodrie-dominated backbone of the national side. Completing the defence were full-backs Steve Nicol and Arthur Albiston, of Liverpool and Manchester United respectively. Nicol's was a particularly versatile talent, being unable to find room for itself in defence for his club side. Ex-Ranger Jim Bett, exiled to Lokeren of Belgium, occupied the left-hand berth in midfield. Ahead of him, the twinkling toes of Ibrox hero Davie Cooper earned an international recall after five seemingly endless years, the reward for the extra motivation instilled by Jock Wallace's messianic return to Rangers.

The main public interest focused on two Celtic babes. Fair-haired Mo Johnston had been a Watford player the previous week. Coming north for £400,000 to the club of his dreams, he now pulled on a Scottish navy shirt for the fifth time as he continued his rapid rise to stardom. His midfield colleague Paul McStay, although still a few days short of his twentieth birthday, was already a Celtic prodigy. His recall to Stein's eleven was the only change from the slayers of Yugoslavia.

As for the Icelanders, who could tell what to expect? They had never faced Scotland before. Their players performed for prestige – no fee being paid for international appearances – though seven of the side were earning their living as pros in the bright lights of West Germany, Holland and Belgium. Sigurvinsson had just helped Stuttgart lift the German championship. One of their home-based stars, the Akranes midfielder Sigi Jonsson, was reportedly attracting the spies of Rangers and Aberdeen.

The game began and the instant scare was Scotland's, as Gudjohnsson powered his way towards Leighton, producing a scrambling save at the keeper's right post.

More predictably, Iceland then fell back on a 'catch us if you can' policy. Their defenders were tough and blond, fitting descendants of their warrior Berserker forbears. McStay, Bett, and the revitalised Cooper all tried their luck, and when Souness's free kick cannoned off the defensive wall the ball broke sweetly to McLeish on the blind side, but the effort was cleared.

Squeals for a Scottish penalty were heard when Atli Edvaldsson – brother of an ex-Celtic player – brushed the ball with his elbow. But the goal which separated the teams after twenty-two minutes was altogether more satisfying. Dalglish's short corner enabled Cooper to tease his way past an Icelandic obstruction and flight the ball beyond the far post towards McStay. The youngster planted his header firmly into the ground, from where it reared up like an exploding shell and flew inside Bjarni Sigurdsson's near upright. It was McStay's baptismal Scottish goal.

Scotland now began to blossom. Dalglish's wriggling slalom and chip deserved better than to brush the wood, before McStay crowned the match with a moment to savour. Forty minutes had elapsed when Dalglish turned the ball to him forty yards out. Touching it ahead, McStay powered his shot inside the top corner as if the ball was wired to an invisible hoist. The boy-wonder threw back his head to milk the heavens' applause.

Stung into action, Iceland surged forward on the reflex. Leighton clung on to Edvaldsson's close-range flick to ensure his team's two-goal interval margin. Upon the resumption Souness, twice, might have made the game safe when well positioned. Both efforts were thwarted, and Hampden sucked in its breath when Leighton plunged at Petursson's feet to frustrate a promising Icelandic attack.

Midway through the half Dalglish, his job done, gave way to Charlie Nicholas – a precociously gifted player with Celtic, now a wayward one with Arsenal. The switch soon showed its reward. Miller journeyed down the right and chipped a perfect floating centre parallel with the goal-line. The ball dropped beyond the groping Sigurdsson and on to the head of the in-rushing Nicholas, who could hardly miss. Before the end McStay's hat-trick aspirations were foiled by the crossbar. Afterwards Jock Stein was a well contented man. One down: five to go.

SCOTLAND (2)3   ICELAND (0)0
    McStay 2, Nicholas

SCOTLAND: J Leighton (Aberdeen), S Nicol (Liverpool), A Albiston (Man U), G Souness (Sampdoria, capt.), A McLeish (Aberdeen), W Miller (Aberdeen), K Dalglish (Liverpool) (*sub* C Nicholas, Arsenal), P McStay (Celtic), M Johnston (Celtic), J Bett (Lokeren), D Cooper (Rangers).

ICELAND: Sigurdsson, Thrainsson, Edvaldsson, Bergs, Margeirsson, Jonsson, Gudlaugsson, Gudjohnsson, Petursson, Sigurvinsson, Sveinsson.

Wednesday, 14 November 1984
SCOTLAND v SPAIN   Hampden 74,000

The hors d'oeuvre had been tasty: now the main course was dished up to a packed banqueting hall. Hampden was crammed to the rafters with 74,000

Richard Gough (Dundee United) in training at Girvan. Richard represented Scotland four times in the qualifying rounds for the 1986 World Cup finals.

all-ticket customers. Spain travelled to Glasgow as runners-up in the European Championships, having lost with distinction to the host nation, France, in the summer. Scotland was all a-buzz.

Spain were infrequent visitors to Scotland: this being only the fourth occasion. On the first, in 1957, Scotland had triumphed dazzlingly in a World Cup eliminator. But a draw in 1965 and a defeat in 1974 meant that it was now close on thirty years since Hampden had witnessed a sunk Spanish armada. On the personal front, a few recent skirmishes were about to be resumed. Liverpool's Souness, Dalglish and Nicol had squared up to Urquiaga, Urtabi and Goicoechia of Atletico Bilbao in the European Cup the previous autumn. Goicoechia was known as 'The Butcher of Bilbao' following a grotesque foul, shown on TV, on Diego Maradona.

Jock Stein was aware of his own embarrassment of riches. Several of his established internationals wouldn't even find a place on the bench. Spanish coach Miguel Munoz expressed his surprise – and relief – that there was still no room in the Scotland line-up for Gordon Strachan, revitalised at Old Trafford. Munoz had fond memories of Hampden, having been manager of the Real Madrid team which enraptured the world in that stadium in the European Cup Final of 1960.

Just in case Scotland became too cocky, their Under-21 side was roundly beaten 2-0 by Spain's youngsters on the Tuesday. And after weighing up all the odds regarding the seniors, the *Guardian* condescendingly decreed: 'Taking the opposition into account, the Scots should not regard a draw as a disaster'.

The popular pundits were unanimous in predicting Spain's stultifying attitude to the match. They were unanimously wrong. The visitors set out determined to put their creative touches to proper use. Spain had, in fact, scored in all but one of their previous dozen away matches, and Gordillo's easy bypassing of Nicol, followed by Victor's threatening shot at Leighton, caused early flutters among Scottish commentators.

But the pundits equally misjudged – and underplayed – Scottish ingenuity. Spain's red shirts and blue shorts were soon inexorably backpeddling, not by choice, but in face of relentless tartan attacks. The Iberian man-for-man marking was soon stretched to breaking point. Kenny Dalglish – winning his 96th cap despite a secret knee injury – was his team's principal architect. One moment he was wrong-footing his shadow, Camacho; the next, spearing a shot beyond Arconada's far post.

Souness and Bett were other inspirational Scots. Bett, patrolling every inch of Hampden, sent over the 29th-minute cross which seemed sure to herald a goal. But the closely shackled Davie Cooper, better at juggling with the ball than heading it, connected all wrong and it bounced back into play off an upright.

Cooper was distracted by his miss for only four minutes before contributing to a spectacular goal. His corner was flicked on by McLeish for Nicol to rake in a blistering volley. Arconada, the experienced Spanish keeper and captain, was a player much revered by undiscerning sports writers. In truth he was a tension-racked performer whose international career was littered with banana skins. Now he plunged to parry Nicol's effort, succeeded only in pushing himself out of the firing line, and left the ball to bounce unattended on the goal-line. Johnston reacted fastest, diving to nod the ball over the line when it was no more than twelve inches off the ground.

Nine minutes later Scotland contrived a second, even more satisfying goal. Bett materialised on the right, collected Miller's pass, and retained his balance despite an elephantine Spanish challenge. His measured centre was headed irresistibly home by Johnston, unimpeded by two defenders positioned between him and the goal.

After the break Emilio Butragueno replaced the semi-fit Rincon as Spain committed themselves to attack. Gordillo began to take the eye, while Urtabi squandered one inviting chance. Camacho was cautioned for his umpteenth clattering of Dalglish before despatching the 68th-minute free kick which brought a surprise Spanish score. Central defender Goicoechia's header was cleanly struck, but was directed almost vertically downwards in front of Leighton. The keeper was caught – literally – on the hop. An eminently savable header bounced up over his shoulder, leaving Leighton with mud on his knees and egg on his face.

Scottish confidence plummeted, then soared with a stunning third goal. Dalglish, on the right edge of the Spanish box, shimmied his way across the face of the goal, drawing three defenders in turn. When finally it seemed he must release the ball he swivelled to strike a murderous shot across Arconada and up into the far junction. The scorer threw his arms wide as if to embrace the universe. He had just equalled Denis Law's all-time scoring record of thirty goals for Scotland.

Afterwards a crestfallen Munoz conceded that this was the best Scottish team he had ever seen. 'It was a masterpiece of technique,' he admitted, and he spoke nothing short of the truth. Scotland's finest all-round performance in many years seemed to have prized the door to Mexico half open.

SCOTLAND (2)3   SPAIN (0)1
   Johnston 2, Dalglish   Goicoechia

SCOTLAND: J Leighton (Aberdeen), S Nicol (Liverpool), A Albiston (Man U), G Souness (Sampdoria, capt.), A McLeish (Aberdeen), W Miller (Aberdeen), K Dalglish (Liverpool), P McStay (Celtic), M Johnston (Celtic), J Bett (Lokeren), D Cooper (Rangers).

SPAIN: Arconada, Urquiaga, Maceda, Goicoechia, Camacho, Senor, Urtabi (Carrasco), Victor, Gordillo, Santillana, Rincon (Butragueno).

Wednesday, 27 February 1985
SPAIN v SCOTLAND   Seville 68,000

The winter of Scottish contentment lasted long, their confidence standing at an all-time high. The media occasionally went overboard in exaggerated praise. One commentator suggested that the incumbent eleven constituted the best Scottish team in history. But Scotland had flattered at home before – and often. A trip to Spain was, in the vernacular, a whole new ball game. It was, in any case, five long years since Scotland had avoided defeat on the soil of any European country outside Britain. Scottish over-confidence, in other words, was a vastly inflated commodity.

Preparations for the big match were far from amicable. For months beforehand the Spanish authorities would not confirm the choice of venue: then it was announced as the Sanchez Pizjuan Stadium in Seville, an arena renowned for its patriotic fervour in times of need. The crowd were separated from the players by no more than the width of a matador's cape. Spain had not lost any of fifteen internationals played in the Sanchez Stadium over a period of sixty years. To compound matters, some of the Scottish squad's training sessions were disrupted by unruly local gate-crashers.

On account of a match which the hosts dare not lose, all Spanish league engagements were postponed. Not so in Scotland, where half the national team featured in a bruising top-of-the-table clash involving Celtic and Aberdeen. No wonder Spanish eyebrows were raised at this manifest disregard for key players' welfare – not to mention Scotland's strange sense of priorities.

Jock Stein was not in the least surprised to learn that Miguel Munoz had axed five players – including the entire strike force – from the team humbled at Hampden. Stein, himself, was all set to field his magic eleven, except that a virus had cruelly laid low Steve Nicol and Kenny Dalglish. It was only an hour before kick-off that this double misfortune was made public.

Nicol's absence was comfortably filled by the versatile Richard Gough of Dundee United. Dalglish's replacement was Steve Archibald, a more forward player who, since his transfer to Barcelona, could provide the dubious advantage of a 'fifth columnist'. Archibald ('Archee' to the Catalonians of eastern Spain) creditably topped the Spanish League's goalscoring charts. Less creditably, he had scored on only four of his twenty-three matches for his country. Stein's reshuffled team now included just a token Anglo – Arthur Albiston of Manchester United.

The Seville crowd were fiercely partisan, pelting Leighton with oranges, toilet rolls and other sundries before and during the match. Almost before play had begun Gough was booked for bisecting Gordillo near the halfway line, but fortunately the game never lived up to its violent potential.

Given the group placings, a draw would have been a worthy result for Scotland. Yet the team did not put up the shutters. In the first half Scotland saw plenty of the ball, but unfortunately they were about as creative as a dead bull.

Spain shaded the honours of an uninspiring half. Indeed, only a coat of paint denied them a goal after only seven minutes. Goicoechia's instant drive caught Leighton in a tizzy. He could only repulse the ball whence it came. As it fell the sprawling Clos headed it back beyond the mortified keeper and past the upright.

Scotland, for their part, could boast no such near misses. The isolated shimmy and turn from Bett was their only sign of invention in that first period. The players were performing in direct proportion to their distance from Arconada. The defence looked sound enough: the midfield – so dominant at Hampden – was lacklustre in Seville; while the attacking duo of Johnston and Archibald were simply irrelevant to the proceedings. The evidence of the first half told that Scotland would be most unlikely to score in the second: but could they keep Spain at bay for the duration?

Scotland learned the answer before Stein's cautionary words had had time to fade. The elusive Butragueno's intelligent burst from his own half sent Senor clear on the right. His cross was tailor-made for McLeish or Miller to repel. Alas they were inexplicably absent and debutant Francisco Clos, having come so near in the first half, headed defiantly beyond Leighton.

One sensed the inevitable now. There was no way back for Scotland. First McStay, then Archibald, were belatedly pulled off. Strachan and Nicholas stripped off their tracksuits. In his eight-minute stint Nicholas

Mo Johnston (Celtic) is thwarted in his attempt at goal in the qualifying match against Spain at Hampden Park on 14th November 1984. The Scots won 3-1. Mo Johnston scored twice and Kenny Dalglish scored the other. Goicoechia countered for Spain.

alone looked likely to prize gaps in the Spanish rearguard. Yet Arconada remained a virtual spectator to the end, and it was Spain who came nearer to adding to the scoresheet as Scotland slid miserably from the match. Souness, culpably casual throughout, climaxed his own indiscretions with a crass professional foul.

Afterwards the Scottish press charged to the rescue. The Spaniards, apparently, were cheats, criminals. The intimidating activities of the crowd had, would you believe, unnerved seasoned professionals accustomed to the hatreds generated by soccer at home and abroad. The truth was that Scotland were as disappointing, individually and collectively, as they had been inspired at Hampden. The press tried to twist a 0-1 defeat into a good result. It wasn't. But, nevertheless, the setback did not appear to harm unduly Scotland's prospects of qualifying.

SPAIN (0)1   SCOTLAND (0)0
    Clos

SPAIN: Arconada, Gerardo, Camacho, Maceda, Goicoechia, Gordillo, Senor, Roberto, Butragueno, Gallego, Clos.

SCOTLAND: J Leighton (Aberdeen), R Gough (Dundee U), A Albiston (Man U), G Souness (Sampdoria, capt.), A McLeish (Aberdeen), W Miller (Aberdeen), S Archibald (Barcelona) (*sub* C Nicholas, Arsenal), P McStay (Celtic) (*sub* G Strachan, Man U), M Johnston (Celtic), J Bett (Lokeren), D Cooper (Rangers).

Wednesday, 27 March 1985
SCOTLAND v WALES   Hampden 62,000

The defeat in Seville appeared to have harmed nothing that could not be quickly rectified. No lasting damage had been done. The following month Scotland played hosts to Wales, whose own chances of qualifying appeared dashed by losses in Iceland and then, heavily, in Spain.

Scotland were well accustomed to slaying the Welsh dragon at Hampden, to whom they had not lost since 1951. For Wales even to score at Hampden was an achievement in itself, and not since 1967 had they had the temerity to breach the Scottish rearguard more than once. In February 1984, in the last meeting within the framework of the now defunct Home International Championships, Wales went down 2-1. With Dalglish and Nicol happily restored to full health, Jock Stein had no hesitation in reverting to the line-up which had served him so well in the two previous home fixtures.

Wales were – outside the valleys – widely written off in this, the one hundredth, meeting between the two countries. Only an outright win could keep their hopes alive. But how could a team which had been beaten in Iceland and which fielded one full-back, Slatter, playing in the Third Division reserves, and another, Joey Jones, acting as a makeshift centre-half, possibly hope to contain Scotland's aristocrats? Wales' slender chances seemed to rest on a vital trio. In goal, Neville Southall was performing week in, week out, with the consistent excellence that would shortly help Everton to become English champions and earn Southall the sports writers' 'Footballer of the Year' award. In attack, the ominous threat posed by Ian Rush was familiar enough, but his side-kick was quickly becoming the revelation of British soccer. Manchester United's thick-thighed, curly-cropped Mark Hughes formed the other half of one of the most potentially lethal strike forces in Europe.

Scottish commentators, nevertheless, seemed none too perturbed. John Greig, for one, explained that the result was practically a foregone conclusion. All Scotland needed to do was sever the connecting lines to Rush and Hughes, and Wales would be emasculated. The home victory that Greig and many others anticipated would effectively end the Welsh challenge and nudge Scotland that bit nearer Mexico.

The press, searching for gossipy titbits to enliven the pre-match atmosphere, latched on to Graeme Souness's ghosted autobiography, which offered unflattering appraisals of certain of his Scottish colleagues. But all was smiles and handshakes – before the cameras at least.

Those same sports correspondents who had been keen to put a fine gloss on the team's failure in Seville could find no comforting scapegoats this time, as Scotland slumped to their worst performance of the current campaign. There were no late illnesses to blame; no orange-hurling Spaniards to accuse of unfair intimidation. Stein's favoured eleven were knocked out of their stride with embarrassing ease by a Welsh team which was readily equipped for a physical battle and to stifle any hint of Scottish flair.

The midfield of Souness, McStay and Bett – only recently compared favourably with the heroes of yesteryear – were ragged beyond belief. Not only was the supply to the Scottish front runners intermittent, at best, but Rush and Hughes enjoyed a much greater sight of the ball than they could have bargained for. Launching themselves at every Welsh punt upfield, the terrible twins constantly buffeted Miller and McLeish with the kind of attrition that eventually reduces battlements to rubble.

The first half was British football at its worst. Huff and puff, bags of energy, with not a touch of class in sight. No worthwhile scoring opportunities had been manufactured at either end when, in the 37th

Jim Leighton looks on anxiously as Willie Miller heads clear. An
incident from the match played at Hampden Park on 27th March
1985. Wales shocked Scotland by winning 1-0 through a goal by Rush.

minute, Wales scored a stunning goal. It owed everything to Welsh aggression and a memorable strike of the ball. Mike England, the Welsh manager, had warned before the game that Ian Rush needed only a split second's freedom, and would need to be policed constantly.

England was right. McLeish was positioned to head clear when he was clattered by the muscular frame of Mark Hughes. The Welshman had little hope of winning the ball, but every hope of disconcerting the centre-half. The ball rebounded from McLeish's chest and into the path of the one man who could exploit the half-chance. Rush smashed the half-volley in a blur inside Leighton's near post. According to the letter of the law, Hughes' challenge was of questionable legality: in the spirit of a match with no quarter asked, few Scots were going to complain. Rush's first-ever goal against Scotland was a gem.

The second half predictably saw Scotland pounding forward. Johnston missed a gaping goal when rounding Southall but shooting wide in what was Scotland's first genuine chance of the match. Predictably, too, the temperature of battle rose, climaxing with Souness's horrendous two-footed thrust in the direction of Peter Nicholas' throat. A judge might have sent Souness to prison: the Belgian referee, Ponnet, did not even send him from the field.

Changes were needed. Hansen replaced Albiston, pushing Nicol forward and leaving only three permanent defenders. Then the inert McStay was substituted by Charlie Nicholas, who miskicked immediately. At the death Johnston's powerful angled shot was contemptuously saved by Southall – the first save he had had to make – and the final whistle sounded. Scotland had lost at home in the World Cup for only the fourth time – following defeats by England in 1950 and 1954, and Poland in 1965. The refrain of 'What a load of rubbish' announced the first occasion in Group 7 that the home side had failed to win.

SCOTLAND (0)0   WALES (1)1
                                    Rush

SCOTLAND: J Leighton (Aberdeen), S Nicol (Liverpool), A Albiston (Man U) (*sub* A Hansen, Liverpool), G Souness (Sampdoria, capt.), A McLeish (Aberdeen), W Miller (Aberdeen), K Dalglish (Liverpool), P McStay (Celtic) (*sub* C Nicholas, Arsenal), M Johnston (Celtic), J Bett (Lokeren), D Cooper (Rangers).

WALES: Southall, Slatter, J Jones, Ratcliffe, Jackett, Phillips, James, Nicholas, Thomas, Hughes, Rush.

Tuesday, 28 May 1985
ICELAND v SCOTLAND   Reykjavik 15,000

Wales' effrontery in overturning the laws of history was a devastating blow to Scotland. In the space of ninety minutes the Scots had tumbled from being favourites to reach Mexico to being outsiders. Both remaining matches were away from home, and three points were still needed. The Welsh, having knocked Group 7 off its feet at Hampden, then proceeded to stand it on its head when crushing Spain 3-0 in Wrexham. With the finishing line in sight Wales now led the pack.

Scotland travelled to the Laugardalsvollur National Stadium in Reykjavik with a bagful of woes unimaginable during the heady autumn of 1984. The team was in tatters and would need major surgery. The Scottish cause was further hampered by a regrettable clash of fixtures. On the previous Saturday Scotland played host to England for the honour of the Rous Trophy. In any ordered sense of priorities the Scottish players would have held something in reserve for the more pressing task awaiting them in Iceland, except that such thoughts are totally alien to the Scottish psyche. In the event all went well: England were beaten and Scotland sustained no injuries.

More damaging to Jock Stein's plans was Liverpool's inconsiderateness in reaching the ill-fated European Cup Final. The Anfield contingent – Dalglish, Nicol and Hansen – would therefore be engaged elsewhere. As a final indignity the Everton pair of Graeme Sharp and Andy Gray were unable to fly out with the Scottish party, being held back for a rearranged league fixture. Through no fault of his own Stein's team selection, one way or another, was thrown into confusion.

Eventually, only Leighton, McLeish, Miller, Bett and Souness remained of the eleven which had captured the nation's plaudits earlier in the season. The Dundee United pairing of Gough and Malpas filled the full-back berths, Gordon Strachan and Celtic's Roy Aitken buttressed the midfield, leaving up front Sharp and Gray to do for Scotland what they had been doing all season for Everton – for whom they had shared forty-four goals. It was Sharp's first cap; Gray's twentieth – ten years after his first.

Despite the short hop across the north Atlantic, Iceland's football inhabited another world from Scotland's. Their manager, Tony Knapp – an ex-pro with Leicester and Southampton – had still not ruled out Iceland's chances of causing an upset in Group 7. If they could beat Wales without the assistance of their unavailable expatriate players, why couldn't they dispose of Scotland with them? Some indication of Icelandic strengths was displayed when Scotland's under-21 team were beaten 2-0 the previous evening.

Once a helpful parachutist had descended into the centre circle bearing the match ball the game could commence. The Scottish players, unrecognisable in their playing performance against Wales, were now unrecognisable in their new strip. Lemon shirts invited unkind fruity comparisons, while the blue shorts sported a hideous lemon hoop as if the entire team had sat down on a newly painted yellow park bench.

Jim Leighton wore all grey, but there was nothing drab about him as he turned in the most sparkling performance of his three-year international career. Within four minutes he clung on to the first of Iceland's promising goal attempts.

The play was fast and furious, with more chances created at either end than in any of Group 7's matches to date. Gray was set up by Strachan and Bett on the left, but his sideways flick flew straight at Gudmundsson. Sharp and Souness were the next to try their luck as Scotland began to impose themselves.

The game would be remembered for several incidents, any of which could have turned the outcome. The first of these arrived midway through the first half when Sigi Jonsson (having eventually signed for Sheffield Wednesday) was laid out by Souness. After an age Jonsson was stretchered off and Soviet referee Milchenko belatedly took the name of the Scottish captain. Souness was booed loudly thereafter, and Scotland were never again able to recapture their earlier promise.

Within ten minutes they ought to have fallen behind. A ball threaded diagonally through Scotland's penalty box reached Petursson, who was instantly brought to earth by Aitken. Petursson was no more than six yards from goal. Doubling the distance from the penalty spot proved too great a handicap for Icelandic captain Thordarsson, for Leighton flung himself far to his left to bring off a save way beyond the call of duty. When the ensuing corner conspiratorially bounced back off the near post before being safely gathered, one sensed that the warrior Norse gods were losing the battle for beneficent divine intervention. Christian prayers seemed to be having greater effect.

Early in the second half Gudmundsson flapped ineffectually at a Souness centre, leaving Bett to lean into a muscular volley which left the crossbar with a mighty headache. Iceland, however, continued to prosper. McLeish hooked off the line from Edvaldsson, and almost immediately Leighton had to tip over a thirty-yarder from Gudlaugsson. The area in front of Miller and McLeish seemed to have been deserted, as time without number Iceland broke through the middle to bear down on an overworked central defence. The out-of-touch Gray trudged off to be replaced by Archibald.

Then, in an extraordinary climax, Strachan's angled centre reached the far post and was swept imperiously home by Bett. Only four minutes remained, but within seconds Gudlaugsson controlled a cross on his chest, found himself in the clear and shot criminally wide of Leighton's right post. The entire Iceland team clutched their heads, and well they might. Scotland greeted their victory with joy and embarrassment in equal measure. 'We stole it,' admitted Denis Law, while Rod Stewart – Scotland's self-proclaimed No 1 fan – agreed: 'We were a wee bit lucky,' he chuckled.

ICELAND (0) 0   SCOTLAND (0) 1
                                               Bett

ICELAND: Gudmundsson, Thrainsson, Sigi Jonsson (Torfason), Bergs, Petursson, Saevar Jonsson, Gudlaugsson, Edvaldsson, Thordarsson (Gretarsson), Thorbjornsson, Sveinsson.

SCOTLAND: J Leighton (Aberdeen), R Gough (Dundee U), M Malpas (Dundee U), R Aitken (Celtic), A McLeish (Aberdeen), W Miller (Aberdeen), G Strachan (Man U), G Souness (Sampdoria, capt.), A Gray (Everton) (*sub* S Archibald, Barcelona), J Bett (Lokeren), G Sharp (Everton).

Tuesday, 10 September 1985
WALES v SCOTLAND   Cardiff 39,500

The Welsh team had been direct victims of Scotland's poached result in Iceland, for the Scots had leapfrogged above them on goal difference. In June, Spain then came from behind to win in Reykjavik, which left all three countries locked on six points with one match to play. Scotland needed only a draw in Wales to secure runners-up spot. Should they win it would, in all probability, guarantee qualification, for Spain would then need to thrash the brave Norsemen by five clear goals to finish top of the pile.

The summer was also spent counting the cost of the tragedies of Bradford and Brussels. Heightened security considerations ruled out Wales' 'lucky' ground, Wrexham, and the Arms Park rugby stadium, leaving the British shoot-out to be staged at Ninian Park.

The press concentrated on the Welsh revenge factor: the need to repay Joe Jordan's infamous handball at Anfield in 1977. The Wales line-up, Mike England's strongest, contained two survivors from that night – Micky Thomas and Joey Jones. Jock Stein's preparations were again disrupted by absentees. Dalglish was ruled out with a septic knee, Hansen and Archibald also withdrew, and Mo Johnston failed to shake off a thigh strain. Souness was suspended, the result of his cautions against Wales and Iceland. Willie Miller took over the captaincy. With Jim Bett now on Aberdeen's payroll, the four-man Dons contingent would be the only Scottish ever-presents throughout Group 7.

Jock Stein made only two changes to the starting formation in Iceland. Nicol came in for Souness, and instead of the bludgeoning hammer of Andy Gray, Stein opted for the whiplash of Chelsea's David Speedie. The possessor of quick legs and an even quicker temper, Speedie had already earned one premature departure in the new season.

Comedians joked about Scotland's new strike-force: how could they fail with names like Sharp and Speedie? Others were concerned at their lack of experience. Both possessed just a solitary cap; neither had ever played alongside the other; and Sharp had just emerged from a spell in Everton's reserves.

In fact, taken as a whole, the Scots outfit compared badly in terms of experience with their opponents, having an aggregate of 181 caps as against 302. The Welsh players between them had a stock of thirty international goals – eleven to Ian Rush. Scotland's tally was only six. With a nose for the prevailing winds, the bookies fancied Wales.

Only twelve thousand tickets were officially allocated to the Scots, a ludicrous under-estimate of those inside the ground. Wales kicked off in a cauldron of noise and immediately Mark Hughes began laying about him, felling McLeish (twice) and Miller. McLeish exacted revenge on Rush and was promptly booked by Dutch referee Keizer.

Scotland's tactics were for McLeish to police Rush, Gough to stick close to Hughes, and leave Miller free to mop up where necessary. The opening exchanges were tense and even, but after eleven minutes Sharp raced into the six-yard box to shoot into the side netting. It might have been 0-1. Two minutes later it was 1-0. On the left touchline Peter Nicholas collected a throw and turned into the theoretically unbreachable wall of Aitken and Nicol. But the wall crumbled, the tackles made of straw. Nicholas was clear, and his drilled low cross was hammered by Mark Hughes through Miller's straining legs and beyond the helpless Leighton. Ninian Park blew steam.

Scotland sagged, the wind knocked out of them. On twenty minutes Wales nearly scored a second. A spirited move climaxed in Robbie James' header floating tantalisingly wide of Leighton's upright. The Scottish goalkeeper, impenetrable in Reykjavik, was more fragile in Cardiff. Twice within seconds he was summoned from his goalmouth to punch clear, failing to make decisive contact on either occasion. Then, right on the interval, he inexplicably allowed an innocuous punt upfield to bounce away off his shins. The situation was retrieved only with a last-gasp plunge at Hughes' feet.

As the players reappeared, Leighton stayed behind, nursing an eye injury. His deputy was Alan Rough, an apparition from a seemingly bygone age. Rush was shortly booked, his victim Strachan was substituted by Davie Cooper, and Rush promptly failed to connect with an inviting deflection off Hughes.

Cooper's brief was to penetrate Wales' suspect right flank. His first touch produced a corner, and it was not long before his audacious slalom along the bye-line created space for a flashing low cross which was frantically whacked clear of the goalmouth. Cooper's virtuosity symbolised his team's revival, but, worryingly for them, Scottish pressure was not being translated into scoring opportunities. Wales seemed to be holding out comfortably enough, though Speedie fleetingly escaped his shadow until brusquely tackled a yard outside the box.

Then, with only nine minutes left, the fates intervened. Wheeling on to Sharp's downward header, Speedie hooked the ball hard against Phillips' arm. The referee, to Welsh dismay, awarded a penalty and Cooper, admirably cool, struck the ball home off Southall's left hand. Lightning *had* struck Wales twice. The best that could be said of the decision was that it was not so scandalous as that at Anfield. But it was still cruelly misjudged, for Phillips was so close to Speedie as to rule out evasive action. Be that as it may, Scotland were level, and Speedie might even have sealed a win when thwarted by Southall with only the keeper to beat. Scotland greeted the final whistle with delirium. A smiling Miller told a TV camera: 'Sure it was a penalty'. But as someone once observed: 'Well he would, wouldn't he?' – but what if it was *his* arm?

Unbeknown to all, Scottish fortune would pay a fearful price. An agitated Jock Stein, harassed by over-zealous photographers, collapsed at the game's conclusion and within half an hour was dead. Celebrations turned to numbing grief.

WALES (1)1   SCOTLAND (0)1
  Hughes   Cooper (pen)

WALES: Southall, Van Den Hauwe, Ratcliffe, Jackett, James (Lovell), Phillips, Nicholas, Thomas (Blackmore), Rush, Hughes.

SCOTLAND: J Leighton (Aberdeen) (*sub* A Rough, Hibs), R Gough (Dundee U), M Malpas (Dundee U), R Aitken (Celtic), A McLeish (Aberdeen), W Miller (Aberdeen, capt.), S Nicol (Liverpool), G Strachan (Man U) (*sub* D Cooper, Rangers), G Sharp (Everton), J Brett (Aberdeen), D Speedie (Chelsea).

Wednesday, 20 November 1985
SCOTLAND v AUSTRALIA   Hampden 61,000

The death of Jock Stein hung like a pall over the Scottish nation. The mind searched for men of comparable stature in the history of Scottish football – and drew a blank. But the show must go on: Scotland were not yet in Mexico.

The SFA were in no rush to appoint a successor, knowing that to act in haste would doubtless lead them to repent at leisure. Yet all along there was only one real candidate. Alex Ferguson, of course, had sat as Stein's right-hand man for the past year. At Pittodrie he had manufactured the most potent force in Scottish football. He was the obvious man for the post, even though his commitments to Aberdeen meant he would combine both jobs until such time as Scotland's interest in the 1986 World Cup terminated.

Spain, meanwhile, had squeezed past Iceland to qualify for Mexico. Scotland thereby faced one final hurdle, a two-edged play-off against the winners of the Oceania group. Whether that would be Israel, Australia, New Zealand or Taiwan was not settled until early November. The pundits favoured Israel: the results favoured Australia.

Although they had featured in the 1974 World Cup finals, Australia were hardly a front-line soccer power. Cricket, tennis, rugby and Australian Rules football still provided their staple sporting diet. For the past three years Australia had been managed by Yugoslav-born Frank Arok. He was caricatured in the Scottish press as something of a wild man. 'Mad dog' was the most common epithet, while the whole Australian team bore the affectionate, if patronising, tag of 'socceroos'. They were a cosmopolitan assortment of part-timers and foreign imports. Included in their line-up were three Scots – David Mitchell (recently of Rangers), Ken Murphy and Joe Watson. These were collectively dubbed the 'Jockeroos', players who had failed to make the grade in Scottish football and gone to find their ray of sunshine elsewhere. For good measure Australia's assistant manager was also a Scot, Eddie Thomson, once of Hearts.

Arok had fostered his players' strengths – muscle rather than finesse – to put together an outfit strong on defensive resilience if short on attacking flair. Throughout his period of office he had yet to see his team dance in defeat to the tune of more than two goals. The only pointer to the Hampden match was a visit Australia had made to Rangers exactly twelve months earlier, when – according to Arok – he had anticipated the World Cup encounter to come. Rangers won 2-1. Now that the gloves were off, Arok put his hopes on a draw, preferably – in the light of the away goals rule – a scoring draw. Scotland supporters, predictably, depending on the degree of inebriation, set their sights on anything from a two-goal victory to something approaching infinity.

There was one new name on Ferguson's team-sheet. During his years with St Mirren Frank McAvennie had been a promising striker in a modest team. Since transferring to West Ham in the close season he had successfully auditioned as the reincarnation of Denis Law, scoring frequently – and with style. For the past year Scotland's chief failing had been their miserable scoring rate. Ferguson looked to him and the recalled Dalglish (now manager of Liverpool, winning his 99th cap) as a new and potentially lethal strikeforce. With both Cooper and Strachan included, Scotland were instructed to stretch their opponents by utilising the full width of Hampden's pitch.

Any sober thoughts of a double-figure scoreline disappeared as soon as Australia erected their yellow-shirted, multiple-tiered defensive blockade. The outcome might have been different had not Miller, free to venture forward at will, shot wide as the ball broke to him. It was, as they say, a 'defender's' shot. Scotland proceeded to weave their pretty patterns, but there was always one extra Aussie obstacle in the way. The battle was entirely confined to the Australian half, but then, out of nothing, Mitchell was clean through and bearing down on Leighton. The keeper raced out to clear.

The visitors conceded corners, free kicks and bookings in abundance – everything but a goal. Cooper slipped the ball back to Souness who blasted in a shot which school-teacher Terry Greedy clutched in falling to his left. It was the first save he had been asked to make, and his only one of an anti-climactic first half. Neither Cooper nor Strachan were able to promote telling crosses, except on the one occasion when Aitken, under close Australian surveillance, dived to head narrowly wide. As the interval approached, shots were bouncing off the big socceroos as if on a frantic game of pinball.

Straight from the restart Aitken miskicked, and Strachan's shot was so feeble it wouldn't have troubled his grandma. There grew uncomfortable feelings of doubt – Mexico seemed more distant than Mars. Then, after fifty-eight minutes of profitless endeavour, Scotland scored. McAvennie was clipped as he chased a through ball. The free kick was central, twenty yards out. Greedy positioned his wall to guard one half of the goal, yet inexplicably left the other exposed as Cooper powered the ball inside the vacant post.

Two minutes later Mexico looked nearer than Manchester. McLeish headed back Greedy's clearance, Dalglish nodded sideways, and the quicksilver McAvennie sprung the trap. The ball was flicked over the advancing Greedy's head, leaving the ecstatic scorer to punch the air in the inimitable manner of a certain Denis Law.

Scotland ought to have landed the K.O. punch. Greedy smothered Dalglish's close-range effort before the exhausted striker was replaced by Graeme Sharp. Obliged to emerge from their shell, Australia forced two unproductive corners, but they were left sighing with relief as, first, Sharp's header looped past a post, and again as McAvennie completely misread the ball in front of an unprotected net. At half-time 2-0 would have seemed a priceless result, but McAvennie's post-match expression of anguish told of his inner torment. He could have sealed Scotland's place in Mexico, but they would now have to live through the fires of Melbourne.

SCOTLAND (0)2   AUSTRALIA (0)0
   Cooper, McAvennie

SCOTLAND: J Leighton (Aberdeen), S Nicol (Liverpool), M Malpas (Dundee U), G Souness (Sampdoria, capt.), A McLeish (Aberdeen), W Miller (Aberdeen), K Dalglish (Liverpool) (*sub* G Sharp, Everton), G Strachan (Man U) (*sub* J Bett, Aberdeen), F McAvennie (West Ham), R Aitken (Celtic), D Cooper (Rangers).

AUSTRALIA: Greedy, Davidson, Jennings, Yankos, Ratcliffe, O'Connor (Dunn), Watson (Patikas), Mitchell, Kosmina, Murphy, Crino.

Wednesday, 4 December 1985
AUSTRALIA v SCOTLAND   Melbourne 35,000

By early December Scotland and Australia were vying for the 24th and final vacancy in Mexico. The whole sporting world – outside Britain – was rooting for Australia to make it. Sympathy with the underdog was partly responsible, but also the more tangible reason that Australia ought to prove less troublesome opposition to the other assembled nations – one of whom would need to drop down the seedings list to make up the complement of six rank outsiders should Scotland deprive Australia of that privilege.

The Scotland squad prepared to embark on the furthest journey any European team had been asked to make in the cause of World Cup qualification. The bill, around £100,000, would be peanuts if Scotland survived. The real concern was not the money but the attitude of certain major English clubs who, as ever, reasoned that league points were more important than the World Cup dreams of a sister nation. Because of the necessity for adequate acclimatisation down under, released players might be unavailable for two successive Saturdays. There was talk of five-figure sums to compensate English clubs for borrowed players. Had Scotland tucked a four-goal lead under their belts at Hampden, the loss of key Anglos could have been shrugged off. Nevertheless, Dalglish and Strachan stayed behind, with Souness flying out from Italy to join the rest of the squad with a day to spare.

For two weeks the British press relished Frank Arok's use of the 'verbals'. He didn't intend to make life pleasant for the Scots, scheming to play the second leg on a rubbish-tip at the stroke of noon – when the heat would, he hoped, reduce Scotland to jelly. Poor Arok did not get his way. The match went ahead at 8 pm in Melbourne's picturesque Olympic Stadium. The pitch was perfect, the weather sublime, and Scotland enjoyed the noisy, partisan support of thousands of Scottish emigrants. It was, said Ferguson, like playing at Wembley.

He made three team changes, all of them enforced. Richard Gough's extra height in defence ensured his inclusion in place of the absent Nicol; Paul McStay took over from Strachan; and David Speedie's natural aggression was asked to compensate for Dalglish's natural skill. The Australian team showed two changes.

Erudite man that he is, Ferguson probably turned to Shakespeare in his pre-match deliberations: whether 'twas nobler in the mind to chase an away goal and qualify with style, or hang on and hope for some outrageous fortune. The Aussies had no recourse to slings and arrows, but they had guts, and Scotland found themselves experiencing early blows to their self-esteem. Patikas, an anonymous substitute at Hampden, quickly established himself as the quickest player on view. His pace and Murphy's calm authority gave Australia an ascendancy in midfield they maintained throughout the match.

Forty-yard back-passes to Leighton did not endear the visitors to the ex-colony. A flare thrown on the pitch and crowd disturbances behind a goal sadly demonstrated that loutishness ranked high among Britain's invisible exports.

In retrospect, the game was memorable for a mere handful of incidents. Its most intense phase was midway through the first half. Leighton twice took his life in his hands, plunging into a mêlée of flying bodies like a bouncer breaking up a pub brawl. The trainer who arrived to minister to his wounds doubtless poured warm words into his ear. Scotland were living dangerously, and never more so than in Australia's next attack. On the right touchline Mitchell sold McLeish a neat dummy and streaked away from his marker for the one and only time. The cross dropped towards the six-yard line where John Kosmina had positioned himself in splendid isolation. Had his powerful header been directed into the corner, Australia would have been ahead. Instead it flew towards Leighton, whose alert reflexes enabled him to palm it out. The goalkeeper had done well, but it was an expensive miss.

A goal at that stage would have put Scotland on the tightrope. McStay restored their dignity with a surging run from inside his own half, climaxing with a swirling shot touched over by Terry Greedy. Souness, looking bleary-eyed and performing as if on an early breakfast, mistook an opponent for a fried egg and earned himself a booking.

Leighton opened the second half with a further demonstration of his keen reactions, parrying Patikas' thunderous angled volley. Cooper brought an incredulous Scottish bench to their feet when knocked to the floor without a penalty for his pains. That same bench then held their breath as the ball was conveyed to the other end where Patikas fired in a grass-trimming centre that eluded everybody in front of Leighton.

On the hour Scotland manufactured their second and final piece of creative play (added to McStay's) to illuminate what was, for them, a sterile ninety minutes. A cleverly worked free-kick saw McLeish head across the box where either McAvennie or Speedie might have scored but for the hindering presence of the other. The ball lobbed onto the bar and behind.

Scotland were not yet safe, and substitute Odzakov took upon himself the role of Australia's saviour. His thirty-yard free kick was of sufficient velocity to necessitate a replacement crossbar – had it passed three inches lower. Encouraged, he then brushed aside two gossamer Scottish tackles to put himself in the clear. Leighton duly spread himself and the shot rolled wide. Australia knew at that moment they must have angered the gods: they were not destined for Mexico, and the game slumbered to a close. In fourteen months Scotland had been asked to compete from the Arctic Circle to the other side of the world. Next stop, Mexico. If only Jock knew.

AUSTRALIA (0)0   SCOTLAND (0)0

AUSTRALIA: Greedy, Davidson, Jennings, Yankos, Ratcliffe, Crino (Odzakov), Dunn (Farina), Murphy, Patikas, Kosmina, Mitchell.

SCOTLAND: J Leighton (Aberdeen), R Gough (Dundee U), M Malpas (Dundee U), G Souness (Sampdoria, capt.), A McLeish (Aberdeen), W Miller (Aberdeen), D Speedie (Chelsea) (*sub* G Sharp, Everton), P McStay (Celtic), F McAvennie (West Ham), R Aitken (Celtic), D Cooper (Rangers).

World Cup Qualifying Group 7:

		AWAY				HOME					
	P	W	D	L	F	A	W	D	L	F	A	PTS
SPAIN	6	3	0	0	6	1	1	0	2	3	7	8
SCOTLAND	6	2	0	1	6	2	1	1	1	2	2	7
Wales	6	2	1	0	·6	2	1	0	2	1	4	7
Iceland	6	1	0	2	2	3	0	0	3	2	7	2

Scotland qualified after play-off with Australia

Other group results

Iceland v Wales	1-0
Spain v Wales	3-0
Wales v Iceland	2-1
Wales v Spain	3-0
Iceland v Spain	1-2
Spain v Iceland	2-1

Scotland appearances and goal-scorers:
World Cup qualifying rounds 1986

	A	G		A	G	
Leighton J	8	–	Johnston M	4	2	
McLeish A*	8	–	Malpas M	4	–	
Miller W*	8	–	Strachan G*	4(1)	–	
Souness G*†	7	–	Sharp G	4(2)	–	
Bett J	7(1)	1	Nicholas C	3(3)	1	
Cooper D	7(1)	2	McAvennie F	2	1	
McStay P	5	2	Speedie D	2	–	
Nicol S	5	–	Archibald S*	2(1)	–	
Aitken R	4	–	Gray A*†	1	–	
Albiston A†	4	–	Hansen A*	1(1)	–	
Dalglish K*†$	4	1	Rough A*†	1(1)	–	
Gough R	4	1	caps	99	10	goals
23 players						

Scottish League	55
English League	30
Italian League	7
Belgian League	5
Spanish League	2
	99

Bracket signifies appearance was as a substitute
*Appeared in 1982 World Cup
†Appeared in 1978 World Cup
$Appeared in 1974 World Cup

Prospects for Mexico

The indelible mark of Jock Stein can be seen imprinted on Scotland's qualifying campaign for both the 1982 and 1986 World Cups. The records are almost identical. In qualifying for Spain, Scotland's eight matches produced nine goals scored and four conceded. In qualifying for Mexico, eight matches produced ten goals scored and four conceded. Scotland, in other words, are a team suffering from a chronic goal-scoring headache. This is balanced by a defensive record which bears comparison with anything in Scottish history, and which ensures that the team plays in fear of no-one.

The performances in the 1982 finals, however, led to much head-scratching. The team which had qualified with a miserly attitude to goals – at both ends of the pitch – suddenly threw open the vaults – again at both ends. Especially worrying was Scotland's failure to prosper despite taking a 1-0 lead in each of their matches. It is to be hoped that they will not fritter away similar advantages in Mexico.

Scotland have also acquired a much sought-after knack, the ability to obtain a desired result without playing well. In the 1982 eliminators Scotland took advantage of results that might easily, given a less favourable run of the ball, have gone against them. The same is even more apparent this time around. Scotland needed only to overcome Iceland, Wales and Australia to join Spain in Mexico, yet they made desperately heavy weather of the task. Many fair-minded observers are agreed that Scotland could easily have suffered – perhaps even deserved to suffer – narrow defeats in Reykjavik, Cardiff, and Melbourne. It is a refreshing change to observe a 'lucky' Scotland team. But luck is not a dispensation from on high. It is earned. Teams make their own luck, and more often than not it stems from confidence. Self-doubt breeds so-called bad luck, and in Alex Ferguson Scotland have the man to banish those doubts.

His deeper problem is to inject weight into an attack which has spluttered ineffectually since the still vivid defeat of Spain in November 1984. A sequence of undistinguished performances since then shows no sign, as yet, of improvement. In the finals avoidance of defeat will not ensure progress, as Scotland painfully learned in 1974 and England in 1982. There is also the deeper psychological hurdle. When have Scotland ever really done themselves justice away from their beloved Hampden?

The draw for the Mexico finals – pitching Scotland against West Germany, Uruguay and Denmark in Group E – could not be described as

212

generous. The Germans, out of sorts of late, will doubtless be as formidable as ever when the time comes. Their record in the World Cup makes chilling reading: champions in 1954 and 1974; runners-up in 1966 and 1982; third in 1970; fourth in 1958. It was West Germany who scuppered Scotland's chances of participating in the previous Mexico finals, in 1970. Not for 27 years have Scotland beaten them, securing just three draws from the last five meetings.

As for Uruguay, it was they who humiliated Scotland in Switzerland in 1954 – 7-0 still standing as Scotland's heaviest World Cup defeat. Goals by John Robertson and Davie Dodds at Hampden in 1983 permitted Scotland some belated revenge, and eight of that side might find themselves included in the party for Mexico.

Uruguay's achievements in the World Cup are remarkable in themselves, never mind for a country with a population of less than three million. World Cup-winners in 1930 and 1950, and fourth in both 1954 and 1970, Uruguay are also the current South American champions – an honour which has escaped Brazil since 1949. Small wonder that Uruguay will be one of the most fancied teams in Mexico.

Group E would be demanding enough for Scotland on account of West Germany and Uruguay alone. Having to face Denmark, too, makes a mockery of the whole seeding principle. Scotland's eleventh-hour elimination of Australia meant that a sixth 'minnow' had to be found to make up the quota of one per group. To their chagrin Denmark were downgraded, for the simple reason that these will be their first ever World Cup finals, despite the opinion of many good judges – Alex Ferguson among them – that the Danes are probably the best team in Europe. Over the years Scotland have won eight out of nine versus Denmark, a meaningless statistic against the semi-finalists in the 1984 European Championships, whose gifted players are scattered to the winds around the Continent. Denmark, another country with a population smaller than Scotland's, provide further evidence that small can be beautiful in football.

The clash with the Danes in the first match of Group E is not without a wry sense of justice. Denmark have Scotland to thank for being dumped into FIFA's trash-bag, ensuring them a tough programme in whichever group they were allocated, and they could be forgiven a desire to clarify on the field the rightful identity of Group E's 'minnow'.

The inclusion of the Danes may impede Scotland's cause in another way. The 1986 World Cup finals will embark on yet another organisational innovation. Only eight of the 24 competing nations will be sent home after the first phase. The surviving 16 will enter a straight knock-out all the way to the Final. Those 16 places will be determined by the six group winners;

the six group runners-up; and the four best-placed teams who finish third.

By 'best-placed' is meant those who earn the most points. If points are level it will be down to goal difference. If goal difference is identical, the country scoring most goals will progress. In a four-team group it is possible to finish third with as many as four points (as Scotland did in 1974) or as few as one. Other teams in other groups will be aiming to pick up cheap points from their respective minnows. The four constituents of Group E will be denied the chance of easy pickings, theoretically putting its third-placed team at a disadvantage with other sections. Scotland, all things considered, will be most unlikely to progress to the second round with less than three points.

The handicap of sharing a group with Denmark is partially reduced by the finals' timetable. Group E will be the last to run its course, so that by the time Scotland face Uruguay on Friday 13 June their fate could still be in their own hands. At worst, they will have the waterline for the third-placed teams clearly in their sights.

On reflection the composition of Group E, while undeniably onerous, will not necessarily diminish Scotland's prospects. Only Uruguay of their three initial opponents will not be inconvenienced by the heat, and the high altitude of Queretaro and Nezahualcoyotl (a suburb of Mexico City), where Group E will be contested, will distribute its hazards without favour. Scotland might even be relieved that there are no Zaires, Irans, New Zealands or Australias to foul up against. Put simply, Scotland have everything to gain and nothing to lose, and will quite possibly thrive on the challenge.

If Scotland do survive Group E, what next? The winners of that section entertain the runners-up from Group D (Brazil? Spain? Northern Ireland?). The second-placed team from Group E move north to Monterrey to face the winners of Group F (England? Poland? Portugal?). If, on the other hand, Scotland finish third and still qualify, they will be asked to play the winners of either Group A or D. Once in the knock-out stages anything can happen, and Scotland could march on ... and on.

Appendix 1

Clubs supplying players capped by Scotland in the World Cup 1950-86 (including qualifying rounds and final stages — excluding World Cup finals 1986)

Club	*Caps*	*Players*
Celtic	114	McGrain 16, Evans 10, McNeill 10, Dalglish 9 (+17 for Liverpool), Collins 7 (+1 for Leeds), Crerand 5 (+3 for Man U), Hay 5, McStay 5, Murdoch 5, R Aitken 4, Fernie 4, T Gemmell 4, Hughes 4, M Johnston 4, J Johnstone 4, Lennox 3, Provan 3, McPhail 2, Mochan 2, Chalmers 1, Connelly 1, Haughney 1, Hunter 1, J Kennedy 1, Macari 1 (+3 for Man U), McKay 1, Simpson 1. *27 players*
Rangers	112	Caldow 12, Greig 12, Jardine 8, Cooper 7, McKinnon 7, G Young 7, Baxter 6 (+1 for Sunderland), Cox 6, T Forsyth 6, W Henderson 5, D Wilson 5, Baird 4, Brand 4, Stein 4, McColl 3, Shearer 3, Waddell 3, Woodburn 3, Provan 2, Scott 2 (+1 for Everton), Forrest 1, W Johnston 1 (+3 for WBA), McMillan 1. *23 players*
Aberdeen	59	Miller 16, McLeish 14, Leighton 8, Strachan 7 (+4 for Man U), Harper 3, S Kennedy 3, Bett 2 (+5 for Lokeren), Leggat 2, F Martin 2, Clark 1, McGarr 1. *11 players*
Liverpool	54	Dalglish 17 (+9 for Celtic), Hansen 10, Souness 9 (+7 for Sampdoria), Younger 6, Nicol 5, Liddell 3, St John 2, Lawrence 1, Yeats 1. *9 players*
Leeds United	50	Bremner 15, Jordan 9 (+4 for Man U; 2 for AC Milan), F Gray 6, (+5 for Nott'm F), Lorimer 6, Harvey 5, E Gray 4, McQueen 4, Collins 1 (+7 for Celtic). *8 players*
Manchester United	44	Buchan 9, Law 6 (+2 for Torino; 3 for Man C), Morgan 6, Albiston 4, Holton 4, Jordan 4 (+9 for Leeds; 2 for AC Milan), Strachan 4 (+7 for Aberdeen), Crerand 3 (+5 for Celtic), Macari 3 (+1 for Celtic), F Burns 1. *10 players*
Hibernian	28	Blackley 3, McLeod 3, Ormond 3, Reilly 3, G Smith 3, Turnbull 3, Brownlie 2, R Johnstone 2, N Martin 2 (+1 for Sunderland), Cormack 1, W Hamilton 1, Rough 1 (+17 for Partick), Stanton 1. *13 players*
Nottingham Forest	25	J Robertson 11, F Gray 5 (+6 for Leeds), K Burns 4 (+ 2 for Birmingham), A Gemmill 3 (+2 for Derby; 4 for Birmingham), Imlach 2. *5 players*

215

Club	Caps	Players
Partick Thistle	24	Rough 17 (+1 for Hibs), McKenzie 4, Davidson 2, A Forsyth 1. *4 players*
Tottenham Hotspur	24	Archibald 9 (+2 for Barcelona), Gilzean 8, W Brown 5 (+1 for Dundee), White 2. *4 players*
Manchester City	19	Hartford 10 (+3 for Everton), Donachie 6, Law 3 (+2 for Torino; 6 for Man U). *3 players*
Dundee	15	Cowie 6, A Hamilton 5, W Brown 1 (+5 for Spurs), Cooke 1 (+5 for Chelsea), H Robertson 1, Ure 1. *6 players*
Chelsea	15	McCreadie 8, Cooke 5 (+1 for Dundee), Speedie 2. *3 players*
Blackpool	14	Mudie 7, A Brown 4, Farm 3. *3 players*
Everton	12	Sharp 4, Hartford 3 (+10 for Man C), Gray 1 (+6 for Wolves; 1 for A Villa), A Parker 1 (+1 for Falkirk), Rioch 1 (+4 for Derby), A Scott 1 (+2 for Rangers), A Young 1. *7 players*
Dundee United	12	Gough 4, Malpas 4, Narey 3, Sturrock 1. *4 players*
Derby County	10	Rioch 4 (+1 for Everton), Steel 3, A Gemmill 2 (+3 for Nott'm F; 4 for Birmingham), Masson 1 (+3 for QPR). *4 players*
Birmingham City	9	A Gemmill 4 (+2 for Derby; 3 for Nott'm F), Herriot 3, K Burns 2 (+4 for Nott'm F). *3 players*
Arsenal	8	Nicholas 3, G Graham 2, Herd 2, Forbes 1. *4 players*
Ipswich Town	8	Wark 6, Brazil 2. *2 players*
Preston North End	8	Docherty 6, Cunningham 2. *2 players*
Clyde	7	Ring 4, A Robertson 2, Linwood 1. *3 players*
Wolverhampton Wanderers	7	A Gray 6 (+1 for A Villa; 1 for Everton), Curran 1. *2 players*
Hearts	6	D Mackay 2, Murray 2, Bauld 1, Ford 1. *4 players*
Coventry City	5	Hutchison 4. Carr 1. *2 players*
Charlton Athletic	5	Hewie 5. *1 player*

Club	Caps	Players	
East Fife	4	G Aitken 2 (+1 for Sunderland), Fleming 1, Morris 1.	3 players
West Brom. Albion	4	W Johnston 3 (+1 for Rangers), Fraser 1.	2 players
West Ham	4	McAvennie 2, Stewart 2.	2 players
Kilmarnock	3	C Forsyth 1, McLean 1, McGrory 1.	3 players
Sunderland	3	G Aitken 1 (+2 for East Fife), Baxter 1 (+6 for Rangers), N Martin 1 (+2 for Hibs).	3 players
Burnley	3	Aird 2, Blacklaw 1.	2 players
Motherwell	3	Quinn 2, Pettigrew 1.	2 players
St Mirren	3	W Thomson 2, Telfer 1.	2 players
Airdrieonians	3	Leslie 3.	1 player
Morton	3	Cowan 3.	1 player
Q.P.R.	3	Masson 3 (+1 for Derby).	1 player
Aston Villa	2	Evans 1, A Gray 1 (+6 for Wolves; 1 for Everton).	2 players
Newcastle United	2	Brennan 2.	1 player
Portsmouth	2	J Henderson 2.	1 player
Sheffield Utd.	2	Colquhoun 2.	1 player
Bolton Wanderers	1	Moir 1.	1 player
Dunfermline	1	Connachan 1.	1 player
Falkirk	1	A Parker 1 (+1 for Everton).	1 player
Huddersfield	1	Watson 1.	1 player
Leicester City	1	Gibson 1.	1 player
Norwich City	1	Bone 1.	1 player
Third Lanark	1	Mason 1.	1 player

Overseas Clubs

Club	Caps	Players	
Sampdoria (Italy)	7	Souness 7 (+9 for Liverpool).	*1 player*
Lokeren (Belgium)	5	Bett 5 (+2 for Aberdeen).	*1 player*
Barcelona (Spain)	2	Archibald 2 (+9 for Spurs).	*1 player*
AC Milan (Italy)	2	Jordan 2 (+9 for Leeds; 4 for Man U).	*1 player*
Torino (Italy)	2	Law 2 (+3 for Man C; 6 for Man U).	*1 player*

Total 763 caps

N.B. A Gemmill, A Gray, Jordan and Law played World Cup football for Scotland while with *three* different clubs; G Aitken, Archibald, Baxter, Bett, W Brown, K Burns, Collins, Cooke, Crerand, Dalglish, F Gray, Hartford, W Johnston, Macari, N Martin, Masson, A Parker, Rioch, Rough, A Scott, Souness and Strachan while with *two* different clubs.

Appendix 2

Scottish World Cup appearances from the Scottish League, English League and Overseas Leagues (including qualifying rounds and final stages – excluding World Cup finals 1986)

World Cup	Scottish League	English League	Overseas Leagues	% Scottish League	Total Caps	
1950	26	7	–	(82%)	33	
1954	35	20	–	(64%)	55	
1958	52	25	–	(68%)	77	
1962	45	8	2	(82%)	55	
1966	39	27	–	(59%)	66	
1970	38	34	–	(53%)	72	(inc. 6 subs)
1974	35	49	–	(42%)	84	(inc. 7 subs)
1978	25	61	–	(29%)	86	(inc. 9 subs)
1982	49	85	2	(36%)	136	(inc. 15 subs)
1986	55	30	14	(56%)	99	(inc. 11 subs)
Totals:	399	346	18		763	(inc. 48 subs)

N.B. Until Jock Stein reversed the trend in the 1982 and '86 World Cups, the percentage of players drawn from the Scottish League had fallen steeply, from 82% for the 1962 World Cup, down to 29% under Ally MacLeod in the 1978 World Cup.

Appendix 3

Scottish World Cup captains 1950-86 (including qualifying rounds and final stages – excluding World Cup finals 1986)

	World Cups	No. matches captained
Billy Bremner	(1970,74)	12
Graeme Souness	(1982,86)	9
George Young	(1950,54,58)	7
Archie Gemmill	(1978,82)	6
Eric Caldow	(1962)	5
Bruce Rioch	(1978)	4
Billy McNeill	(1966)	3
Danny McGrain	(1982)	3
Willie Cunningham	(1954)	2
Tommy Docherty	(1958)	2
Tommy Younger	(1958)	2
Asa Hartford	(1982)	2
Sammy Cox	(1954)	1
Bobby Evans	(1958)	1
Denis Law	(1966)	1
Jim Baxter	(1966)	1
John Greig	(1966)	1
Davie Hay	(1974)	1
Don Masson	(1978)	1
Willie Miller	(1986)	1
		65 matches

Appendix 4

Scotland World Cup goal-scorers 1950-86 (including qualifying rounds and final stages – excluding World Cup finals 1986)

Goals	Name	Matches	World Cups
7	Joe Jordan	15	(1974,78,82)
7	Kenny Dalglish	26	(1974,78,82,86)
6	Colin Stein	4	(1970)
6	Jackie Mudie	7	(1958)
5	Denis Law	11	(1962,66,70,74)
4	John Robertson	11	(1978,82)
3	Henry Morris	1	(1950)
3	Ian St John	2	(1962)
3	Ralph Brand	4	(1962)
3	John Wark	6	(1982)
3	Alan Gilzean	8	(1966,70)
2	Charlie Fleming	1	(1954)
2	Alex Young	1	(1962)
2	David Herd	2	(1962)
2	Lawrie Reilly	3	(1950,54)
2	Willie Waddell	3	(1950,54)
2	Allan Brown	4	(1954)
2	Mo Johnston	4	(1986)
2	Bobby Murdoch	5	(1966,70)
2	Paul McStay	5	(1986)
2	Peter Lorimer	6	(1970,74)
2	Davie Cooper	7	(1986)
2	Bobby Collins	8	(1958,66)
2	Archie Gemmill	9	(1978,82)
2	Billy McNeill	10	(1962,66,70)
2	John Greig	12	(1966,70)
1	Jimmy Bone	1	(1974)
1	Steve Chalmers	1	(1966)
1	Davie Gibson	1	(1966)
1	Alec Linwood	1	(1950)
1	Jimmy Mason	1	(1950)
1	Paul Sturrock	1	(1982)
1	Jackie Henderson	2	(1954)
1	Bobby Johnstone	2	(1954)

Goals	Name	Matches	World Cups
1	Frank McAvennie	2	(1986)
1	John McPhail	2	(1950,54)
1	Jimmy Murray	2	(1958)
1	Archie Robertson	2	(1958)
1	Joe Harper	3	(1974,78)
1	David Narey	3	(1982)
1	Charlie Nicholas	3	(1986)
1	Davie Provan	3	(1982)
1	Alec Scott	3	(1958,62,66)
1	Gordon Smith	3	(1958)
1	Billy Steel	3	(1950)
1	Sam Baird	4	(1958)
1	Tommy Gemmell	4	(1970)
1	Eddie Gray	4	(1970,78)
1	Jim Holton	4	(1974)
1	Lou Macari	4	(1974,78)
1	Don Masson	4	(1978)
1	Jimmy Johnstone	4	(1966,70)
1	Willie Henderson	5	(1966,70)
1	John Hewie	5	(1958)
1	Davie Wilson	5	(1962,66)
1	Willie Morgan	6	(1974)
1	Jim Bett	7	(1986)
1	Gordon Strachan	11	(1982,86)
1	Steve Archibald	11	(1982,86)
1	Asa Hartford	13	(1978,82)
1	Billy Bremner	15	(1966,70,74)
1	Graeme Souness	16	(1978,82,86)

+3 own-goals

119 goals

Appendix 5

Scotland World Cup goalkeepers and goals conceded 1950-86 (including qualifying rounds and final stages – excluding World Cup finals 1986)

Name	World Cups	Appearances	Goals Conceded	Average per match
D. Harvey	(1974)	5	2	0.40
J. Leighton	(1986)	7½	4	0.53
J. Cowan	(1950)	3	3	1.00
J. Herriot	(1970)	3	3	1.00
R. Clark	(1974)	1	1	1.00
C. Forsyth	(1966)	1	1	1.00
A. Hunter	(1974)	1	1	1.00
T. Lawrence	(1970)	1	1	1.00
R. Simpson	(1970)	1	1	1.00
A. Rough	(1978,82,86)	17½	19	1.09
W. Brown	(1958,62,66)	6	8	1.33
L. Leslie	(1962)	3	5	1.67
E. McGarr	(1970)	1	2	2.00
W. Thomson	(1982)	1*	2	2.00
T. Younger	(1958)	6	13	2.17
G. Farm	(1954)	3	8	2.67
A. Blacklaw	(1966)	1	3	3.00
E. Connachan	(1962)	1	4	4.00
F. Martin	(1954)	2	8	4.00

*Billy Thomson's other appearance, as a ten-minute substitute, is overlooked for present purposes.

Scotland's 19 World Cup goalkeepers can be contrasted with England, Wales and Northern Ireland, none of whom have called upon more than 11 goalkeepers in the World Cup.

	keepers	World Cup matches	goals conceded
Scotland	19	65	89
England	11	69	61
Wales	11	49	66
N Ireland	10	62	80

Including all Scotland's World Cup fixtures between 1950 and 1966, a clean-sheet was recorded only three times out of 26 matches.

223

Before the introduction of Alan Rough in 1976, Scotland had called upon seventeen goalkeepers in forty World Cup games, giving them on average barely two caps per man. England have used in total only eleven goalkeepers in 69 World Cup games, at an average of over six per man.

Appendix 6

Full record of Scotland and the other British nations in the World Cup 1950-86
(including qualifying rounds and final stages – excluding World Cup finals 1986)

SCOTLAND			P	W	D	L	F	A
Qualifying	Home		26	18	4	4	59	26
rounds	Away		24	11	4	9	38	30
	Neutral (play-off)		1	0	0	1	2	4
World Cup								
finals 1954,58,74,78,82			14	3	5	6	20	29
		Total	65	32	13	20	119	89

ENGLAND			P	W	D	L	F	A
Qualifying	Home		19	14	5	0	57	12
rounds	Away		21	12	4	5	51	20
World Cup								
finals 1950,54,58,62,66,70,82			29	13	8	8	40	29
		Total	69	39	17	13	148	61

Taking into account England's staging of the 1966 World Cup finals, England's complete home record in all World Cups is:

	P	W	D	L	F	A
	25	19	6	0	68	15

NORTHERN IRELAND			P	W	D	L	F	A
Qualifying	Home		25	16	4	5	45	25
rounds	Away		27	3	9	15	16	38
World Cup								
finals 1958,82			10	3	4	3	11	17
		Total	62	22	17	23	72	80

WALES			P	W	D	L	F	A
Qualifying	Home		23	12	3	8	38	26
rounds	Away		21	3	3	15	13	36
World Cup								
finals 1958			5	1	3	1	4	4
		Total	49	16	9	24	55	66

225

Appendix 7

Scotland appearances and goal-scorers in the World Cup 1950-86 (including qualifying rounds and final stages – excluding World Cup finals 1986) (Bracket indicates that the appearance was as a substitute)

	1950		1954		1958		1962		1966		1970		1974		1978		1982		1986	
Appearances	A	G	A	G	A	G	A	G	A	G	A	G	A	G	A	G	A	G	A	G
26 Dalglish, Kenny													7(1)	1	7	3	8(2)	2	4	1
18 Rough, Alan															7		10		1(1)	
16 McGrain, Danny													5		3		8(1)			
16 Miller, Willie																	8(1)		8	
16 Souness, Graeme															1		8	1	7	
15 Bremner, Billy									3		6		6							
15 Jordan, Joe													5(1)	3	7	2	3	2		
14 McLeish, Alex																	6(1)		8	
13 Hartford, Asa															7(2)	1	6(1)			
12 Caldow, Eric					7		5													
12 Greig, John									6		6									
11 Gray, Frank																	11			
11 Archibald, Steve																	9(2)	1	2(1)	
11 Law, Denis							2		4		2	2	1	3						
11 Robertson, John															1		10	4		
11 Strachan, Gordon																	7	1	4(1)	
10 Evans, Bobby	2		3		5															

Appearances	1950 A	1950 G	1954 A	1954 G	1958 A	1958 G	1962 A	1962 G	1966 A	1966 G	1970 A	1970 G	1974 A	1974 G	1978 A	1978 G	1982 A	1982 G	1986 A	1986 G
10 Hansen, Alan																	9		1(1)	
10 McNeill, Billy									3		3(1)	1								
9 Buchan, Martin													4		5(1)					
9 Gemmill, Archie															5(1)	2	4			
8 Collins, Bobby					6		2													
8 Crerand, Pat							5		3											
8 Gilzean, Alan									2		6(1)	3								
8 Gray, Andy															1		6(3)			
8 Jardine, Sandy													5		3					
8 Leighton, Jim																	8			
8 McCreadie, Eddie									4		4									
7 Baxter, Jim							5		2											
7 Bett, Jim																			7(1)	1
7 Cooper, Davie																			7(1)	2
7 McKinnon, Ronnie									2		5									
7 Mudie, Jackie					7	2														
7 Young, George	3		2		2															
6 Brown, Bill					1		1		4											
6 Burns, Kenny													2		4(1)					
6 Cooke, Charlie									1		5(1)									
6 Cowie, Doug			4		2															
6 Cox, Sammy	3		3																	
6 Docherty, Tommy			2		4															
6 Donachie, Willie													1		5					
6 Forsyth, Tom													1		5(1)					

Appearances	1950 A	1950 G	1954 A	1954 G	1958 A	1958 G	1962 A	1962 G	1966 A	1966 G	1970 A	1970 G	1974 A	1974 G	1978 A	1978 G	1982 A	1982 G	1986 A	1986 G
6 Lorimer, Peter											1(1)		5	2						
6 Morgan, Willie													6	1						
6 Wark, John																	6	3		2
6 Younger, Tommy					6															
5 Hamilton, Alec							1		4											
5 Harvey, David													5							
5 Hay, Davie													5							
5 Henderson, Willie									4		1	1								
5 Hewie, John					5	1														
5 McStay, Paul																			5	
5 Murdoch, Bobby									2		3	2								
5 Nicol, Steve																			5	
5 Rioch, Bruce															5					
5 Wilson, Davie							4		1	1										
4 Aitken, Roy																			4	
4 Albiston, Arthur																			4	
4 Baird, Sam					4	1														
4 Brand, Ralph							4	3												
4 Brown, Allan			4	2																
4 Fernie, Willie			2		2															
4 Gemmell, Tommy											4	1								
4 Gough, Richard																			4	
4 Gray, Eddie											3	1			1					
4 Holton, Jim													4	1						
4 Hughes, John									3		1									
4 Hutchison, Tom													4(2)							

Appearances	1950 A	1950 G	1954 A	1954 G	1958 A	1958 G	1962 A	1962 G	1966 A	1966 G	1970 A	1970 G	1974 A	1974 G	1978 A	1978 G	1982 A	1982 G	1986 A	1986 G
4 Johnston, Mo																			4	2
4 Johnston, Willie									1						3					
4 Johnstone, Jimmy									1				1	1						
4 Macari, Lou													1		3(1)					
4 Malpas, Maurice															4				4	
4 Masson, Don															4	1				
4 McKenzie, John			4	4																
4 McQueen, Gordon															4					
4 Ring, Tommy					4															
4 Sharp, Graeme											4(1)								4(2)	
4 Stein, Colin												6								
3 Aitken, George	2		1																	
3 Blackley, John													2							
3 Cowan, Jimmy	3		3																	
3 Farm, George					3															
3 Harper, Joe													2(1)	1						
3 Herriot, Jim											3									
3 Kennedy, Stuart													1(1)	1	2		1(1)			
3 Lennox, Bobby											3(1)									
3 Leslie, Lawrie							3													
3 Liddell, Billy	2		1		2															
3 McColl, Ian	1						3													
3 McLeod, John																				
3 Martin, Neil									3											
3 Narey, David																	3(1)	1		

Appearances	1950		1954		1958		1962		1966		1970		1974		1978		1982		1986	
	A	G	A	G	A	G	A	G	A	G	A	G	A	G	A	G	A	G	A	G
3 Nicholas, Charlie																			3(3)	1
3 Ormond, Willie			3																	
3 Provan, Davie (Celtic)																	3			
3 Reilly, Lawrie	2	1	1	1																
3 Scott, Alec					2	1			1											
3 Shearer, Bobby							3													
3 Smith, Gordon					3	1														
3 Steel, Billy			3	1																
3 Turnbull, Eddie					3	1														
3 Waddell, Willie	2	1	1																	
3 Woodburn, Willie	3																			
2 Aird, John			2																	
2 Brazil, Alan																	2(1)			
2 Brennan, Frank	2																			
2 Brownlie, John													2							
2 Colquhoun, Eddie													2							
2 Cunningham, Willie					2															
2 Davidson, Jimmy			2																	
2 Graham, George													2	1						
2 Henderson, Jackie					2															
2 Herd, David							2	2												
2 Imlach, Stuart					2															
2 Johnstone, Bobby			2	1																
2 Leggat, Graham					2	2														
2 Mackay, Dave					2	2														

Appearances	1950		1954		1958		1962		1966		1970		1974		1978		1982		1986	
	A	G	A	G	A	G	A	G	A	G	A	G	A	G	A	G	A	G	A	G
2 McAvennie, Frank																			2	1
2 McPhail, John	1		1																	
2 Martin, Fred			2																	
2 Mochan, Neil			2																	
2 Murray, Jimmy					2	1														
2 Parker, Alec					2															
2 Provan, Dave (Rangers)									2											
2 Quinn, Pat							2													
2 Robertson, Archie					2	1														
2 Speedie, David																			2	
2 Stewart, Ray																	2			
2 St John, Ian							2	3												
2 Thompson, Billy																	2(1)			
2 White, John							2													
1 Bauld, Willie	1																			
1 Blacklaw, Adam									1											
1 Bone, Jimmy													1							
1 Burns, Francis											1									
1 Carr, Willie													1(1)							
1 Chalmers, Steve									1	1										
1 Clark, Bobby													1							
1 Connachan, Eddie							1													
1 Connelly, George													1							
1 Cormack, Peter											1									
1 Curren, Hugh											1									
1 Evans, Allan																	1			

Appearances	1950 A	1950 G	1954 G	1954 A	1958 G	1958 A	1962 G	1962 A	1966 G	1966 A	1970 G	1970 A	1974 G	1974 A	1978 G	1978 A	1982 G	1982 A	1986 G
1 Fleming, Charlie	1																		
1 Forbes, Alec			2	1															
1 Ford, Donald														1(1)					
1 Forrest, Jim														1					
1 Forsyth, Alec														1					
1 Forsyth, Campbell										1									
1 Fraser, Doug												1							
1 Gibson, Davie									1	1									
1 Hamilton, Willie				1															
1 Haughney, Mike																			
1 Hunter, Ally														1					
1 Kennedy, Jim																			
1 Lawrence, Tommy										1									
1 Linwood, Alec	1																		
1 McGarr, Ernie												1							
1 McGrory, Jackie										1									
1 McKay, Duncan								1											
1 McLean, Tommy												1							
1 McMillan, Ian	1																		
1 Mason, Jimmy	1																		
1 Moir, Willie	3																		
1 Morris, Henry	1														1(1)				
1 Pettigrew, Willie				1															
1 Robertson, Hugh												1							
1 Simpson, Ronnie												1							
1 Stanton, Pat												1							

Appearances	1950 A	G	1954 A	G	1958 A	G	1962 A	G	1966 A	G	1970 A	G	1974 A	G	1978 A	G	1982 A	G	1986 A	G
1 Sturrock, Paul																	1	1		
1 Telter, Willie			1																	
1 Ure, Ian			1				1													
1 Watson, Jimmy										1										
1 Yeats, Ron							1	2												
1 Young, Alex				1												2				
own-goals																				
TOTAL: 763 caps	33		55		77		55		66		72		84		86		136		99	
TOTAL: 48 subs	–		–		–		–		–		(6)		(7)		(9)		(15)		(11)	
TOTAL: 65 games	3		5		7		5		6		6		7		7		11		8	
TOTAL: 119 goals		10		8		14		12		8		18		11		11		17		10
TOTAL: 176 players																				

N.B. Kenny Dalglish has some way to go before matching the achievement of Northern Ireland goalkeeper Pat Jennings, who so far has played in 37 World Cup matches between 1964 and 1986, and who is the only British player to have appeared in *six* World Cups.

Although, up to 1986, Denis Law and Kenny Dalglish are the only Scottish players to have appeared in four World Cups, Willie Johnston also played in two competitions twelve years apart – 1966 and 1978.

Appendix 8

Results of the World Cup finals 1930–82

a.e.t. means 'after extra time'

1930 URUGUAY

					P	W	D	L	F	A	PTS
Pool 1:	France v Mexico	4-1	ARGENTINA		3	3	0	0	10	4	6
	Argentina v France	1-0	Chile		3	2	0	1	5	3	4
	Chile v Mexico	3-0	France		3	1	0	2	4	3	2
	Chile v France	1-0	Mexico		3	0	0	3	4	13	0
	Argentina v Mexico	6-3									
	Argentina v Chile	3-1									
Pool 2:	Yugoslavia v Brazil	2-1	YUGOSLAVIA		2	2	0	0	6	1	4
	Yugoslavia v Bolivia	4-0	Brazil		2	1	0	1	5	2	2
	Brazil v Bolivia	4-0	Bolivia		2	0	0	2	0	8	0
Pool 3:	Romania v Peru	3-1	URUGUAY		2	2	0	0	5	0	4
	Uruguay v Peru	1-0	Romania		2	1	0	1	3	5	2
	Uruguay v Romania	4-0	Peru		2	0	0	2	1	4	0
Pool 4:	USA v Belgium	3-0	USA		2	2	0	0	6	0	4
	USA v Paraguay	3-0	Paraguay		2	1	0	1	3	5	2
	Paraguay v Belgium	1-0	Belgium		2	0	0	2	0	4	0

Semi-finals: Argentina v USA 6-1
Uruguay v Y'slavia 6-1

World Cup Final: Uruguay v Argentina 4-2

1934 ITALY

First Round: Italy v USA 7-1
Czechoslovakia v Romania 2-1
Germany v Belgium 5-2
Austria v France 3-2 (after extra-time)
Spain v Brazil 3-1
Switzerland v Holland 3-2
Sweden v Argentina 3-2
Hungary v Egypt 4-2

Second Round: Germany v Sweden 2-1
Austria v Hungary 2-1
Italy v Spain 1-1 1-0 (after replay)
Czechoslovakia v Switz'land 3-2

Semi-finals: Czechoslovakia v Germany 3-1
Italy v Austria 1-0

Third-place match: Germany v Austria 3-2

World Cup Final: Italy v Czechoslovakia 2-1 (after extra-time)

1938 FRANCE

First Round:	Switzerland v Germany	1-1	4-2 (after replay)
	Cuba v Romania	3-3	2-1 (after replay)
	Hungary v Dutch East Indies	6-0	
	France v Belgium	3-1	
	Czechoslovakia v Holland	3-0	(after extra-time)
	Brazil v Poland	6-5	(after extra-time)
	Italy v Norway	2-1	(after extra-time)
Second Round:	Sweden v Cuba	8-0	
	Hungary v Switzerland	2-0	
	Italy v France	3-1	
	Brazil v Czechoslovakia	1-1	2-1 (after replay)
Semi-finals:	Italy v Brazil	2-1	
	Hungary v Sweden	5-1	
Third-place match:	Brazil v Sweden	4-2	
World Cup Final:	Italy v Hungary	4-2	

1950 BRAZIL

					P	W	D	L	F	A	PTS
Pool 1:	Brazil v Mexico	4-0	BRAZIL		3	2	1	0	8	2	5
	Yugoslavia v Switzerland	3-0	Yugoslavia		3	2	0	1	7	3	4
	Yugoslavia v Mexico	4-1	Switzerland		3	1	1	1	4	6	3
	Brazil v Switzerland	2-2	Mexico		3	0	0	3	2	10	0
	Brazil v Yugoslavia	2-0									
	Switzerland v Mexico	2-1									
Pool 2:	Spain v USA	3-1	SPAIN		3	3	0	0	6	1	6
	England v Chile	2-0	England		3	1	0	2	2	2	2
	USA v England	1-0	Chile		3	1	0	2	5	6	2
	Spain v Chile	2-0	USA		3	1	0	2	4	8	2
	Spain v England	1-0									
	Chile v USA	5-2									
Pool 3:	Sweden v Italy	3-2	SWEDEN		2	1	1	0	5	4	3
	Sweden v Paraguay	2-2	Italy		2	1	0	1	4	3	2
	Italy v Paraguay	2-0	Paraguay		2	0	1	1	2	4	1
Pool 4:	Uruguay v Bolivia	8-0	URUGUAY		1	1	0	0	8	0	2
			Bolivia		1	0	0	1	0	8	0
Final Pool:	Uruguay v Spain	2-2	Final positions:								
	Brazil v Sweden	7-1	1st URUGUAY		3	2	1	0	7	5	5
	Uruguay v Sweden	3-2	2nd Brazil		3	2	0	1	14	4	4
	Brazil v Spain	6-1	3rd Sweden		3	1	0	2	6	11	2
	Sweden v Spain	3-1	4th Spain		3	0	1	2	4	11	1
	Uruguay v Brazil	2-1									

1954 SWITZERLAND

			P	W	D	L	F	A	PTS
Group 1:	Yugoslavia v France	1-0	BRAZIL	2	1	1	0	6	1	3
	Brazil v Mexico	5-0	YUGOSLAVIA	2	1	1	0	2	1	3
	France v Mexico	3-2	France	2	1	0	1	3	3	2
	Brazil v Yu'slavia (a.e.t.)	1-1	Mexico	2	0	0	2	2	8	0

Group 2:	Hungary v S. Korea	9-0	HUNGARY	2	2	0	0	17	3	4
	W. Germany v Turkey	4-1	W. GERMANY	2	1	0	1	7	9	2
	Hungary v W. Germany	8-3	Turkey	2	1	0	1	8	4	2
	Turkey v S. Korea	7-0	South Korea	2	0	0	2	0	16	0
	W. Germany v Turkey	7-2	(play off)							

Group 3:	Austria v Scotland	1-0	URUGUAY	2	2	0	0	9	0	4
	Uruguay v Czech'vakia	2-0	AUSTRIA	2	2	0	0	6	0	4
	Austria v Czechoslovakia	5-0	Czechoslovakia	2	0	0	2	0	7	0
	Uruguay v Scotland	7-0	Scotland	2	0	0	2	0	8	0

Group 4:	England v Bel'm (a.e.t.)	4-4	ENGLAND	2	1	1	0	6	4	3
	Switzerland v Italy	2-1	SWITZERLAND	2	1	0	1	2	3	2
	England v Switzerland	2-0	Italy	2	1	0	1	5	3	2
	Italy v Belgium	4-1	Belgium	2	0	1	1	5	8	1
	Switzerland v Italy	4-1	(play-off)							

Quarter-finals:	W. Germany v Y'slavia	2-0
	Hungary v Brazil	4-2
	Austria v Switzerland	7-5
	Uruguay v England	4-2

Semi-finals:	West Germany v Austria	6-1
	Hungary v Uruguay	4-2	(after extra-time)
Third-place		
match:	Austria v Uruguay	3-1

World Cup Final:	W. Germany v Hungary	3-2

1958 SWEDEN

			P	W	D	L	F	A	PTS
Group 1:	W. Germany v Argentina	3-1	W. GERMANY	3	1	2	0	7	5	4
	N. Ireland v Czech'vakia	1-0	N. IRELAND	3	1	1	1	4	5	3
	W. Germany v Czech'ia	2-2	Czechoslovakia	3	1	1	1	8	4	3
	Argentina v N. Ireland	3-1	Argentina	3	1	0	2	5	10	2
	W. Germany v N. Ireland	2-2								
	Czechoslovakia v Arg'tina	6-1								
	N. Ireland v Czech'vakia	2-1	(play-off; after extra-time)							

Group 2:	France v Paraguay	7-3	FRANCE	3	2	0	1	11	7	4
	Y'slavia v Scotland	1-1	YUGOSLAVIA	3	1	2	0	7	6	4
	Yugoslavia v France	3-2	Paraguay	3	1	1	1	9	12	3
	Paraguay v Scotland	3-2	Scotland	3	0	1	2	4	6	1
	France v Scotland	2-1								
	Y'slavia v Paraguay	3-3								

Group 3:	Sweden v Mexico	3-0	SWEDEN	3	2	1	0	5	1	5
	Hungary v Wales	1-1	WALES	3	0	3	0	2	2	3
	Wales v Mexico	1-1	Hungary	3	1	1	1	6	3	3
	Sweden v Hungary	2-1	Mexico	3	0	1	2	1	8	1
	Sweden v Wales	0-0								
	Hungary v Mexico	4-0								
	Wales v Hungary	2-1	(play-off)							

Group 4:	England v USSR	2-2	BRAZIL	3	2	1	0	5	0	5
	Brazil v Austria	3-0	USSR	3	1	1	1	4	4	3
	England v Brazil	0-0	England	3	0	3	0	4	4	3
	USSR v Austria	2-0	Austria	3	0	1	2	2	7	1
	Brazil v USSR	2-0								
	England v Austria	2-2								
	USSR v England	1-0	(play-off)							

Quarter-finals:	France v N Ireland	4-0
	W. Ger. v Y'slavia	1-0
	Sweden v USSR	2-0
	Brazil v Wales	1-0

Semi-finals:	Brazil v France	5-2
	Sweden v W. Germany	3-1
Third-place match:	France v W. Germany	6-3

World Cup Final:	Brazil v Sweden	5-2

1962 CHILE

				P	W	D	L	F	A	PTS
Group 1:	Uruguay v Colombia	2-1	USSR	3	2	1	0	8	5	5
	USSR v Yugoslavia	2-0	YUGOSLAVIA	3	2	0	1	8	3	4
	Y'slavia v Uruguay	3-1	Uruguay	3	1	0	2	4	6	2
	USSR v Colombia	4-4	Colombia	3	0	1	2	5	11	1
	USSR v Uruguay	2-1								
	Y'slavia v Colombia	5-0								

Group 2:	Chile v Switzerland	3-1	W. GERMANY	3	2	1	0	8	5	5
	West Germany v Italy	0-0	CHILE	3	2	0	1	5	3	4
	Chile v Italy	2-0	Italy	3	1	1	1	3	2	3
	W. Ger. v Switz'land	2-1	Switzerland	3	0	0	3	2	8	0
	W. Germany v Chile	2-0								
	Italy v Switzerland	3-0								

Group 3:	Brazil v Mexico	2-0	BRAZIL	3	2	1	0	4	1	5
	Czechoslovakia v Spain	1-0	CZECH'VAKIA	3	1	1	1	2	3	3
	Brazil v Czechoslovakia	0-0	Mexico	3	1	0	2	3	4	2
	Spain v Mexico	1-0	Spain	3	1	0	2	2	3	2
	Brazil v Spain	2-1								
	Mexico v Czechoslovakia	3-1								

Group 4:	Argentina v Bulgaria	1-0	HUNGARY	3	2	1	0	8	2	5
	Hungary v England	2-1	ENGLAND	3	1	1	1	4	3	3
	England v Argentina	3-1	Argentina	3	1	1	1	2	3	3
	Hungary v Bulgaria	6-1	Bulgaria	3	0	1	2	1	7	1
	Argentina v Hungary	0-0								
	England v Bulgaria	0-0								

Quarter-finals:	Y'slavia v W. Germany	1-0
	Brazil v England	3-1
	Chile v USSR	2-1
	Czechoslovakia v Hungary	1-0

Semi-finals:	Brazil v Chile	4-2
	Czechoslovakia v Y'slavia	3-1

Third-place match:	Chile v Yugoslavia	1-0

World Cup Final:	Brazil v Czechoslovakia	3-1

1966 ENGLAND

				P	W	D	L	F	A	PTS
Group 1:	England v Uruguay	0-0	ENGLAND	3	2	1	0	4	0	5
	France v Mexico	1-1	URUGUAY	3	1	2	0	2	1	4
	Uruguay v France	2-1	Mexico	3	0	2	1	1	3	2
	England v Mexico	2-0	France	3	0	1	2	2	5	1
	Uruguay v Mexico	0-0								
	England v France	2-0								
Group 2:	W. Ger. v Switz'land	5-0	W. GERMANY	3	2	1	0	7	1	5
	Argentina v Spain	2-1	ARGENTINA	3	2	1	0	4	1	5
	Spain v Switzerland	2-1	Spain	3	1	0	2	4	5	2
	Argentina v W. Ger.	0-0	Switzerland	3	0	0	3	1	9	0
	Arg'tina v Switz'land	2-0								
	W. Germany v Spain	2-1								
Group 3:	Brazil v Bulgaria	0-0	PORTUGAL	3	3	0	0	9	2	6
	Portugal v Hungary	3-1	HUNGARY	3	2	0	1	7	5	4
	Hungary v Brazil	3-1	Brazil	3	1	0	2	4	6	2
	Portugal v Bulgaria	3-0	Bulgaria	3	0	0	3	1	8	0
	Portugal v Brazil	3-1								
	Hungary v Bulgaria	3-1								
Group 4:	USSR v North Korea	3-0	USSR	3	3	0	0	6	1	6
	Italy v Chile	2-0	N. KOREA	3	1	1	1	2	4	3
	Chile v North Korea	1-1	Italy	3	1	0	2	2	2	2
	USSR v Italy	1-0	Chile	3	0	1	2	2	5	1
	North Korea v Italy	1-0								
	USSR v Chile	2-1								

Quarter-finals:	England v Argentina	1-0
	W. Ger. v Uruguay	4-0
	Portugal v N. Korea	5-3
	USSR v Hungary	2-1
Semi-finals:	W. Germany v USSR	2-1
	England v Portugal	2-1
Third-place match:	Portugual v USSR	2-1
World Cup Final:	England v West Germany	4-2 (after extra-time)

1970 MEXICO

				P	W	D	L	F	A	PTS
Group 1:	Mexico v USSR	0-0	USSR	3	2	1	0	6	1	5
	Belgium v El Salvador	3-0	MEXICO	3	2	1	0	5	0	5
	USSR v Belgium	4-1	Belgium	3	1	0	2	4	5	2
	Mexico v El Salvador	4-0	El Salvador	3	0	0	3	0	9	0
	USSR v El Salvador	2-0								
	Belgium v Mexico	0-1								
Group 2:	Uruguay v Israel	2-0	ITALY	3	1	2	0	1	0	4
	Italy v Sweden	1-0	URUGUAY	3	1	1	1	2	1	3
	Uruguay v Italy	0-0	Sweden	3	1	1	1	2	2	3
	Israel v Sweden	1-1	Israel	3	0	2	1	1	3	2
	Sweden v Uruguay	1-0								
	Israel v Italy	0-0								
Group 3:	England v Romania	1-0	BRAZIL	3	3	0	0	8	3	6
	Brazil v Czechoslovakia	4-1	ENGLAND	3	2	0	1	2	1	4
	Romania v Czech'vakia	2-1	Romania	3	1	0	2	4	5	2
	Brazil v England	1-0	Czechoslovakia	3	0	0	3	2	7	0
	Brazil v Romania	3-2								
	England v Czechoslovakia	1-0								
Group 4:	Peru v Bulgaria	3-2	W. GERMANY	3	3	0	0	10	4	6
	W. Ger. v Morocco	2-1	PERU	3	2	0	1	7	5	4
	Peru v Morocco	3-0	Bulgaria	3	0	1	2	5	9	1
	W. Ger. v Bulgaria	5-2	Morocco	3	0	1	2	2	6	1
	W. Germany v Peru	3-1								
	Bulgaria v Morocco	1-1								

Quarter-finals:	Uruguay v USSR	1-0 (after extra-time)
	Italy v Mexico	4-1
	Brazil v Peru	4-2
	W. Ger. v England	3-2 (after extra-time)
Semi-finals:	Italy v West Germany	4-3 (after extra-time)
	Brazil v Uruguay	3-1
Third-place match:	W. Ger. v Uruguay	1-0
World Cup Final:	Brazil v Italy	4-1

1974 WEST GERMANY

Group 1:				P	W	D	L	F	A	PTS
	W. Germany v Chile	1-0	E. GERMANY	3	2	1	0	4	1	5
	E. Ger. v Australia	2-0	W. GERMANY	3	2	0	1	4	1	4
	W. Ger. v Australia	3-0	Chile	3	0	2	1	1	2	2
	E. Germany v Chile	1-1	Australia	3	0	1	2	0	5	1
	E. Ger. v W. Ger.	1-0								
	Chile v Australia	0-0								
Group 2:	Brazil v Yugoslavia	0-0	YUGOSLAVIA	3	1	2	0	10	1	4
	Scotland v Zaire	2-0	BRAZIL	3	1	2	0	3	0	4
	Brazil v Scotland	0-0	Scotland	3	1	2	0	3	1	4
	Yugoslavia v Zaire	9-0	Zaire	3	0	0	3	0	14	0
	Scotland v Y'slavia	1-1								
	Brazil v Zaire	3-0								
Group 3:	Holland v Uruguay	2-0	HOLLAND	3	2	1	0	6	1	5
	Sweden v Bulgaria	0-0	SWEDEN	3	1	2	0	3	0	4
	Holland v Sweden	0-0	Bulgaria	3	0	2	1	2	5	2
	Bulgaria v Uruguay	1-1	Uruguay	3	0	1	2	1	6	1
	Holland v Bulgaria	4-1								
	Sweden v Uruguay	3-0								
Group 4:	Italy v Haiti	3-1	POLAND	3	3	0	0	12	3	6
	Poland v Argentina	3-2	ARGENTINA	3	1	1	1	7	5	3
	Argentina v Italy	1-1	Italy	3	1	1	1	5	4	3
	Poland v Haiti	7-0	Haiti	3	0	0	3	2	14	0
	Argentina v Haiti	4-1								
	Poland v Italy	2-1								
Group A:	Brazil v E. Germany	1-0	HOLLAND	3	3	0	0	8	0	6
	Holland v Argentina	4-0	Brazil	3	2	0	1	3	3	4
	Holland v E. Ger.	2-0	East Germany	3	0	1	2	1	4	1
	Brazil v Argentina	2-1	Argentina	3	0	1	2	2	7	1
	Holland v Brazil	2-0								
	Argentina v E. Ger.	1-1								
Group B:	Poland v Sweden	1-0	W. GERMANY	3	3	0	0	7	2	6
	W. Ger. v Y'slavia	2-0	Poland	3	2	0	1	3	2	4
	Poland v Yugoslavia	2-1	Sweden	3	1	0	2	4	6	2
	W. Ger. v Sweden	4-2	Yugoslavia	3	0	0	3	2	6	0
	Sweden v Yugoslavia	2-1								
	W. Ger. v Poland	1-0								

Third-place
match: Poland v Brazil   1-0

World Cup Final: West Germany v Holland   2-1

1978 ARGENTINA

				P	W	D	L	F	A	PTS
Group 1:	Italy v France	2-1	ITALY	3	3	0	0	6	2	6
	Argentina v Hungary	2-1	ARGENTINA	3	2	0	1	4	3	4
	Italy v Hungary	3-1	France	3	1	0	2	5	5	2
	Argentina v France	2-1	Hungary	3	0	0	3	3	8	0
	France v Hungary	3-1								
	Italy v Argentina	1-0								
Group 2:	W. Ger. v Poland	0-0	POLAND	3	2	1	0	4	1	5
	Tunisia v Mexico	3-1	W. GERMANY	3	1	2	0	6	0	4
	Poland v Tunisia	1-0	Tunisia	3	1	1	1	3	2	3
	W. Ger. v Mexico	6-0	Mexico	3	0	0	3	2	12	0
	Poland v Mexico	3-1								
	W. Ger. v Tunisia	0-0								
Group 3:	Austria v Spain	2-1	AUSTRIA	3	2	0	1	3	2	4
	Brazil v Sweden	1-1	BRAZIL	3	1	2	0	2	1	4
	Austria v Sweden	1-0	Spain	3	1	1	1	2	2	3
	Brazil v Spain	0-0	Sweden	3	0	1	2	1	3	1
	Spain v Sweden	1-0								
	Brazil v Austria	1-0								
Group 4:	Peru v Scotland	3-1	PERU	3	2	1	0	7	2	5
	Holland v Iran	3-0	HOLLAND	3	1	1	1	5	3	3
	Scotland v Iran	1-1	Scotland	3	1	1	1	5	6	3
	Holland v Peru	0-0	Iran	3	0	1	2	2	8	1
	Peru v Iran	4-1								
	Scotland v Holland	3-2								
Group A:	West Germany v Italy	0-0	HOLLAND	3	2	1	0	9	4	5
	Holland v Austria	5-1	Italy	3	1	1	1	2	2	3
	Italy v Austria	1-0	West Germany	3	0	2	1	4	5	2
	Holland v W. Ger.	2-2	Austria	3	1	0	2	4	8	2
	Holland v Italy	2-1								
	Austria v W. Ger.	3-2								
Group B:	Brazil v Peru	3-0	ARGENTINA	3	2	1	0	8	0	5
	Argentina v Poland	2-0	Brazil	3	2	1	0	6	1	5
	Poland v Peru	1-0	Poland	3	1	0	2	2	5	2
	Argentina v Brazil	0-0	Peru	3	0	0	3	0	10	0
	Brazil v Poland	3-1								
	Argentina v Peru	6-0								

Third-place match:	Brazil v Italy	2-1	
World Cup Final:	Argentina v Holland	3-1	(after extra-time)

1982 SPAIN

				P	W	D	L	F	A	PTS
Group 1:	Italy v Poland	0-0	POLAND	3	1	2	0	5	1	4
	Peru v Cameroon	0-0	ITALY	3	0	3	0	2	2	3
	Italy v Peru	1-1	Cameroon	3	0	3	0	1	1	3
	Poland v Cameroon	0-0	Peru	3	0	2	1	2	6	2
	Peru v Poland	1-5								
	Italy v Cameroon	1-1								
Group 2:	W. Ger. v Algeria	1-2	W. GERMANY	3	2	0	1	6	3	4
	Chile v Austria	0-1	AUSTRIA	3	2	0	1	3	1	4
	W. Germany v Chile	4-1	Algeria	3	2	0	1	5	5	4
	Algeria v Austria	0-2	Chile	3	0	0	3	3	8	0
	Algeria v Chile	3-2								
	W. Ger. v Austria	1-0								
Group 3:	Argentina v Belgium	0-1	BELGIUM	3	2	1	0	3	1	5
	Hungary v El Sal'dor	10-1	ARGENTINA	3	2	0	1	6	2	4
	Argentina v Hungary	4-1	Hungary	3	1	1	1	12	6	3
	Belgium v El Sal'dor	1-0	El Salvador	3	0	0	3	1	13	0
	Belgium v Hungary	1-1								
	Arg'tina v El Sal'dor	2-0								
Group 4:	England v France	3-1	ENGLAND	3	3	0	0	6	1	6
	Czechoslovakia v Kuwait	1-1	FRANCE	3	1	1	1	6	5	3
	England v Czechoslovakia	2-0	Czechoslovakia	3	0	2	1	2	4	2
	France v Kuwait	4-1	Kuwait	3	0	1	2	2	6	1
	France v Czechoslovakia	1-1								
	England v Kuwait	1-0								
Group 5:	Spain v Honduras	1-1	N IRELAND	3	1	2	0	2	1	4
	Y'slavia v N. Ireland	0-0	SPAIN	3	1	1	1	3	3	3
	Spain v Yugoslavia	2-1	Yugoslavia	3	1	1	1	2	2	3
	Hondur. v N. Ireland	1-1	Honduras	3	0	2	1	2	3	2
	Honduras v Y'slavia	0-1								
	Spain v N. Ireland	0-1								
Group 6:	Brazil v USSR	2-1	BRAZIL	3	3	0	0	10	2	6
	Scotland v N Zealand	5-2	USSR	3	1	1	1	6	4	3
	Brazil v Scotland	4-1	Scotland	3	1	1	1	8	8	3
	USSR v New Zealand	3-0	New Zealand	3	0	0	3	2	12	0
	USSR v Scotland	2-2								
	Brazil v New Zealand	4-0								
Group A:	Belgium v Poland	0-3	POLAND	2	1	1	0	3	0	3
	Belgium v USSR	0-1	USSR	2	1	1	0	1	0	3
	Poland v USSR	0-0	Belgium	2	0	0	2	0	4	0
Group B:	W. Ger. v England	0-0	W. GERMANY	2	1	1	0	2	1	3
	W. Germany v Spain	2-1	England	2	0	2	0	0	0	2
	England v Spain	0-0	Spain	2	0	1	1	1	2	1

1982 SPAIN *continued*

				P	W	D	L	F	A	PTS
Group C:	Argentina v Italy	1-2	ITALY	2	2	0	0	5	3	4
	Argentina v Brazil	1-3	Brazil	2	1	0	1	5	4	2
	Italy v Brazil	3-2	Argentina	2	0	0	2	2	5	0
Group D:	Austria v France	0-1	FRANCE	2	2	0	0	5	1	4
	Austria v N. Ireland	2-2	Austria	2	0	1	1	2	3	1
	France v N. Ireland	4-1	N Ireland	2	0	1	1	3	6	1

Semi-finals: Italy v Poland 2-0
W. Germany v France 3-3 (after extra-time: Germany won on penalties)

Third-place
match: Poland v France 3-2

World Cup Final: Italy v West Germany 3-1

The 1986 World Cup Finals Programme

Date	City	Stadium	Group	Fixtures	Result/scorers
Sat 31 May	Mexico City	Aztec	A	Bulgaria v Italy	
Sun 1 June	Leon	Leon	C	Canada v France	
	Guadalajara	Jalisco	D	Spain v Brazil	
Mon 2 June	Mexico City	Olympic '68	A	Argentina v South Korea	
	Irapuato	Irapuato	C	USSR v Hungary	
	Monterrey	University	F	Morocco v Poland	
Tue 3 June	Mexico City	Aztec	B	Belgium v Mexico	
	Guadalajara	3rd March	D	Algeria v N. Ireland	
	Monterrey	Technological	F	Portugal v England	
Wed 4 June	Toluca	Toluca	B	Paraguay v Iraq	
	Queretaro	Corregidora	E	Uruguay v West Germany	
	Nezahualcoyotl	Neza '86	E	SCOTLAND v Denmark	
Thu 5 June	Puebla	Cuauhtemoc	A	Italy v Argentina	

Date	City	Stadium	Group	Fixtures	Result/scorers
	Mexico City	Olympic '68	A	South Korea v Bulgaria	
	Leon	Leon	C	France v USSR	
Fri 6 June	Irapuato	Irapuato	C	Hungary v Canada	
	Guadalajara	Jalisco	D	Brazil v Algeria	
	Monterrey	Technological	F	England v Morocco	
Sat 7 June	Mexico City	Aztec	B	Mexico v Paraguay	
	Guadalajara	3rd March	D	N. Ireland v Spain	
	Monterrey	University	F	Poland v Portugal	
Sun 8 June	Toluca	Toluca	B	Iraq v Belgium	
	Queretaro	Corregidora	E	West Germany v SCOTLAND	
	Nezahualcoyotl	Neza '86	E	Denmark v Uruguay	
Mon 9 June	Leon	Leon	C	Hungary v France	
	Irapuato	Irapuato	C	USSR v Canada	
Tue 10 June	Puebla	Cuauhtemoc	A	South Korea v Italy	

Date	City	Stadium	Group	Fixtures	Result/scorer
	Mexico City	Olympic '68	A	Argentina v Bulgaria	
Wed 11 June	Mexico City	Aztec	B	Iraq v Mexico	
	Toluca	Toluca	B	Paraguay v Belgium	
	Guadalajara	3rd March	F	Portugal v Morocco	
	Monterrey	University	F	England v Poland	
Thu 12 June	Guadalajara	Jalisco	D	N Ireland v Brazil	
	Monterrey	Technological	D	Algeria v Spain	
Fri 13 June	Queretaro	Corregidora	E	Denmark v West Germany	
	Nezahualcoyotl	Neza '86	E	SCOTLAND v Uruguay	

2nd Round

Date	City	Stadium	Group	Fixtures	Result/scorer
Sun 15 June	Mexico City	Aztec	8	1st B v 3rd A or C or D	
	Leon	Leon	4	1st C v 3rd A or B or F	
Mon 16 June	Puebla	Cuauhtemoc	1	1st A v 3rd C or D or E	
	Guadalajara	Jalisco	5	1st D v 3rd B or E or F	

Date	City	Stadium	Group	Fixtures	Result/scorers
Tue 17 June	Mexico City	Olympic '68	6	2nd A v 2nd C	
	Monterrey	University	7	1st F v 2nd E	
Wed 18 June	Mexico City	Aztec	2	2nd F v 2nd B	
	Queretaro	Corregidora	3	1st E v 2nd D	

Quarter-Finals

Sat 21 June	Guadalajara	Jalisco	C	5 v 6	
	Monterrey	University	D	7 v 8	
Sun 22 June	Puebla	Cuauhtemoc	B	3 v 4	
	Mexico City	Aztec	A	1 v 2	

Semi-Finals

Wed 25 June	Guadalajara	Jalisco		C v D	
	Mexico City	Aztec		A v B	

Third Place Match

Sat 28 June	Puebla	Cuauhtemoc			

World Cup Final

Sun 29 June	Mexico City	Aztec